Critical Essays on Frank Norris

Critical Essays on
Frank Norris

Don Graham

G. K. Hall & Co. • **Boston, Massachusetts**

Library of Congress Cataloging in Publication Data
Main entry under title:

Critical essays on Frank Norris.

(Critical essays on American literature)
Includes index.
1. Norris, Frank, 1870-1902—Criticism and interpretation—Addresses,
essays, lectures. I. Graham, Don, 1940-   II. Title.
PS2473.C7   813'.4   80-21426
ISBN 0-8161-8307-4

CRITICAL ESSAYS ON AMERICAN LITERATURE

This series seeks to publish the most important reprinted criticism on writers and topics in American literature along with, in various volumes, original essays, interviews, bibliographies, letters, manuscript sections, and other materials brought to public attention for the first time. Don Graham's volume on Frank Norris is not only the first comprehensive collection of criticism on this writer ever published, it is one of the fine anthologies of scholarship in American literature. Professor Graham's introduction is itself an important overview of Norris's work and critical responses to it. In addition, he offers reprinted essays by many of the leading Norris scholars, including Donald Pizer, Joseph Katz, Warren French, Charles Child Walcutt, and others, along with an original essay on *The Octopus* by Joseph R. McElrath, Jr. We are confident that this collection will make a permanent and significant contribution to American literary scholarship.

JAMES NAGEL, GENERAL EDITOR
Northeastern University

For Lois

CONTENTS

ACKNOWLEDGMENTS

I wish to thank a number of people who helped me in various ways during the preparation of this book. One is Irene Moran of the Bancroft Library, Berkeley, California, who as usual was efficient and prompt in supplying me with information I could not have obtained otherwise. Another is my colleague William J. Scheick, who gave me some valuable tips along the way. A third is Karen McCormick, who performed tedious clerical chores with dispatch and good humor. Finally, there is Joseph R. McElrath, Jr., of Florida State University, who generously shared his copies of reviews of Norris's novels and early responses to Norris's death. I am also grateful to the University Research Institute of the University of Texas for a Summer Research Award which provided generous support for this undertaking.

INTRODUCTION

Frank Norris survives today on the basis of two novels—*McTeague* and *The Octopus*—one short story, "A Deal in Wheat," and one or two literary essays, "A Plea for Romantic Fiction" or "Zola as a Romantic Writer." The number of works is not impressive until we recall what remains alive by some of his contemporaries. Harold Frederic, for example, is known almost exclusively by one novel, *The Damnation of Theron Ware*. The same is true of Hamlin Garland for *Main-Travelled Roads*, despite efforts to enlarge his stature through reprinting such works as *Rose of Dutcher's Coolly*. Or there is Henry Blake Fuller, an interesting but still largely unknown writer of the period beside whom Norris is, in terms of visibility, a towering figure. Yet when Norris is compared with other luminaries of the Nineties, Stephen Crane, Theodore Dreiser (counting *Sister Carrie*, 1900, as of the Nineties), and the previous generation, Henry James, Mark Twain, W. D. Howells, suddenly he is eclipsed, overshadowed in the minds of literary critics by the "major" writers. Norris occupies, then, that curious, ambiguous space between minor and major. Neither a Henry Blake Fuller nor a Stephen Crane, he is, however, as much as Crane or anybody of the period, an American original.

Norris's uncertain status is well mirrored in the treatment he receives in recent anthologies of American literature. In four major surveys, works by Norris appear in only two: "A Deal in Wheat" (*America in Literature*, II, 1978), and "A Deal in Wheat" and "A Plea for Romantic Fiction" (*Anthology of American Literature*, II, 1974). Both *The American Tradition in Literature* (1974) and *American Literature: The Makers and the Making* (II, 1973) reprint nothing by Norris, though the latter does contain a four-page summary of his career. Of course one can argue that Norris is not represented best by short works, but to omit him completely seems to be a severe judgment indeed.

Norris's uncertain status is evident too in the tone that critics adopt in talking about even his most highly regarded works. In a recent article on *McTeague*, for example, the author begins thus: "For most readers the first impression of Frank Norris's *McTeague* (1899) must surely be that it is a novel almost embarrassing in its obviousness—in its simple characterization, melodramatic plot, ponderous style, and jejune philosophizing."[1] This tendency to write about Norris from a stance of suspended embarrassment is very curious indeed. One explanation has been offered by two favorably-disposed Norris critics: "It sometimes seems that if Norris were not 'historically important' few commentators would have bothered to comment at all."[2] But the same pair offer a more fruitful possibility when they point out that "the experiment of coming to grips with a writer who was considered unique in his own time and who might still merit the description is only seventy years old."[3]

To look back upon the contemporary reception of Norris and to follow the fluctuating course of his critical fortunes since then is to see both the accomplishments and the unfinished prospects of Norris criticism. The young writer who adopted a variety of personal styles, from self-named boy Zola to fraternity booster to *pater familias* to Novelist, confounded classifiers, pigeon-holers, and categorizers in his time. In the words of a contemporary reviewer, his novels seemed in their "wide difference from each other [to be] an unprecedented thing in literature."[4] What was true in Norris's time is true now: there is at present no "image of stasis" in Norris studies.[5]

The picture of Norris presented in the following selections is something of a revisionist image intended to express a multi-faceted Norris, not the naive naturalist too often presented in the past. Rather than following a simple chronological order, the pieces have been organized according to appropriate categories. (A) biography; (B) reviews; (C) studies of relatively minor aspects of his oeuvre—journalism and the so-called "popular" novels, *Moran of the Lady Letty, Blix,* and *A Man's Woman;* (D) studies of the major-novels—*McTeague, The Octopus, The Pit,* and *Vandover and the Brute;* and (E) broader-scoped studies of the total configuration of his works.

Since there are several previous bibliographical surveys of Norris scholarship available, the present one will give some attention to major earlier work while stressing developments since 1973, the closing date for the last such study. *Frank Norris: A Reference Guide* (1974), edited by Jesse S. Crisler and Joseph R. McElrath, Jr., is an indispensable aid. Arranged chronologically, it begins with the earliest mention of Norris, in 1892, and runs through 1973, containing a highly reliable listing with brief neutral summaries of reviews, articles, and books. It also contains a valuable revisionist essay by the editors that reassesses, on the basis of many reviews they uncovered for the volume, the lively and often favorable response that Norris's works elicited from contemporary reviewers. An excellent companion piece is McElrath's thorough analysis of some forty-odd dissertations written on Norris ("Frank Norris," 1975).[6] A second helpful overview is William B. Dillingham's essay in *Fifteen American Authors Before 1900* (1971). This piece supersedes Warren French's earlier, briefer survey in 1967, "Frank Norris (1870–1902)."[7]

Two more sources of annotated commentary on Norris scholarship are Dillingham's book, *Frank Norris: Instinct and Art* (1969) and French's *Frank Norris* (1962).

Although no selections below deal with primary bibliography, a word needs to be said about this phase of Norris studies. The most substantial attempt to compile a definitive bibliography was made by Kenneth A. Lohf and Eugene P. Sheehy's *Frank Norris: A Bibliography* (1959). The operative word is *attempt*, because immediately subsequent to its publication appeared William White's "Frank Norris: Bibliograph-ical Addenda" (1959).[8] More important are two bibliographies prepared by Joseph Katz: "The Shorter Publications of Frank Norris: A Checklist" (1973) and "The Elusive Criticism Syndicated by Frank Norris" (1973).[9] These in turn are expected to be superseded by Katz's and Robert A. Morace's *Frank Norris: A Bibliographical Checklist*, which is scheduled for publication. Anyone anticipating a "definitive" bibliography should, however, heed the words of Crisler and McElrath: "There is no definitive bibliography of Frank Norris, nor will one ever exist."[10]

The textual situation is less promising. A ten-volume *Complete Edition* appeared in 1928, but it was both incomplete and commercially cavalier about editorial procedures. Over ten years ago Warren French stressed the need for a standard edition that would meet the criteria of the MLA Center for American Editions.[11] So far that need has not been remedied. *Frank Norris of "The Wave"* (1931) contains journalistic sketches and stories not included in the *Complete Edition*. The most important source for Norris's literary essays, also incomplete, is Donald Pizer's *The Literary Criticism of Frank Norris* (1964). Also important are Norris's student themes written at Harvard; these appear, with a valuable introduction by James D. Hart, in *A Novelist in the Making: A Collection of Student Themes and the Novels* Blix *and* Vandover and the Brute (1970). There is also need for a new edition of Norris's letters. Since 1956 when Franklin Walker's slender edition, *The Letters of Frank Norris*, was published, numerous new letters have been found. With regard to popular markets, Norris is currently being well served, with paperback editions of *McTeague, The Octopus*, and *Vandover and the Brute* available.

On the biographical side, Norris has been both blessed and cursed by an excellent first biography, Franklin Walker's *Frank Norris: A Biography* (1932). Drawing upon interviews, contemporaneous accounts, letters, and other sources, Walker fashioned an interpretation that has influenced Norris studies ever since. In Walker's presentation Norris was an exuberant, boyish, and endearing amateur who wrote too much too fast and died too young. Walker's book in effect consolidated the image of Norris as a brash and engaging youth up from middle-class culture that had characterized Charles Caldwell Dobie's biographical sketch in his preface to *McTeague* in the *Complete Edition* (VII, 1928). Since Walker, there has been some piecemeal original biographical research that has added new facts to our knowledge of Norris's life, but there remains the need for a newly researched, factual and interpretive biography. As William B. Dillingham has pointed out, a major source for such an undertaking is the interviews and other documents at the Bancroft Library that formed the basis of Walker's study.[12] Dillingham himself, in his *Frank Norris: Instinct and Art* (1969), has shed new light upon Norris's training in London and Paris during the years 1887–89 when he was studying to be a painter. Other new biographical facts have appeared in brief notes. Joseph R. McElrath, Jr., for example, clarifies the chronology of Norris's whereabouts during one of the least documented periods of his life, his trip to Cuba during the Spanish-American War ("Norris's Return From Cuba," 1973).[13] Similarly, Don Graham has uncovered evidence that points to Norris's standing in San Francisco society and his amateur skills as an actor ("Frank Norris, Actor," 1976).[14] Another piece of local information, discovered by James D. Hart, is that Norris was a member of the Bohemian Club, a very important social club in San Francisco ("Frank Norris, California Author," 1973).[15] Such findings, plus new information contained in letters found since Walker's edition, plus the kind of facts about Norris's parents that could be unearthed through research, plus a complete rethinking of the data in Walker's book, all suggest that a new biography would be one of the most useful contributions that could be made to Norris studies.

In addition to factual biographical studies, there have been several interpretive biographical essays that deserve mention. The most interesting is Maxwell Geismar's spirited portrait of Norris in *Rebels and Ancestors* (1953). For Geismar, Norris's vitality derives from two sources: his success in transcending the restrictions and limited viewpoint of his class to report what was truly going on in *fin de siècle* America, and his introspective analysis of brute instincts within himself that, as in the first case, helped liberate him from the pale affirmations of genteel fiction. A less convincing interpretation of Norris's life occurs in Kenneth Lynn's *The Dream of Success* (1955), wherein Norris's relations with his actress-mother and businessman-father, about which there is little hard evidence, are speculatively assigned crucial roles in Norris's representation of male-female experience in his fiction. Implicit in both these accounts is the familiar assumption that Norris was essentially an intuitive, emotional personality who never properly matured.

Of the several early biographical essays written in the years immediately following his death, two deserve special mention. Denison Hailey Clift's "The Artist in Frank Norris" (1907), which contains the kind of local information that Walker relied heavily upon for his biography, is particularly valuable for its identification of San Francisco locales and incidents recorded in the fiction.[16] Bailey Millard's "A Significant Literary Life" (1903) is important for its interpretive approach to the facts of Norris's life. Millard stresses Norris's profound feelings for nature and the West as revealed in his actions and temperament in the years just before his death.[17] Another valuable account by one of Norris's contemporaries, though not published until much later, is Ernest Peixotto's "Romanticist Under the Skin" (1933).[18] The essays by Clift and Millard, plus other memoirs and numerous obituaries, have been conveniently brought together in Joseph R. McElrath, Jr.'s recent compilation, "Frank Norris: Early Posthumous Responses" (1979).[19] McElrath has used these sources, combined with a shrewd reading of Norris's works, to offer a stimulating reinterpretation of the career. "Frank Norris: A Biographical Essay" (1978), reprinted below, argues persuasively that Norris experienced a considerable growth in maturity in the years following his marriage and the consolidation of his commitment to serious writing.

Although not strictly biographical, other new work has contributed to revising the picture of Norris, in Joseph Katz's words, as a person "perennially young, a writer talented with boyish exuberance . . . but lacking the discipline that would have tamed it into something more."[20] Katz's bibliographical study of Norris's journalism leads him to see Norris as a "professional" who, compared with the traditional image, is "more serious, more versatile, and more prolific."[21] Taking another tack, Don Graham's "Frank Norris and *Les Jeunes*: Architectural Criticism and Aesthetic Values" (1978) explores the community of opinions shared by Norris and his friends with regard to public taste in the 1890s, thereby revealing Norris's informed perception of San Francisco's aesthetic ambience in the period.[22] The unavoidable implication of such recent work is that from a biographical and cultural standpoint there is still much to be learned about Norris.

The small sampling of reviews reprinted here is part of an emerging revisionist understanding of how Norris was regarded by his contemporary reviewers. These reviews offer in miniature what will be treated much more comprehensively in Joseph R. McElrath, Jr.'s forthcoming volume, *Frank Norris: The Critical Reception*. In an important introduction to their *Frank Norris: A Reference Guide* Crisler and McElrath have demonstrated the inaccuracy of several long-standing misconceptions about Norris's early reputation. First, Norris did not receive a "cold reception" prior to the publication of *The Octopus*, nor did this work represent a major breakthrough for the cause of realism.[23] Second, Norris's minor works, almost universally held in low esteem today, won considerable favor among contemporary reviewers. Howells, for example, praised *Moran of the Lady Letty* for its "being so boldly circumstanced in the light of common day."[24] Another work that should be consulted with regard to Norris's contemporary reception is the first critical book on Norris, Ernest Marchand's still valuable *Frank Norris, A Study* (1942).

The reviews reprinted below begin with a sparkling response by fellow Californian Geraldine Bonner to *Moran of the Lady Letty* (1898). Howells and Bonner were by no means the sole admirers of Norris's first book. Well over half of the reviews listed in *Frank Norris: A Reference Guide* are quite favorable. Norris's second novel, *McTeague* (1899), aroused a firestorm of praise and disapproval. The controversy surrounding *McTeague* is well represented in the debate sparked by John D. Barry's excited and insightful review in the *Literary World*. Shortly after his review appeared, it was answered in the same publication by Edward and Madeline Vaughn Abbot who, while conceding Barry's claim that Norris was a powerful writer, rejected categorically Norris's "grossness for the sake of grossness." Among the most eloquent champions of *McTeague* were, again, Howells, and a young journalist named Willa Cather. Howells recognized in *McTeague* the promise of a "continental American fiction" that he had glimpsed in *Moran of the Lady Letty*. Cather's review contains one of the most prescient remarks ever registered about Norris's work. Contrasting his method with the characteristic tendencies of fiction in his day, she put her finger on one of his major strengths: "This power of mature and comprehensive description is very unusual among the younger American writers. Most of them observe the world through a temperament, and are more occupied with their medium than the objects they watch."[25]

If *McTeague* shocked some Norris readers, *Blix* (1899) caught many by surprise. It seemed improbable that such an amiable romance could have come from the same hand that had produced the depressing, sordid *McTeague*. In a wonderful vernacular tone Willa Cather exulted over Norris's creation of a "red-blooded newspaper man," the first of its kind in American fiction. Like many other reviewers, she was struck by Norris's "versatility." Also of particular interest is the anonymous review in the *Washington Times* that rates *Blix* as the best work yet of a completely original American talent who in rapid succession had produced three works that shared only one trait, their "fidelity to nature."

Norris's next novel, *A Man's Woman* (1900), proved to be as shocking as *McTeague*, with one reviewer after another taking exception to explicit surgical details in the celebrated amputation scene. Universally held in the lowest esteem today, *A Man's Woman* was by no means so regarded when it came out. There were as many favorable as unfavorable reviews, although they tended to be briefer and less analytically interesting than those that had greeted *McTeague*. *A Man's Woman* sold better than either of Norris's previous novels.[26]

The Octopus (1901) saw the consolidation of Norris's growing stature as a writer of significance. Western and Eastern critics alike recognized the epic national intentions of the novel and responded with some of the broadest praise yet bestowed upon Norris. Reviews of *The Octopus* that remain vital today are those which identified issues that continue to engage present-day criticism of Norris's work. One of the most frequent questions raised about the novel is whether it is philosophically consistent. The question was first addressed, with a negative answer, in a review by Wallace Rice. Another critically prescient review was Frederic T. Cooper's, which identified two critical problems that are still alive: the blend of realism and romance, in his view an uneasy blend; and the allegorical machinery that to his mind had got out of hand. Overall, reviews of *The Octopus* reflect a lively engagement with a novelist perceived to have great if mixed powers.

Reviews of *The Pit* (1902) may have been affected somewhat by the impact of Norris's sudden death. Many reviews contained an elegiac note, and even an unfavorable review seemed to reflect in its title the mood of fervent loss that permeated most reviews: "A Dispassionate Examination of Frank Norris's Posthumous Novel." As with *The Octopus*, reviewers who detected minor faults often had only the highest praise for the novel as a whole, for Norris's insight into large forces underpinning American life, for his ability to invest such abstractions with vividness and drama. There were even some reviewers who ranked *The Pit* ahead of *The Octopus*, finding evidence in the second volume of the wheat trilogy of a firmer control, a surer mastery of characterization and symbolism.[27] On the whole, however, the reviews of *The Pit* were less lively and less critically engaging than were those of several of the earlier novels.

By 1914 when *Vandover and the Brute* appeared, there was nothing particularly new or shocking about Norris's brand of realism. As one reviewer observed, "It shows how far we have traveled from the standards of twenty years ago that *Vandover and the Brute* will find few readers to-day to question its morality, or even its propriety."[28] The recollection of Norris's untimely death colored many reviews, most of which devoted considerable space to relating the supposed strange circumstances of the manuscript's survival, a story concocted by Norris's brother, Charles

Norris. As with everything Norris wrote, opinions about *Vandover's* worth varied wildly, one reviewer calling it a novel "of which any writer might be proud,"[29] another saying that its youthful author, had he lived, "would have rewritten . . . or burned" this novel.[30]

Following Norris's death, several retrospective overviews were published. One of the most noteworthy was by William Dean Howells, who took the occasion to assert Norris's importance. Howells's opinion still has the power to surprise, for he rated Norris ahead of Stephen Crane: "What Norris did, not merely what he dreamed of doing, was of vaster frame, and inclusive of imaginative attention far beyond those of the only immediate contemporary to be matched with him."[31] This piece is also interesting for its increased estimation of *McTeague,* a novel that Howells had already strongly praised. A similarly lofty appraisal was made by Hamlin Garland. Reprinted below, Garland's essay identifies several permanently interesting elements of Norris's fiction. Of particular interest in the light of many contemporary and subsequent misreadings of *The Octopus* is Garland's firm perception that the farmers in the novel are "immense land lords, oppressors in their own right."

Studies of Norris's minor works have not been numerous. Of the three modes—popular novel, short fiction, and journalism—the novels have kindled the most interest. The best sustained discussion of the "middle trilogy" (*Moran of the Lady Letty, Blix,* and *A Man's Woman*) is Donald Pizer's "The Masculine-Feminine Ethic in Frank Norris's Popular Novels" (1964), reprinted below. While acknowledging that none of these novels is ever likely to be "rediscovered," Pizer believes that they merit study because of what they reveal about Norris's attitudes and what they disclose about the major novels. Pizer shows how in each work the central issue is the achievement of a proper masculinity through the dynamic interaction of male and female roles. Beyond Pizer's essay and brief discussions of the popular novels in book-length studies of Norris,[32] there has been a handful of articles published on these novels. One is John R. Sherwood's description of Norris's borrowings from accounts of polar explorations for many of the incidents in *A Man's Woman* ("Norris and the *Jeannette,*" 1958).[33] A second is James R. Giles's analysis of the theme of *Moran of the Lady Letty* as a complex psychology of "beneficial atavism," a process by which a character achieves maturity through the integration of instincts and civilizing factors ("Beneficial Atavism in Frank Norris and Jack London," 1969).[34] In a pair of recent articles Joseph R. McElrath, Jr., has taken fresh looks at *Moran* and *Blix.* In "The Erratic Design of *Moran of the Lady Letty*" (1977) McElrath concedes that *Moran* was written as a pot-boiler and remains an "unsatisfactory" work, but denies that it is the "cheap book" that many critics have charged.[35] By closely examining the management of point of view in *Moran,* McElrath discloses the possibility that Norris was deliberately parodying the conventions of romance-adventure fiction at the expense of the genteel audience which the work sought to titillate. McElrath's brief essay on *Blix* ("Allegory in Frank Norris's *Blix*: Its Relevance to *Vandover,*" 1979) examines another frequently derided element in Norris's fiction, the tendency to allegorize in a heavy-handed manner.[36] Granting that Norris's technique in *Blix* may be anything but subtle, McElrath still finds useful points to make in analyzing the use of nature as a measurement of health and sanity in this novel as in *The Octopus.*

There are even fewer studies of Norris's short fiction. Indeed, only minor source studies of a few individual stories have been published.[37] For the full body of Norris's considerable short story production, there is a useful unpublished survey of techniques and themes in Charles Kaplan's dissertation ("Frank Norris and the Craft of Fiction," 1952). Norris's journalism is another area of his work that needs attention. Only a few efforts have been directed at this side of his output. One is Joseph Kwiat's "The Newspaper Experience: Crane, Norris, and Dreiser" (1953), a study predicated upon a misperception of the nature of Norris's job with the *Wave.*[38] As Joseph Katz has demonstrated in his rejoinder, "Frank Norris and 'The Newspaper Experience,'" (1971), Norris never worked as a reporter for a daily newspaper as did Crane and Dreiser, and hence the skills he acquired were closer to those of a magazinist than a reporter.[39] Far and away the best work done on Norris's journalism is Robert A. Morace's "The Writer and His Middle Class Audience: Frank Norris, A Case in Point" (1980), reprinted below. Following Katz's lead in seeing Norris as a professional, Morace shows in detail how Norris varied his persona to fit the needs of his audience as well as transforming potentially dull material into lively, effective nonfiction.

Since the 1940s, *The Octopus* has been the most critically alive of Norris's novels, which is to say it has engendered the most articles, the most disagreement about its meanings and artistry. But in the past few years *McTeague* has come on to challenge *The Octopus* in producing reevaluations and interesting criticism. An indispensable source for coming to terms with *McTeague* is the Norton Critical Edition (1977), edited by Donald Pizer. This volume provides a reliable text and contains fascinating primary source material, including San Francisco newspaper accounts of the crime upon which Norris based the murder of Trina, as well as reprinting Norris's Harvard themes dealing with the roughhewn dentist. The volume also contains a generous offering of criticism. Much of this material, however, never takes us very far from the long-standing source-oriented approach to Norris, and that spells two things: Zola and Naturalism. Still it is good to have such articles in one place. The last section contains articles written through 1974, by such leading Norris critics as Maxwell Geismar, Richard Chase, Donald Pizer, and William B. Dillingham. Only one piece, however, Joseph H. Gardner's "Dickens, Romance, and *McTeague*: A Study in Mutual Interpretation" (1974) is exciting. By means of a careful comparatist approach, Gardner shows how Norris employed an essentially Dickensian mode in developing the grotesque yet all-too-human side of McTeague and especially Trina. What Gardner demonstrates is a possible ground for Norris's "peculiar modernity" in the writer's linking of sex and money.

The Norton Critical Edition is but one indicator of a renewed interest in *McTeague* in the 1970s. In 1975 alone, for example, four articles on *McTeague* were published. Although it might seem that approaching the novel from its naturalistic context would yield little that is new, Louis J. Budd's "Objectivity and Low Seriousness in American Naturalism" (1975) belies such an impression. Using *McTeague* as the centerpiece of a wide-ranging discussion of naturalism's unique contribution to fiction, Budd shows how Norris's compassion for the disenfranchised lower middle class had to be expressed in a tonal strategy that avoided both irony and sentimentality. Budd's approach, which applies rhetorical analysis to reveal "bold directions in tone," achieves a fresh perspective on naturalism by focusing on technique rather than ideology.[40] Another naturalistically-centered approach can be seen in Lewis Fried's "The Golden Brotherhood of *McTeague*" (1975), which substitutes economic determinism for heredity and environment as the all-shaping external force in *McTeague*. Though Fried's article contains some provocative remarks on isolated elements, such as Norris's almost Marxist portrait of the Jew as an alienated economic entity, the article is too brief and too general to constitute a sustained reading of the novel.[41]

Other recent critical approaches to *McTeague* represent further attempts to see the novel from new perspectives. Joseph R. McElrath, Jr.'s "The Comedy of Frank Norris's *McTeague*" (1975) concentrates on tone but, unlike Budd's findings, emphasizes the presence of farcical humor, not the creation of a compassionate attitude. McElrath's is a corrective piece directed at critics overly impressed by the pathetic and/or tragic nature of the second half of the novel. McElrath instead calls attention to Norris's technique of "ironic inflation" used to create a vaudevillian mood in the novel's first half.[42] Another refreshing recent essay on *McTeague* is achieved by film critic George Wead's study of the relationship of the famous film *Greed* to its source, *McTeague*. In "Frank Norris: His Share of *Greed*" (1977) Wead seeks to counterbalance the extravagant praise lavished upon von Stroheim's film by film critics who claim that the greatness of *Greed* transcends *McTeague* while blaming the film's weaknesses on too faithful a reliance upon Norris's novel. As one example, Wead shows how it is von Stroheim's vision, not Norris's, that builds the film around the theme of greed. By close reference to the text of the novel, Wead develops his case that Norris is a "novelist of remarkable moral complexity."[43]

One of the standard approaches to *McTeague*—and to Norris's work in general—has been the exploration of sources. Donald Pizer's account of the background of *McTeague,* excerpted from his influential *The Novels of Frank Norris* (1966), is the best example of the kind of study that firmly places Norris in the Zolaesque-Naturalistic tradition. Other important source work on *McTeague* preceding Pizer's includes Lars Ahnebrink's *The Beginnings of Naturalism in American Fiction* (1950), which cites many parallels between Norris and Zola; and Robert D. Lundy's unpublished dissertation, "The Making of *McTeague* and *The Octopus*" (1956), which contains a lengthy examination of the Polk Street background and Norris's Harvard themes. More recent source work includes Jesse S. Crisler's unpublished dissertation, "A Critical and Textual Study of Frank Norris's *McTeague*" (1973), which corrects some of Lundy's errors; and William B. Dillingham's *Frank Norris: Instinct and Art* (1969), which develops, as does Pizer's book, the influence of Cesare Lombroso's criminal theories of atavism upon the characterization of McTeague.

McTeague has also provoked a number of other critical approaches, including mythic, formalist, and psychological readings. One of the most controversial pieces is George W. Johnson's exercise in myth criticism, "The Frontier Behind Frank Norris's *McTeague*" (1962).[44] William B. Dillingham, for example, has taken strong exception to Johnson's depiction of McTeague as a Populist victim of city evils.[45] In sharp contrast, Warren French has hailed this essay as one "that no one making a study of Norris should fail to take into consideration."[46] French's own reading of *McTeague* in *Frank Norris* (1962) stresses an opposition between nature and urbane civilization that is similar to Johnson's thesis. Behind Johnson, one should note, lies Richard Chase's Populist interpretation of *McTeague* in his seminal *The American Novel and Its Tradition* (1957).

Suzy Bernstein Goldman's "*McTeague*: The Imagistic Network" (1972) is an example of an image-oriented New Critical approach to the novel.[47] Her identification of several major clusters of images yields some astute points such as, for example, the importance of "sacred objects" to McTeague; and the wealth of obsessive images, such as hands and teeth, comes close to suggesting Freudian implications. But when Goldman implies an intentional imagistic structure, she is perhaps less convincing. Still, her argument exemplifies the virtue of paying close attention to the discrete details of Norris's imagination. Another essay which examines previously overlooked elements in *McTeague* is Don Graham's "Art in *McTeague*" (1975), reprinted below. Concentrating upon the surprising degree of aesthetic documentation in the novel, Graham shows how such references are employed to measure the humanity of the characters and the disappointing culture in which they struggle to exist. An expanded version of this argument, with commentary on Norris's interest in popular culture, appears in Graham's *The Fiction of Frank Norris: The Aesthetic Context* (1978).

The best example of a psychological interpretation is George M. Spangler's "The Structure of *McTeague*" (1978), reprinted below. Spangler identifies a two-part division in the novel, labeling the two halves "realistic narrative" and "surrealistic nightmare," with the dividing point being McTeague's lapses back to sexual dormancy, not long after his marriage to Trina. Drawing upon popular Freudian psychology, Spangler explores "overt" and "latent" meanings in each half, disclosing that the real meaning is different from what the surface meaning suggests. Thus while instincts, especially sexual drives, are authorially denounced as dangerous in the first half, sexual instincts are shown in the action to produce positive, creative effects. Similarly, in the second half, which ostensibly is about greed, the real subject is fear of female sexuality, with Trina's all-consuming greed symbolizing sexual aggressiveness. One weakness of Spangler's approach is his reliance upon a kind of Freudian allegory that is sometimes hard to accept, as for example this interpretation of Marcus Schouler: "[he] represents in Freudian terms the father who punishes for the incestuous wishes underlying castration anxiety." Still, Spangler's effort to find a principle of "rhythmic unity" underlying *McTeague* is commendable.

Since the 1930s, when extended, formal analysis of Norris's works began to appear, *The Octopus* has produced more critical sparks than any of his other works, with the possible recent exception of *McTeague* as noted above. A useful work for reviewing the history of criticism of this novel is *Studies in The Octopus* (1969), compiled by Richard Allan Davison. Davison's little volume reprints reviews, plus excerpts from leading Norris critics through 1963, including Donald Pizer, Warren French, Charles C. Walcutt, and others. The underlying concern of this volume, as indeed of most criticism of *The Octopus* until recently, is whether the novel achieves philosophical coherence, and if so, exactly what its philosophical premises are. Two of the major articles included in

Davison are George W. Meyer's "A New Interpretation of *The Octopus*" (1943) and Donald Pizer's "The Concept of Nature in Frank Norris's *The Octopus*" (1962). Meyer's importance lies in his insistence that the wheat ranchers are self-serving and at least partially responsible for a fate too often blamed entirely upon the railroad by readers and critics eager to see *The Octopus* as a muckraking document. Pizer's essay, one of several that he has written on *The Octopus*, remains the most formidable attempt to explain the intellectual background of Norris's structuring of the novel.[48] Pizer's widely influential thesis is that the symbols and themes of *The Octopus* express a doctrine of evolutionary theism—an optimistic version of Darwinism that Norris came into contact with principally through the teaching of Joseph Le Conte.

As with *McTeague*, considerable source work has been done on *The Octopus*. Robert D. Lundy's study of the economic background, from his unpublished dissertation, "The Making of *McTeague* and *The Octopus*" (1956), provides extensive examples and commentary to show how Norris handled complex economic facts in a dramatic fashion. Also of interest in regard to the economic sources is the early study of the Mussel Slough episode by Irving McKee ("Notable Memorials to Mussel Slough," 1948).[49] Two recent critics have turned from economic and philosophical backgrounds to consider the novel's autobiographical and artistic roots. Charles L. Crow in "The Real Vanamee and His Influence on Frank Norris's *The Octopus*" (1974) shows how Norris used both the personality and writings of his friend Bruce Porter to create the mystic Vanamee.[50] Don Graham in "Studio Art in *The Octopus*" (1973) focuses on the salon artists lampooned in the San Francisco scenes, and identifies the thinly veiled presence of actual figures such as Japanese poet Yone Noguchi.[51] Graham's *The Fiction of Frank Norris: The Aesthetic Context* (1978) contains a much more extensive discussion of the aesthetic sources of *The Octopus*.

Connections between Norris's novel and the French Naturalistic tradition have been remarked upon since the earliest reviews of *The Octopus*. The latest discussion of the subject, Philip Walker's "*The Octopus* and Zola: A New Look" (1967), is disappointing in its failure to move beyond superficial stylistic matters into a much-needed comparatist analysis on the order of Gardner's study of *McTeague* and Dickens.[52] Searching for a new intellectual context in which to evaluate naturalism, James K. Folsom in "The Wheat and the Locomotive: Norris and Naturalistic Esthetics" (1975) adopts a Jungian perspective, with Norris as his major example.[53] The results are mixed. Folsom contends that naturalism often presents a dualistic interpretation of nature and that such dualism characterizes Norris's work from *Moran* through *The Octopus*. With works like *McTeague,* Folsom has nothing useful to say; in fact, his reading of this novel as a parable of greed whose central character is merely an animal is almost atavistically wrong. But with *The Octopus,* the Jungian thesis yields some insights. Folsom argues that ranchers and railroad management alike fail to see nature in its true doubleness, the ranchers ignoring the animal side, and S. Behrman and his cohorts ignoring the vegetable side. Norris's work, however, still awaits an adequate Jungian reading.

Proving that almost nothing has been settled in critical debate about *The Octopus,* two critics have examined the novel in terms of literary modes and reached diametrically opposite conclusions. In *Heroic Fiction: The Epic Tradition and American Novels of the Twentieth Century* (1970) Leonard Lutwack discusses the compatability of four literary forms in *The Octopus*: epic, comedy, tragedy, and romance. Concentrating on the epic, Lutwack finds many Homeric parallels in the novel, some of which seem forced and unconvincing as, for example, comparing Magnus Derrick to "a kind of Agamemnon."[54] Lutwack faults Norris only for stylistic lapses into bombast, seeing no serious problems in the combination of literary modes. But in a long article published the same year as Lutwack's analysis, William L. Vance adopted a more rigorous genre approach, and reached opposite conclusions about the artistic coherence of *The Octopus.* Vance discusses in great detail the presence of five fictional modes: Allegorical Melodrama, Naturalism, Tragedy, Realism, and Romance. It is the last, employed to tell the story of the shepherd Vanamee, that in Vance's judgment disrupts the rest. His article, "Romance in *The Octopus,*" reprinted below, is a model of responsible negative criticism.

The most fruitful positive reexaminations of *The Octopus* since Pizer's groundbreaking work of the 1950s and 1960s are both reprinted below. Richard Allan Davison's "Frank Norris's *The Octopus*: Some Observations on Vanamee, Shelgrim and St. Paul" (1975) explores the formal structure of the work in the light of Norris's own ideas about Aristotelian form. Davison also explicates a moral theme completely different from the old view of Norris's characters as operating in a deterministic universe. In Davison's view Norris "portrays a complex world whose inhabitants are clearly responsible for their actions." Davison locates the source of his moral optimism in the teachings of Christianity, particularly St. Paul, as filtered through the musings of Vanamee. What Davison accomplishes, in effect, is to reinforce Pizer's argument of coherency based upon evolutionary themes with a coherency based upon conventional Christian imagery and motifs. Another "Christian" reading of *The Octopus* is offered by Joseph R. McElrath, Jr. in an essay published here for the first time, "Frank Norris's *The Octopus*: The Christian Ethic as Pragmatic Response." McElrath tackles head-on the continuously vexing problem of seeing Presley and Vanamee as spokesmen for a cosmic optimism when so many facts previously recorded in the novel contravene such a view. McElrath's solution is that Norris presented a macrocosmic complexity that could not be resolved, but that he also presented a specific, practical view of what an individual character, working within the small sphere of his own emotions and intellect, could do about his moral nature. In the most complete analysis yet made of Annixter, McElrath demonstrates how this character's experiential discovery of *agapè* fulfills an ethic that derives ultimately from the Sermon on the Mount. A further strength of McElrath's reading is its grounding in Norris's biography and oeuvre.

Though *The Pit* has had its admirers, from Owen Wister to recent critics such as Larzer Ziff, it has never generated anything like the exegetical interest provoked by *McTeague* or *The Octopus*.[55] Besides chapters in book-length studies of Norris, only a handful of articles have dealt with *The Pit*. One is Charles Kaplan's "Norris's Use of Sources in *The Pit*" (1953), a study of parallels between the career of Joseph Leiter, an actual wheat speculator, and that of Norris's fictional Curtis Jadwin.[56] Another more loosely focused study is Michael Millgate's "The Novelist and the Businessman: Henry James, Edith Wharton, Frank Norris" (1959), which compares *The Pit*, in Millgate's view an underrated novel, with Zola's *L'Argent*.[57] A general appreciation of the novel appears in James D. Hart's introduction to a reprint of *The Pit* (1970).

In the late 1970s an upsurge of interest in *The Pit* is discernible. An important precursor of this trend is Warren French, whose chapter on *The Pit* from his book *Frank Norris* (1962) is reprinted below. Unlike his fellow critics Donald Pizer and William B. Dillingham who also wrote books on Norris during the 1960s, French feels that *The Pit* signalled a growth in personal and artistic maturity on Norris's part. Of particular importance in French's interpretation is his emphasis upon Laura Jadwin as the central element in the novel. In three recent studies *The Pit* receives respectful explicative attention. A chapter of Don Graham's *The Fiction of Frank Norris: The Aesthetic Context* (1978) is devoted to considering the dramatic structure of the novel. Graham traces the motif of role-playing as exemplified in Laura Jadwin's actions and explores the consequences of her heavy investment in aesthetic and sensuous pleasures. A similar emphasis on the novel's heroine informs Joseph Katz's "Eroticism in American Literary Realism" (1977), which uses *The Pit* to highlight a discussion of how writers of Realism brought sexuality into fiction by means of subtle, oblique details and symbolism.

Excerpted below, Katz's demonstration of adultery between Laura and the artist Sheldon Corthell is a superb bit of explication. Richard Allan Davison's "A Reading of Frank Norris's *The Pit*" (1979) follows the method of his approach to *The Octopus* in that it carefully considers Norris's probable intentions, then examines in close detail the characterization and structure.[58] As in his reading of *The Octopus,* Davison finds not naturalistic themes but those drawn from a half-Stoic, half-Christian tradition that stresses individual moral responsibility.

Vandover and the Brute, Norris's first or last novel depending upon how one views the curious circumstances of its early composition and posthumous publication, has stimulated less criticism than *McTeague* or *The Octopus,* but criticism of keener interest than that generated by *The Pit.* As early as 1948, *Vandover* was the subject of a major essay by Charles Child Walcutt. His "The Naturalism of *Vandover and the Brute,*" excerpted below, examines *Vandover* as a modern tragedy that falls short of achieving truly tragic stature because of too strident didacticism and an incomplete presentation of the external forces that destroy the protagonist. While Walcutt believes that Norris's power derives in large part from the interplay of free will and scientific determinism, Stanley Cooperman locates the tension between hero and fate in a totally different context. In "Frank Norris and the Werewolf of Guilt" (1959), Cooperman places *Vandover* and *McTeague* against a Christian background, specifically within a Calvinist duality of body and spirit.[59] Cooperman's thesis is more interesting than his demonstration, since he oversimplifies the novels by quoting didactic passages out of context.

A very valuable corrective to Cooperman's practice, all too common in the criticism of Naturalistic writers, appears in Donald Pizer's "The Problem of Philosophy in the Novel" (1970).[60] Pizer shows how Naturalistic novelists such as Dreiser and Norris employed scientific content and imagery not for their value as raw ideas but as metaphors to describe psychological states. Pizer uses a social-Darwinist passage from *Vandover* to demonstrate that conventional scientific metaphors are being used to represent the hero's fear, not to exhibit the author's naive thinking. An earlier article by Pizer is quite different in thrust and more typical of his always reliable approach to Norris. "Evolutionary Ethical Dualism in Frank Norris's *Vandover and the Brute* and *McTeague*" (1961) is a genesis-oriented study that examines the emergence of the *Vandover* plot in the Harvard themes, then explores Norris's use of contemporary scientific data to develop the motif of paresis, the disease symbolized in the novel by lycanthropy. Pizer also analyzes various strengths and weaknesses of structure and language in *Vandover.*[61] An indispensible source for further study of the Harvard themes as well as the thorny problem of the composition and publication of the novel is James D. Hart's long introduction to *A Novelist in the Making: A Collection of Student Themes, and the Novels* Blix *and* Vandover and the Brute (1970).

As with *The Pit*, *Vandover* has come in for renewed attention in the past few years. In a new paperback edition of *Vandover* (1978) Warren French proposes in his introduction that Norris, along with Stephen Crane and Kate Chopin, should be seen as novelists belonging to a short but intense period of decadent revolt. Thus *Vandover*, like *The Awakening*, is a novel about the loss of energy, the lack of drive that animates the heroes of quite different writers like Horatio Alger and Henry James. French's new assessment supersedes his chapter on *Vandover* in *Frank Norris* (1962), which less convincingly depicts *Vandover* as an expression of Norris's commitment to anti-urban Populism. Two other recent studies of *Vandover* explore different elements to arrive at strikingly similar conclusions. In *The Fiction of Frank Norris: The Aesthetic Context* (1978) Don Graham veers away from conventional naturalistic interpretations to argue that Vandover's defeat arises from a failure of imagination and sensibility within himself. Graham tracks the growth and decline of Vandover's sensibility as reflected in a wealth of aesthetic objects and symbols. In "Frank Norris's *Vandover and the Brute*: Narrative Technique and the Socio-Critical Viewpoint" (1976), reprinted below, Joseph R. McElrath Jr. stresses Norris's complex management of a reflector technique to dramatize the confusions and defeats stemming from Vandover's failure to appreciate the nuances and codes of sexual conduct in a rigid, smug society. Like Graham, McElrath credits Norris with both intelligence and skill.

The section labeled "general overviews" is an eclectic category in which to discuss numerous types of approaches to Norris that either do not fit comfortably into the other categories devised above or that deal with all the works rather than one or two. From the contemporary eulogies of Howells and Garland to the present, a large number of essays devoted to synthesizing past and present opinions about Norris into a "definitive" assessment have been attempted. Not one has accomplished such a purpose; not one has defined the essential Frank Norris. The weaker efforts in this vein tend to rehash previous truisms of Norris criticism without developing new insights or applying carefully defined critical principles to the analysis of texts. Two examples may be cited from among many. H. E. Francis's "A Reconsideration of Frank Norris" (1959) does little more than make the oft-repeated points that Norris confused his novelistic impulses with his moralistic ones and possessed both a youthful and a romantic nature.[62] Bryant N. Wyatt's "Naturalism as Expediency in the Novels of Frank Norris" (1971) is possibly the most reductive essay on Norris and naturalism ever written. According to Wyatt, Norris merely used naturalism as an easy way to explain the themes of his fiction.[63]

On the other hand, some excellent essays on the corpus of Norris's work have been written. One that seeks to systematize Norris as a philosophical thinker—admittedly not an easy task—is Arnold L. Goldsmith's "The Development of Frank Norris's Philosophy" (1958). Although Goldsmith relies somewhat naively upon very minor journalistic pieces, overall he succeeds in tracing a movement in Norris's thought from pessimistic naturalism to a more optimistic stance in his last two novels.[64] A different synthesis is sought in George W. Johnson's "Frank Norris and Romance" (1961), which contains a comprehensive discussion of how Norris integrated romance and realism into a successful texture that united the claims and techniques of two major schools of fiction.[65]

Other broad-gauged approaches should be mentioned to indicate the kind of healthy eclecticism that Norris studies could benefit from in the future. The first, Henry Dan Piper's "Frank Norris and Scott Fitzgerald" (1959), offers conclusive evidence to show Norris's impact upon a major writer of a later generation.[66] The essential relationships established by Piper have been amplified by other articles along the same lines. Richard Astro, for example, traced in great detail the numerous affinities between Fitzgerald's *The Beautiful and Damned* and Norris's *Vandover and the Brute* ("*Vandover and the Brute* and *The Beautiful and Damned*: A Search for Thematic and Stylistic Reinterpretations," (1968).[67] More recently, in a pair of articles S. S. Moorty has stressed, on the one hand in "Norris and Fitzgerald as Moralists" (1976) the common concern with moral action evinced by the two writers, and on the other in "Frank Norris and Scott Fitzgerald: Two Sides on the Same Coin" (1976), the optimism of Norris as contrasted with the pessimism of Fitzgerald.[68] Influence studies of Norris begin and end with Fitzgerald, though William B. Dillingham has pointed out the need for investigating the possible influence of Norris upon such writers as William Faulkner and Willa Cather.[69]

An influential early perspective on Norris is Charles B. Hoffmann's "Norris and the Responsibility of the Novelist" (1955).[70] Hoffmann's essay remains important for its argument that Norris can best be understood by broadening if not eliminating the context of naturalism in order to recognize the large redemptive role played by love in his later novels. Another is William B. Dillingham's "Frank Norris and The Genteel Tradition" (1960). Reprinted below, this is a corrective piece aimed at restoring Norris to the tradition against which he is so often seen as being in total revolt. Dillingham identifies several characteristics of Norris's fiction that link him to the Genteel Tradition, most having to do with his presentation of sexual experience. Another useful corrective essay is Glen A. Love's "Frank Norris's Western Metropolitans" (1976), reprinted below. Love focuses on two often overlooked dimensions of Norris's work: his identity as a Westerner and his positive, complex portrayal of urban life. Love's article is a much needed rebuttal to the widely held view that Norris should be seen as an agrarian-directed Populist.[71]

The present collection, as indicated earlier, is aimed at projecting an emerging picture of Norris as a vital, still undefined, and interesting writer. It would, of course, have been possible to build another kind of collection, presenting him as a museum piece, exhibit B in a Natural History of Naturalism; that Norris is a dead-letter. The present one, it is hoped, is not. Much good work has been done on Norris; much remains to be done.

NOTES

1. George M. Spangler, "The Structure of *McTeague*," *English Studies*, 59 (February, 1978), 48.

2. Jesse S. Crisler and Joseph R. McElrath, Jr., *Frank Norris: A Reference Guide* (Boston: G. K. Hall & Co., 1974), p. xiii.

3. Crisler and McElrath, p. xiii.

4. "A California Novelist," *Washington Times* (October 15, 1899), p. 8, part 2.

5. Crisler and McElrath, p. xiii.

6. *American Literary Realism*, 8 (Autumn 1975), 307–319.

7. *American Literary Realism*, 1 (Fall 1967), 84–89.

8. *Bulletin of Bibliography*, 22 (1959), 227–228.

9. *Proof 3* (1973), pp. 155–220; *Proof 3* (1973), pp. 221–252.

10. *Frank Norris: A Reference Guide*, p. vii.

11. "Frank Norris (1870–1902)," p. 88.

12. "Frank Norris" in *Fifteen American Authors Before 1900: Bibliographic Essays on Research and Criticism*, edited by Robert A. Rees and Earl N. Harbert (Madison: University of Wisconsin Press, 1971), p. 311.

13. *American Literary Realism*, 6 (Summer 1973), 251.

14. *Quarterly News-Letter* of the Book Club of California, 41 (Spring 1976), 38–40.

15. *Bohemian Club Library Notes* (February, 1973), 1–4.

16. *Pacific Monthly*, 17 (March, 1907), 313–332.

17. *Out West*, 18 (January, 1903), 49–55.

18. *Saturday Review of Literature*, 9 (May 15, 1933), 613–615.

19. *American Literary Realism*, 12 (Spring 1979), 1–76.

20. "The Shorter Publications of Frank Norris: A Checklist," p. 155. The per-

sistence of the old image of Norris is evident even in a good book on the period like Larzer Ziff's *The American 1890s: Life and Times of a Lost Generation* (New York: Viking Press, 1966), wherein Norris is treated under the heading of "Life Without Style."

21. "The Shorter Publications of Frank Norris: A Checklist," p. 155.

22. *American Literary Realism*, 11 (Autumn 1978) 235–242.

23. *Frank Norris: A Reference Guide*, p. x.

24. "American Letter," *Literature*, 3 (December 17, 1898), 57.

25. "Books and Magazines," *Pittsburgh Leader*, March 31, 1899, p. 8.

26. *Frank Norris: A Reference Guide*, p. xi.

27. For representative expressions of this opinion, see B. O. Flower, "The Pit," *The Arena*, 29 (April, 1903), 440–442; and "Frank Norris's 'The Pit,'" *The Bookman* (English), 23 (March, 1903), 246–247.

28. Anonymous, "Novel by Frank Norris," *New York Review of Books*, 62 (April 12, 1914), 181–182.

29. E. F. E. [Edwin Francis Edgett], "Norris's Posthumous Novel," *Boston Evening Transcript*, April 22, 1914, p. 8, part 2.

30. Anonymous, "Derelict by Destiny," London *Pall Mall Gazette*, June 16, 1914, p. 9.

31. "Frank Norris," *North American Review*, 175 (December, 1902), 769–770.

32. See, for example, Ernest Marchand, *Frank Norris, A Study* (1942); Warren French, *Frank Norris* (1962); William B. Dillingham, *Frank Norris: Instinct and Art* (1969); and Don Graham, *The Fiction of Frank Norris: The Aesthetic Context* (1978). Pizer's article is reprinted in his *The Novels of Frank Norris* (1966).

33. *Philological Quarterly*, 37 (April, 1958), 242–252.

34. *Western American Literature*, 4 (Spring 1969), 15–27.

35. *American Literary Realism*, 10 (Spring 1977), 114–124.

36. *Markham Review*, 8 (Winter 1979), 25–27.

37. Such source studies include the following: John S. Hill, "Poe's 'Fall of the House of Usher' and Frank Norris's Early Short Stories," *Huntington Library Quarterly*, 26 (October, 1962), 111–112; John S. Hill, "The Influence of Cesare Lombroso on Frank Norris's Early Fiction," *American Literature*, 42 (March, 1970), 89–91; and Joseph R. McElrath, Jr., "A Source for Norris's 'A Deal in Wheat.'" *American Literary Realism*, 11 (Spring 1978), 141. The most interesting source study of a Norris short story is Stephen Tatum's "Norris's Debt in 'Lauth' to LeMattre's 'On The Transfusion of Blood,'" *American Literary Realism*, 11 (Autumn 1978), 243–248. Also of interest is the publication by John K. Swensson of a newly discovered Norris story, "'The Great Corner in Hannibal and St. Jo': A Previously Unpublished Short Story by Frank Norris," *American Literary Realism*, 4 (Summer 1971), 205–226. In "'The Great Corner in Hannibal & St. Jo': Another Look" *American Literary Realism*, 10 (1977), 213–214, Wayne W. Westbrook documents Norris's generally impressive command of stockmarket terminology.

38. *Nineteenth Century Fiction*, 8 (September, 1953), 99–117.

39. *American Literary Realism*, 4 (Winter 1971), 73–77.

40. *Prospects*, edited by Jack Salzman (New York: Burt Franklin and Co., 1975), I, 41–61.

41. *Zeitschrift fur Anglistik und Amerikanistik*, 23 (January, 1975), 36–40.

42. *Studies in American Humor*, 2 (October, 1975), 88–95.

43. *The Classic American Novel and the Movies*, edited by Gerald Peary and Roger Shatzkin (New York: Frederick Ungar, 1977), p. 151.

44. *Huntington Library Quarterly*, 26, (November, 1962), 91–104.

45. "Frank Norris" in *Fifteen American Authors Before 1900: Bibliographic Essays on Research and Criticism*, p. 325.

46. "Frank Norris (1870–1902)," p. 87.

47. *Western American Literature*, 7 (1972), 83–89.

48. Pizer's other essays on *The Octopus* are: "Another Look at 'The Octopus,'" *Nineteenth-Century Fiction*, X (December, 1955), 217–224; and "Synthetic Criticism and Frank Norris; Or, Mr. Marx, Mr. Taylor, and *The Octopus*," *American Literature*, 34 (January, 1963), 532–541.

49. *Pacific Historical Review*, 17 (February, 1948), 19–27.

50. *Western American Literature*, 9 (August, 1974), 131–139.

51. *American Literature*, 44 (January, 1973), 657–666.

52. *Symposium*, 21 (Summer 1967), 155–165.

53. *American Literary Naturalism: A Reassessment*, edited by Yoshinobu Hakutani and Lewis Fried (Heidelberg: Carl Winter, 1975), pp. 57–74.

54. Carbondale: Southern Illinois University Press, 1970, p. 27.

55. See *The American 1890s: Life and Times of a Lost Generation*, p. 271.

56. *American Literature*, 25 (March, 1953), 75–84.

57. *Studi Americani*, 5 (1959), 161–189.

58. *The Stoic in American Literature*, edited by Duane J. MacMillan (Toronto: University of Toronto Press, 1979), 77–94.

59. *Modern Language Quarterly*, 20 (September, 1959), 252–58.

60. *Bucknell Review*, 18 (Spring 1970), 53–62.

61. *PMLA*, 76 (December, 1961), 552–560.

62. *Emory University Quarterly*, 15 (June, 1959), 110–118.

63. *Markham Review*, 2 (February, 1971), 83–87.

64. *Studies in Honor of John Wilcox*, edited by A. Doyle Wallace and Woodburn O. Ross (Detroit: Wayne State University Press, 1958), pp. 175–194.

65. *American Literature*, 33 (March, 1961), 52–63.

66. *Huntington Library Quarterly*, 19 (August, 1956), 393–400.

67. *Modern Fiction Studies*, 16 (Winter 1968), 379–413.

68. *Studies in American Literature: Essays in Honour of William Mulder*, edited by Jagdish Chander and Narindar S. Pradhan (Delhi: Oxford University Press, 1976), pp. 119–126; *Utah Academy Proceedings*, 53 (1976), 29–34.

69. *Frank Norris: Instinct and Art* (Lincoln: University of Nebraska Press, 1969), p. 168, n. 2.

70. *South Atlantic Quarterly*, 54 (October, 1955), 508–515.

71. Another recent article that examines Norris in relation to the West is Donald Pizer's "Frank Norris and the Frontier as Popular Idea in America," *Amerikastudien*, 23 (1978), 230–239. Pizer shows how Norris, like Theodore Roosevelt, combined the thesis of the Anglo-Saxon march with Turner's thesis of unique individualism. The result was a popular synthesis that helped explain America's progress from agrarianism to industrialism.

Frank Norris:
A Biographical Essay

Joseph R. McElrath, Jr.[*]

Images of Norris's personality produced since the 1932 publication of Franklin Walker's *Frank Norris: A Biography*[1] differ in certain minor ways. But, for the most part, biographers and critics have amplified rather than significantly altered the portrait he executed. Ernest Marchand provided a fuller picture of the background of Norris's life and works; Warren French and Donald Pizer more closely examined his thought; and William B. Dillingham described in detail the spontaneous (i.e., "instinctive") nature of Norris's personality and its artistic consequences.[2] Much has been added to our understanding of Norris; but it is in the context of Walker's biography that the "boy Zola" still stands.

This is the situation, and it is likely to remain so because of the *kind* of information Walker had available to him. He interviewed friends and associates of the writer; we no longer have access to such invaluable information sources. There are, however, three bodies of data that can be reexamined today should we wish to call into question or add to Walker's observations. First, there is much information that can yet be excavated from newspapers and periodicals which earlier searchers have overlooked. It is still possible to recover previously unnoticed facts from the late 1880s and the 1890s, and it is simply a matter of time before the more devoted scholars further flesh-out the Norris we now know.[3]

There are, second, the published works by Norris which have not yet been exhausted in terms of their biographical relevance. Don B. Graham, in a forthcoming book, makes it plain that the novels *can* yield new information if the appropriate questions are posed. In focusing on the aesthetic sensibility of Norris, Graham has discovered dimensions of the works and the personality that were long begging to be observed.[4]

Third, there are the early posthumous writings about Norris—essays of a eulogy-memoir character—that truly merit reconsideration. When this body of data is examined in light of what the novels, short stories,

*[*]Reprinted from *American Literary Realism*, 11 (Autumn 1978), 219–234, by permission of *American Literary Realism* and the author.

and journalistic pieces reveal about their author's personality, some interesting facts immediately stand out in relief. The most dramatic fact involves what seems to be a remarkable contradiction in terms. For while the works point to one kind of Norris, the early posthumous writings posit another, different personality. The purpose of this essay, then, is to expand upon Walker's assignment of personality traits and clarify an apparent paradox in Norris's life.

Walker's post-"Jazz Age" biography has recalled to many the sensational characteristics of F. Scott Fitzgerald's public image. Walker's Norris did not leap into fountain pools; but he is depicted as a zany fraternity-boy who never lost his zestful appreciation for college "high jinks." Norris was the "Fiji" who devised the "Pig Dinner" which is still celebrated by the brothers of Phi Gamma Delta. He was the married professional writer of thirty years who sent to an annual fraternity dinner at the Poodle Dog Café in San Francisco a lengthy bit of comical doggerel—"An Exile's Toast"—when business made it impossible for him to attend. He was the father who named a daughter Billy because he thought it would be fun to call the name and have a female appear. (This was, it should be noted, perfectly consistent for a novelist who named one male character Dolly and a female character Lloyd.) When Walker depicts a perpetually boyish Norris, he seems to be right on target.

Norris never "grew up," as contemporary boy-wonders Stephen Crane and Richard Harding Davis never did. All remained distinctly adolescent in their own ways, and they provided models for another generation of American writers that seemed to revel in arrested development: Hemingway and Fitzgerald, of course, come to mind. Norris's adolescent qualities, however, seem more varied and, to a degree, more profound than Walker indicates. Aside from the "high jinks" tendencies, there are other adolescent traits that manifest themselves in the works. Some psychoanalytically-oriented scholars have suggested that Norris's works reveal a continuous, deep-seated rebellion against paternal and maternal domination, which can be explained in Freudian terms.[5] Be that as it may, there is at least a general sense of conscious rebellion pervading his literary career. He flagrantly violated the "laws" of the genteel literary world. He brutally disappointed conventional moral expectations. He was a deliberate, conscious iconoclast; as he slapped the Establishment's face again and again, he proved downright vandalic. In understanding Norris, the "adjusted" middle-aged mind needs to recall the sense of selfhood and power that is experienced by the archetypal adolescent when he breaks a school building window or proclaims invalid the *Weltanschauung* of the previous generation. Norris was such an adolescent in sensibility and in his literary behavior. He intentionally went beyond the bounds of propriety at almost every opportunity; and he frequently did so with a vengeance not noted by Walker.

It has already been argued that the first published novel, *Moran of the Lady Letty*, signifies a frontal assault on the popular adventure-romance readership that Norris felt compelled to write for in 1897–98.[6] To gain entry to the book publishing world, Norris simultaneously wrote for a *Prisoner of Zenda* audience and satirized both the subgenre and the audience for it. In the bizarre plot of *Moran* and the grotesque characterizations of Moran Sternersen, Ross Wilbur, and Josie Herrick, Norris pandered to and lampooned the entertainment-seeking public of his day. When Ross Wilbur punches Moran in the forehead and pins her to the ground, and when she thereby realizes her love for this manly hero, Norris revealed not a sensibility of "high jinks" but one that might be termed "high kinky" in today's parlance. *Moran* is a peculiar book. Norris had an equally peculiar—and pointed—sense of humor.

It was a sense of humor not only flippant but bordering on what is now formally termed the "dark." That is, there are some lines of relationship to be noted between Norris and Joseph Heller, Nathanael West, Ambrose Bierce, and the author of the conclusion of *Maggie*. In an article entiled "The Comedy of Frank Norris's *McTeague*" the less "dark," more vaudevillean comic elements of that novel have been given consideration.[7] But black humor is also to be noted in *McTeague*. The characterizations of Zerkow and Maria Macapa are cases in point. But the most salient indication of Norris's perverse comedic streak is seen in his treatment of Trina's amputation experience. By the close of chapter XVIII, Trina solicits a good deal of sympathy from most readers, despite her degenerative traits. She has become a truly gross creature, a haggish scrubbing woman more repellent than Zerkow. And yet—she is suffering more than anyone should. Her miserable life's center, her gold, has been stolen by McTeague. It is the greatest trauma she could experience at this late stage in the story. Coming out of a prolonged state of dementia triggered by the theft, she receives another crushing blow, delivered by the physician who has examined her swollen hand.

> "Why, this is blood-poisoning, you know," he told her; "the worst kind. You'll have to have those fingers amputated, beyond a doubt, or lose the entire hand—or even worse."

This is serious business. Norris has created a charged, pathetic atmosphere, whereupon he shifts to a totally unanticipated tone and shockingly different point of view for the beginning of the next chapter.

> One can hold a scrubbing-brush with two good fingers and

> the stumps of two others even if both joints of the thumbs are
> gone, but it takes considerable practice to get used to it.[8]

The reader *should* wince; the seasoned student of Norris from his journalist days on *The Wave* through 1899, however, will note a characteristic flourish, and then wince. Trina did not merit such treatment at
that point. Norris's nonchalance is outrageous. But the chilling twist is
consistent with earlier efforts of the kind, as in "A Salvation Boom in
Matabeleland" and "Fantaisie Printaniere," where a crucifixion and the
art of wife-beating are given comic treatment.[9]

Even more shocking is Norris's comedic manipulation of another
amputee in *A Man's Woman,* which was published in book form the
following year. The sadistic elements of *Moran* and the lurid violence
of *McTeague* seem pale beside the excesses of late 1899 in *A Man's
Woman.* The graphic description of physical suffering in the Arctic,
the minute rendering of a surgical procedure, and the braining of a
horse with a geologic hammer are indices of Norris's increasing boldness
as a Realist—or, so he was termed by his contemporaries, as an Ultra-
Realist. But nothing quite equals the deliberately ultra-tasteless fashioning of Richard Ferriss's situation.

Because of frostbite and its gangrenous consequences, Ferriss loses
both of his hands. As in the case of Trina, it is no laughing matter. Ferriss
is developed as a pathetic object—until Norris can no longer resist the
temptation to indulge in the bizarre.

> Ferriss and Bennett sat on opposite sides of the tent, Bennett
> using his knees as a desk, Ferriss trying to free himself from
> the sleeping bag with the stumps of his arms. Upon one of
> these stumps, the right one, a tin spoon had been lashed.[10]

The detail of the spoon is what one *might* expect of a pioneer in the
area of graphic Realism. But the use to which the detail is put leads
one beyond such ordinary categorization. Norris dwells upon it. Building
on the image of a double amputee clumsily struggling to get out of a
sleeping bag, Norris next depicts Ferriss in a revery over his loved one
Lloyd Searight, whom he seems still to hope to woo despite his calami-
tous infirmity. Norris reduces to absurdity the pathetic scene by prompt-
ing the reader to imagine the possible physical consequences of a
successful suit. With faint but actual erotic imagery, he depicts Ferriss
in his love revery as "sitting very erect upon his sleeping bag, drawing
figures and vague patterns in the fur of his deer-skin coat with the tip
of his spoon." It took Frank Norris at the turn of the century to hazard
the Westian possibilities of an imagined tableau in which a double amputee fondles his lover.[11]

But Norris has only begun here. Ward Bennett also loves Lloyd. Because Ferriss concludes that they will soon perish in the Arctic wastes, he nobly lies to Bennett, telling him that Lloyd cares for him. Bennett is ecstatic at the news. He leaps to his feet, thrusts out his hand, crying to Ferriss, "Congratulate me!"

> Ferriss feebly rose, too, and instinctively extended his arm, but withdrew it suddenly. Bennett paused abruptly, letting his hand fall to his side, and the two men remained there an instant, looking at the stumps of Ferriss's arms, the tin spoon still lashed to the right wrist.

The scene of acute embarrassment is no accident. For Norris has set up a situation in which Ferriss's lack of hands is *somehow* forgotten by a best friend, not once but twice. Lloyd does the same as Bennett after Ferriss returns from the Arctic. He is walking through a park when she hails him. He comes to her as she attempts to descend from her carriage. She stalls between the running board and the ground and becomes irritated over Ferriss's lack of gallantry. Ferriss just stands there, feeling embarrassed with his stumps in his pockets. "He raised a shoulder resignedly, and Lloyd, with the suddenness of a blow, remembered that Ferriss had no hands."

If this does not convince one concerning authorial intent and a dark comedic sensibility, he should note the coda with which Norris concludes his unusual performance. As the erstwhile lovers were parting, "Lloyd leaned from the phaeton and looked back. The carriage was just disappearing down the vista of elms and cottonwoods. She waved her hand gayly, and Ferriss responded with the stump of one forearm."

In *The Octopus* (1901) and *The Pit* (1903), there are no sickly descents into the bizarre. Norris continued his interest in fashioning Dickensian character types after *A Man's Woman*; he never suppressed his flair for the eccentric, the grotesque, and the silly. But *A Man's Woman* was the last of its kind. By July of 1899—with four novels finished—he was working on a more seriously ambitious kind of literature, an "epic" of the wheat. Yet, from the early 1890s through 1899, he had given free rein to a markedly rebellious nature manifesting itself in various forms of literary sensationalism. Crane and Davis had devised attention-winning formulas; and Norris attempted to follow their leads with his grimace- and wince-inducing violations of the conventional reader's expectations. As reviews of *McTeague* and *A Man's Woman* indicate, his strategy worked. He was noticed.[12]

It seems, though, to have been not only a strategy. The more violent, amoral, and quirky traits of Norris's personality appear to have been especially suited to what was proving a winning formula. To some degree the personality became the plan. And reference to Stevenson's and Zola's influences on Norris do not explain away the irregular psychology behind *Moran, McTeague,* and *A Man's Woman.* Without the dark humor, *Blix* too is a rebellious book, calling into question social "certainties" of the American 1890s. *Vandover and the Brute* questions the same "certainties" and then goes on to puzzle over the Judaeo-Christian ethos sanctioning such mores. Norris, then, was unconventional. He was a hard-headed and fierce iconoclast, literarily and philosophically. He was innovative in his brave—if sometimes tasteless—choices of subject matter. He despised "society men" and their trivial values; and even in more mature works like *The Octopus* and *The Pit,* he sternly called into question the society of his time.

When one turns from the works to posthumous characterizations of Norris by his friends and associates, however, he finds that no such Frank Norris seems to have existed—at least not in any obvious way. This is the paradox encountered when pairing writings by Norris with early writings about him. The queer grin of the bizarre humorist and the furrowed brow of the social critic disappear, giving way to a benign countenance. The Frank Norris portrayed by his contemporaries (we here exclude book reviewers) was a model citizen in every way. He very much resembles the man that Condy Rivers was in the process of becoming at the close of *Blix.*

There is at least one possible explanation for the posthumous writings' contradiction of the biographical image suggested by the short stories and novels. Between 1901 and 1903 Norris became a serious contender for the honor of having written the long-awaited Great American Novel. *The Octopus* was viewed as having come very close to it; and *The Pit* was described by most reviewers as, at least, one of the greats. The lamentation over his premature demise in 1902 had resulted in the creation of an aura about his recollected visage. But the hagiographic consequences which naturally follow upon the early death of a promising author did not truly get out of hand. It is thus difficult to dismiss the major points commentators made. There is a tone of sincerity in most of the memoirs and eulogies that tends to disarm the cynical historian.

In fact, there is such unanimity in the positive descriptions of Norris's personality that redundancy is a problem when reporting what was, in effect, a choric response to his death. That this critic of society life in *The Octopus* was himself very much a society man of surpassing charm seems a piquant enough fact to merit initial consideration. Bailey Millard, when describing *Blix* as "a story of San Francisco society life," went on to say that the subject was one "which Norris knew well enough, and which, in my opinion, somewhat hampered his genius, as he let the pink teas get too strong a hold upon him."[13] That was undoubtedly true of Norris through the mid-1890s since *Moran* (1898) and *Blix* (1899) are translucently autobiographical in their energetic rejections of pink teas and cotillions. Norris obviously *knew* at first hand the tedium of socializing when depicting its inanities in these two volumes. But while Norris abandoned the larger San Francisco social scene, what Millard termed his "charming personality" was enjoyed by various little circles. It seems that Norris did not shine his brightest at large and formal social functions. Frank Morton Todd related that his "friendships were of the intensive rather than the extensive kind."[14] And an unsigned article in the San Francisco *Chronicle*, complemented this observation with the statement that, "Personally he was a favorite in many small circles, for he preferred to have them small."[15] Thus the sociable young man was not an especially extrovert fellow—not a backslapper and hanger-on. Rather than behave as a social lionizer, he seems to have conducted his polite activities in the manner of those of Van's circle in *Vandover and the Brute* (the early chapters, that is).

It was only in the "unmixed" activities of the fraternity scene that Norris let loose. According to H. M. Wright, Norris "was always ready for any college prank or celebration and never missed a rush or a football game. Indeed he was an enthusiastic spectator of a game on the [Berkeley] campus only a week before his death."[16] Franklin Walker has convincingly described at length this obstreperous side of Norris's personality. At the head of a gang of collegians he could be one of the roughs; but in more formal circumstances he could be equally reserved. In various social settings he knew his place and was sensitive to changing environments. The result was Bailey Millard's being able to assign him the reputation of being both "a man's man" and "a woman's man." To Millard this was the highest compliment imaginable. Norris might mortify the polite male and female reviewers of his books, but when it came to image projection on a personal level he seems to have been able to put everyone at his ease.

Mrs. Robert Louis Stevenson and Gelett Burgess succinctly summarized the personality that they knew when designing a memorial seat to be placed on the path leading to Norris's cabin in the Santa Cruz mountains.[17] The inscription composed for a granite slab reads thus:

FRANK NORRIS

1870–1902

SIMPLENESS AND GENTLENESS AND HONOR

AND CLEAN MIRTH

At this point we should recall the peculiar comedy, the amorality, and the violence of *Moran, McTeague,* and *A Man's Woman.* One familiar with Norris's early works quite naturally pauses over the ascription of "Clean Mirth," simplicity and honor. Norris had embraced Zolaesque Naturalism with obvious abandon in his hours at his desk; never, from his novels, would one presume that he was the good boy described above. The raucous authorial laughter leveled at dim-witted McTeague jars with the concept that anything so refined as "mirth" would ever be associated with Norris's name. But, the fact is, it was.

Moreover, Norris was honorable (in the Victorian sense of that word) to the extent that, as one reads the posthumous essays, he cannot help but recall Richard Harding Davis's young gentlemen-adventurers. Two full statements by long-time acquaintances will serve to delineate this aspect of Norris's public character. Wright is most eloquent:

> A surpassing personal charm, a ready wit, and a capacity for finding joy in life—all these were his in full measure. He was always the same to his friends; he never used people as a means of advancing himself, and he never truckled or toadied to the powerful. He was simple and unaffected and always sincere to his friends and enemies alike, a strong friend and an open enemy.

Todd echoed this high eulogy:

> He was thoroughly a part of his crowd, and never tried to be a larger part than the other fellow. His wit was always well-timed and happy—never studied or pretentious, but simple and natural. . . . he was never guilty of affectation, and he scorned and despised the contemptible masquerade of puffed-up self-indulgence, that wretched, cheating imposition on the artist's suffering friends, called the "eccentricity of genius."

The long list of virtues assigned to Norris by these writers and others ultimately leads to the consideration that he may have been something of a prig in his private life. For example, when Todd describes Norris's reluctance to apply himself to his course of study at Berkeley, he writes, "What he did not like he would not study, any more than he would associate with a man he thought unworthy, and there was an end of it." Another writer was even more specific: "His sense of honor was very acute, in fact it had been called finicky and he often missed chances to do things because he did not consider them quite according to his code."[18] We may here recall the high moral code of gentlemanliness represented by Dolly Haight in *Vandover* and the horrible example of moral failure in the personality of Van. Norris, then, appeared to two observers almost as much an honorable gentleman as the Van Bibber and Travers figures whom Richard Harding Davis so deftly satirized. To some degree, he had the ramrod spine of a polite moralist.[19]

Norris's era, however, was that of Theodore Roosevelt as well as Van Bibber, and Norris had in 1898 satirized his own Van Bibber figure, Ross Wilbur of *Moran*. In *The Octopus* he continued his assault upon exotic social types. In his works he despised such sissies and stuffed-shirts with Rooseveltian gusto. It therefore comes as no surprise when Bailey Millard was careful to insist that, while Norris "could be outspoken enough," he "was never a prig." When the ramrod spine was in evidence, it manifested itself in the manners of "a catholic man" who "did not pose nor preach."[20]

Somewhere between the prig and the libertine stood, stylishly and likeably, Frank Norris the man. That rough but positive generalization about his personality is given sanction by all of the early posthumous writings about him. It does not square with the main thematic thrust of *Vandover and the Brute*, which demonstrates the inadequacies of the honorable, high moral code of Dolly Haight, Turner Ravis, and their circle.[21] But Norris, in personal and social relationships, seems to have appeared so idealistically motivated and mannered as to pass for Dolly's brother-in-arms. The psychological irregularities manifested in the works are contradicted thus in testimony after testimony.

There are two final bits of biographical evidence worth analyzing—and speculating upon—when considering the relationship between Norris's life and works: Norris's marriage and his religiosity. The marriage appears to have been a remarkably stable and fulfilling one—especially for an artist of the *fin de siècle* literary environment. After the lovely courtship more or less accurately recorded in *Blix*, Norris married a woman who proved the "man's woman" whom he had sought to define, directly or by implication, in all of his novels. She supported him emo-

tionally, as Blix did Condy, and seemed quite willing to share his interests. New York, California, Chicago—she moved with him, living his
life. When he unexpectedly died, they were on the threshold of even
better years. He was secure enough to return for good to what he considered his "home" state after the then professionally mandatory sojourn
in the East. He planned to reside in a cabin in the Santa Cruz mountains
and make only occasional business trips to New York City. Concerning
the years of his late apprenticeship and his transient life with Jeannette
Black Norris, the San Francisco *Chronicle* offered a suggestive note:

> He depended greatly on his wife for criticism of his work,
> and had the utmost confidence in her ability. Together they
> read over his work, and the changes which he made in it were
> chiefly at her suggestion. She receives much credit from their
> friends for his later successes.

That she was to accompany him on a trip around the world to gather
material for the never-written third volume of the Epic of the Wheat
testifies to the fact that, while it may not have been a marriage made in
heaven, it was a healthy one. As in *Blix*, this young woman was not only
a lover but a "chum."

By 1902, Norris had real success, a stable family life, and admiring
friends and associates in San Francisco, Chicago, New York, and Boston.
The Octopus had proven the final door through which he passed in his
writing; he had become a junior member of the Establishment which
had rejected him through 1897, when his future seemed unpromising.
By 1902 he was even pontificating on the nature of his profession in
The Critic and the Boston *Evening Transcript*. He had become the
taxpaying bourgeois whom he had derided in *Moran*; if it had been
announced in a literary gossip column that the newly recognized literary
critic and author of *The Octopus* was an Episcopalian churchman, that
fact would have seemed consistent with Norris's new image as a belle-
trist. As it turns out, Norris was not only a tax-payer but a plate-passer.

The Reverend W. S. Rainsford wrote a eulogy that should have
stimulated more interest on the part of Norris biographers long before
now. While other eulogists had anticipated his remarks on the "honesty,
the bravery" of Frank Norris, Rainsford is the only one to mention "the
faith of the man." He continued: "It was my privilege to be counted
among his friends for years. I seldom have met so lovable a man. . . . He
believed with all his soul in the future of democracy, and ever and always
tried to serve his brother man."[22] The author of *McTeague* and *A Man's
Woman* being a high-minded young gentleman is troublesome enough a
notion. But the possibility that Norris was a conventional believer, with
friends in the ministry, is an even more startling one.

Reverend Rainsford came from Toronto to St. George's Episcopal Church in New York City and served as rector from 1883 to 1905. Norris formally became a parishioner at St. George's in 1899, and although he soon traveled to California for research on *The Octopus*, he appears to have been active enough in the church before and after that trip to become well-known to Rainsford. Norris was married at St. George's on February 12, 1900, with the Reverend E. P. Gould as the minister and Frank Nelson Doubleday and Gertrude Norris as the witnesses. A month after the marriage Jeannette became a parishioner. In light of this it seems more than a matter of social form that his funeral took place at St. Luke's Episcopal Church in San Francisco. In fact, other data become suggestive in light of the possibility that Norris was a practicing Episcopalian. While he questioned the extreme religious certainty of the hysterical young lady who dies as the *Mazatlan* is sinking in *Vandover*, one can begin to see signs of a latent or active religiosity in Norris's works once he considers an Episcopalian frame of reference. The novels are replete with Biblical allusions, and *Moran* begins with the imagery of battle, murder, and sudden death which directly echoes the great litany of the Book of Common Prayer. The phrase "the perils of childbirth," which perks young Van's curiosity one Sunday in church, appears in the same litany. And the communion service that a hungover Van attends with Turner Ravis is clearly the Episcopalian. On the strength of these specific observations and the general observation that Norris's grand style was sermon-like and oratorical, it becomes more plausible that—as Richard Davison has recently suggested—*The Octopus* can only be satisfactorily understood from a Pauline perspective.[23] Despite his Naturalistic modernity, Norris may have been in his private life as "square" a figure as the posthumous commentators depict.

How then could he be so blatant an *enfant terrible* in his Naturalistic works? The most logical response to the puzzle is that Norris, at his work, was different from the Episcopalian boy whom Gertrude Norris reared, from the dandy who returned from art study at Paris, from the fraternity boy and social delight who moved effortlessly through San Francisco parlors, and from the successful professional writer who enjoyed and looked forward to continued domestic joy. The Norris of the novels was frantic, frenetic at many moments, in his overblown rhetoric and gorgeous verbal painting. In his literary criticism he rationally celebrated simplicity in art; in his novels he went baroque. He rioted in colors, sounds, and tastes; while sometimes stumbling, his narrative pace is relentless in its emotional haste. The man became vicariously involved in muscular and nervous story-telling to the degree that nit-witted Ross Wilbur's high adventures in *Moran* triggered a desire for identification with him. Hence, the unexpected shifts in authorial tone in that erratic work. That Norris "depended greatly on his wife for criticism" does seem very likely in light of the typical characteristics of his writing. It is difficult to imagine his coolly excising and rephrasing for any length of time. Undoubtedly his most noteworthy act of revision—the marvelous improvement of *Blix* prior to book publication—was facilitated by Jeannette. This is not to suggest that Norris went berserk at his desk. But Poe's "species of fine frenzy" is the phrase that sometimes comes to mind when one views even a mature work like *The Pit*.

Norris's friends—with one exception—did not note this quality in the works, but the turn-of-the-century reviewers did, especially in *A Man's Woman, The Octopus*, and *The Pit*. Norris's friends did not seriously examine the personality in light of the works and identify the temperamental paradox that is at question here. Still, they did provide information supporting the present supposition. The fact of the matter is that writing did not come easy for Norris; it involved a good deal of strain. Isaac F. Marcosson informs us that Norris wrote "as much as 3,000 words a day." Denison Hailey Clift suggests that such labor proved a great pleasure for the author, telling us that Norris's motto was "True happiness is being able to do the work you love."[24] Surviving evidence suggests, to the contrary, that Norris was hardly mellow when pushing his pen. We might keep Vandover's tendency toward the profound delights of play in mind when noting that as early as 1897 Eleanor M. Davenport had related, "It has always been hard for Mr. Norris to shut himself up with pen and paper and say, no, to the calls of a delightfully alive world."[25] This is the major note sounded in posthumous descriptions of his compositional labors. Writing was *not* play.

> When his material [for *The Octopus*] was gathered, he worked continually till his task was done. It was as if he were under the whip.
>
> (H. M. Wright)

> When he had once begun a story, he worked indefatigably so that by the time it was completed he was nearly a nervous wreck.
>
> San Francisco *Chronicle*

> The Stevensonian injunction, "Stick to your folio," was followed by Norris in his latter days, although he often had little nerve for the writing and went to it wearily.
>
> (Bailey Millard)[26]

The one friend who did detect signs of strain in the works was Harry M. East. "You can read between the lines his great consuming, feverish desire to write something worth while, something distinctive that should endure. His mental straining to express himself is apparent in almost everything that he wrote."[27] Frederic Tabor Cooper, who was not an intimate but was the earliest serious student of Norris's art, made the same point. Viewing his total literary output, Cooper concluded, "Such are the books which Norris, with feverish impatience and tireless nervous energy, produced in the few short years that fate allowed him." What Cooper had visualized was this: *Moran* (1898), *McTeague* (1899), *Blix* (1899), *A Man's Woman* (1900), *The Octopus* (1901), *The Pit* (1903), and the stories and essays posthumously collected in three volumes. This was quite a list of works for a span of few years. Cooper, however, did not have the fuller picture of Norris's output that we do now.[28] Norris was more prolific than Cooper knew; he had truly driven himself in the quest for success.

It is not difficult to imagine him emotionally building up a head of steam for each of the rapidly composed works; for the tenor of the novels, the pitch of voice and sometimes spasmodic leaps in narrative pace correspond with such an imagined scene. The overall impression one receives from the bombast and redundancy that are essential characteristics of all the novels is that Norris did write "The End" in a state of exhaustion and was not inclined to review his compositions thoroughly after he had struggled through the last manuscript sheet.

There emerges, then, the picture of a divided personality: the suave, elegant, boyish-looking man of ease; and a more idiosyncratic and excitable creature who ran on nervous energy in private. William Dean Howells never met this second person: he characterized Norris by contrasting him with Stephen Crane, proclaiming that Norris seemed able to realize his professional goals "without the tremor of 'those electrical nerves' which imparted itself from the presence of Stephen Crane."[29] The second Norris of the writing desk and "electrical nerves" did surface in public once, in a much quoted tale retold in 1911 by Frederic Tabor Cooper in *Some American Story Tellers*:

> His friends are still fond of telling of the day when he came to his office trembling with excitement, incapacitated for work, his brain seething with a single thought, the Trilogy of the Wheat. "I have got a big idea, the biggest I ever had," was the burden of all he had to say for many a day thereafter.

That occurred in 1899, and two years of novelistic labor (along with his journalistic work) later, something seems to have burned out, or simply changed, in the man.

That is, although the evidence is minimal, Norris seems to have been beginning a change of perspective and life-style. By 1902, when making his final alterations in *The Pit*, he had given up his more youthful notions of the "romance" of authorship. His Davis- and Crane-inspired lark of reporting from South Africa in 1896 and his zestful reportorial derring-do during the Spanish-American War seem to have lost their attractiveness. His American field-research activities for *The Octopus* and *The Pit* most probably revealed the commonplace realities of rented rooms and restaurants. Davis remained a globe-trotter until his death, but by 1902 Norris had become interested in something else.

This was Todd's opinion. He was a classmate of Norris at Berkeley *and* Harvard, and a long-time friend. In fact, he had attended a reading given by Norris at Berkeley a few weeks before his death. Thus, he was in a position to know what was on Norris's mind during the final days. He wrote,

> And at last the rover came back—the sailor came home from the sea, the hunter home from the hill—gave up his contemplated tour of the world and bought a farm in California; and had the simple, human weakness to say he did it because he was homesick; liked his own people best, and wanted to be with the fellows he used to know.

He had purchased the cabin near Gilroy. Like San Francisco, it too offered what may be termed the hearthside pleasures. Nellie Sanchez related that during his brief stay in the Santa Cruz mountains "his peculiar attraction of person and character had endeared him to all his neighbors, and his memory will ever be enshrined in their hearts." Gilroy, however, offered more than fellowship.

Nature had attracted his attention during the final months. Norris's works reveal that Bailey Millard was missing much when insisting that "All his life he had been a city man, of city habits and of city thoughts." Although Norris was a city dweller, *Moran, Blix,* and *The Octopus* reveal a strong inclination toward and appreciation of non-urban realities. But while Millard seems to err a bit, these novels do support his conclusion: "As a vital and necessary part of his spiritual and artistic growth, [the artist] must at last come to see, as Norris saw, that the sham social life found in such Babels of self-assured greatness as London and New York, and the club-life—the pride of their vain gregariousness —*must* be abandoned for long periods of time."[30] This propagandistic statement tells us at least as much about Millard's anti-urban biases as about Norris's preferences; as with Todd's high-blown rhetoric, though, a fact can be dimly gleaned.

The essential fact was expressed by Norris himself in a late letter to an unidentified friend. Regarding his cabin in the mountains, he declared:

I can shoot deer from my front windows. The quails are a
pest. There's a trout stream just around the corner. We have
the Stevensons for near neighbors. This beats a New York
apartment.[31]

Was this turn to Nature and return to "home" another lark? The
evidence suggests that it was not. Several articles testify to the fact that
Norris intended to write the sequel to *The Pit,* the announced volume
entitled *The Wolf,* at the cabin. Although a projected trilogy on the
Battle of Gettysburg was in his future plans, Nellie Sanchez reports
that he had recently developed a scheme for some stories set in the Gilroy
environment. What was not planned was the continuation of his trip
from New York to San Francisco to New York, around the world. Most
posthumous essays repeat the story of his intention to visit the Mediter-
ranean and India for *Wolf* research purposes. But Todd, who was in
recent contact with Norris, indicated that he had decided against the
trip.[32]

A major factor in the decision to stay at home and send down roots
may have been his close brush with death—something that he liked to
write about melodramatically during his *Moran* days. The literary subject became a reality for Norris when Jeannette was stricken with appendicitis in 1902. It is most tempting to speculate that the serious illness
brought to the fore the question of how Norris was going to spend the
rest of his life. Speculating further, one may imagine Norris asking the
question, what if this had happened during their world cruise? To state
the matter baldly, he almost lost his Blixian "chum." Franklin Walker
provides information from Bruce Porter which may support such speculation.

> While Mrs. Norris was in the hospital, her husband called at
> Bruce Porter's studio, haggard and despairing. He told his old
> friend that his wife had been operated on and was now out of
> danger, but as they lunched together he seemed unable to
> shake off the depression which held him. They walked to the
> hospital together, and outside the door they stood for a mo-
> ment:
> "Bruce, I'm afraid!"
> His friend gave him the formal assurance that all was
> well.
> "Yes—but I'm afraid!"
> "Afraid of what, Frank?"
> "I'm afraid of death!"[33]

Only twice in the novels are we able to infer such "tender-minded" personality traits in the author. (In the main, Norris appeared clearly within

James's "tough-minded" category.) There is *Vandover*, in which a young man remarkably like Frank Norris solicits his sympathy. And there is *Blix*, in which a struggling, young, excitable writer experiences fits of depression and requires a young girl—remarkably like Jeannette Black—to help him sort out his professional and private life. In both cases we view an unstable and somewhat insecure fellow, erratically prone to emotional highs and lows, trying to organize his life.

Norris's marriage occurred between the end of one phase of his professional career and the beginning of a second. The peculiar *bizarreries* of *Moran*, *McTeague*, and *A Man's Woman* were behind him by late 1899. After the marriage came the more conventional attempts at high art in *The Octopus* and *The Pit*. Norris was leveling-out, it seems, when Jeannette's brush with death occurred. It was perhaps no accident that Curtis Jadwin—who greatly appreciates William Dean Howells' *The Rise of Silas Lapham*—was Norris's final full-scale hero. Jadwin's middle-class solidity and his beginning of a new life with his wife at the conclusion of *The Pit* may be of some real biographical relevance. It may be that at his death Norris was finally "growing up" and surrendering to the more enduring pleasure of the American middle-class. *The Octopus* and *The Pit* suggest that his adolescent qualities were evaporating with the approach of middle-age.

Ultimately we do not know exactly what was happening in Norris's personality in 1902. Hard facts are admittedly scarce and speculative gestures are a consequence. Much seems to have been going on at the end. For example, Charles G. Norris told Randolph Edgar in 1916 that the title of the third volume of the Epic of the Wheat was *not* to be *The Wolf* after all.[34] What was it to become? What did the change of mind signify? It was a time of change in Norris's life and the pity of it is that we are not able to view the result of his transition from adolescence to sober maturity.

Notes

1. Garden City, N. Y.: Doubleday & Company, Inc.

2. Marchand, *Frank Norris: A Study* (Stanford: Stanford U Press, 1942); French, *Frank Norris* (New York: Twayne Publishers, Inc., 1962); Pizer, *The Novels of Frank Norris* (Bloomington: Indiana U Press, 1966); and Dillingham, *Frank Norris: Instinct and Art* (Lincoln: U of Nebraska Press, 1969).

3. *Frank Norris: A Reference Guide* (Boston: G. K. Hall & Co., 1975), completed by Jesse S. Crisler and Joseph R. McElrath, Jr., has recently enlarged the canon of writings about Norris. The forthcoming Burt Franklin volume, *Frank Norris: The Critical Reception* by McElrath and Katherine Knight, includes even more new items about Norris and his work. Don B. Graham's "Frank Norris, Actor," *Quarterly*

Newsletter of the Book Club of California, 41 (1976) 38–40, demonstrates what is still possible if one is willing simply to read San Francisco newspapers of the 1890s.

4. Graham's study is a remarkable expansion of his "Aesthetic Experience in the Fiction of Frank Norris." Diss. University of Texas 1971. The U of Missouri Press is preparing to publish it.

5. See especially Dexter M. Roberts, "A Psychological Interpretation of the Social Philosophy in the Work of Frank Norris, American Literary Naturalist." Diss. Stanford University 1967. It is the most ambitious effort of the kind. George W. Johnson does not execute a formal psychoanalytical study, but as a literary historian he comes to similar conclusions concerning tensions and conflicts in Norris's life and works. See "Romance and Realism in the Novels of Frank Norris." Diss. Columbia University 1960.

6. Joseph R. McElrath, Jr., "The Erratic Design of Frank Norris's *Moran of the Lady Letty*," *American Literary Realism* 10 (1977), 114–124.

7. Joseph R. McElrath, Jr., "The Comedy of Frank Norris's *McTeague*," *Studies in American Humor*, 2 (1975), 88–95. This essay argues that the comedy of *McTeague* is not "dark." The present essay modifies that conclusion.

8. *McTeague: A Story of San Francisco*, ed. Donald Pizer (New York: W. W. Norton & Company, Inc., 1977), pp. 196–197.

9. The interpretation of Norris's *Wave* writings is based upon a reading of a virtually complete collection of such pieces compiled by Joseph Katz in 1972. No one has yet published a full collection of *Wave* writings.

10. *A Man's Woman* (New York: Doubleday & McClure Co., 1899), p. 37. Subsequent quotations are derived from this edition, as they appear on pp. 39, 43, 79, and 84.

11. When claiming that Norris was not able to resist a fine opportunity to indulge in the bizarre, I have two prior examples of his unique temperamental tendencies in mind. The first has to do with the fashioning of the sensational conclusion of *McTeague;* Frederic Tabor Cooper relates a relevant anecdote: "When a friend once expostulated with Norris for the gross improbability of that chapter in which a murderer, fleeing from justice into the burning heat of an alkali desert, carries with him a canary that continues to sing after thirty-six hours without food or water, he frankly admitted the absurdity, but said that he had been unable to resist the temptation, because the scene offered such a dramatic contrast. 'Besides,' he added whimsically, 'I compromised by saying that the canary was half-dead, anyhow' " ("Frank Norris," *Some American Story Tellers* [New York: Henry Holt and Co., 1911], pp. 295–330). The second example concerns the ludicrous fist fight between Ross Wilbur and Moran Sternersen. Juliet Wilbor Tompkins claims that Norris designed *Moran* for the sake of staging such a scene ("Introduction," *The Argonaut Manuscript Limited Edition of Frank Norris's Works*, IX [Garden City, N. Y.: Doubleday, Doran & Company, Inc., 1928], vii–x).

N. B. Since most of the posthumous writings about Norris will be referred to more than once, all first citations will include the full pagination. The writings are not especially long and the absence of specific page references should not create serious difficulty. All writings are cited only once, with the exception of Bailey Millard's: he produced two essays.

12. *A Man's Woman* produced a greater outrage in reviews than *McTeague*. The forthcoming *Frank Norris: The Critical Reception* will make available the texts of *McTeague* and *A Man's Woman* reviews.

13. Bailey Millard, "Writer Was Planning to Stay in California This Winter and Complete *The Wolf* when Stricken by Appendicitis," San Francisco *Examiner* (26 October, 1902), p. 18.

14. Frank Morton Todd, "Frank Norris–Student, Author, and Man," *The University of California Magazine*, 8 (November, 1902), 349–356.

15. "Death Ends the Career of Frank Norris," San Francisco *Chronicle* (26 October, 1902), p. 24.

16. H. M. Wright, "In Memoriam—Frank Norris: 1870–1902," *The University of California Chronicle*, 5 (October, 1902), 240–245.

17. Nellie V. de Sanchez, "Books and Writers: Frank Norris' Memorial Seat," *Sunset*, 11 (April, 1904), 560–561.

18. "Death Ends the Career of Frank Norris."

19. There is, of course, a tradition in Norris criticism having to do with his image as an arch-Victorian moralist. See, for example, William B. Dillingham, "Frank Norris and the Genteel Tradition," *Tennessee Studies in Literature*, 5 (1960), 15–24. Norris, that is, has been viewed as a straightforward genteel moralist–a preacher.

20. Bailey Millard, "A Significant Literary Life," *Out West*, 18 (January, 1903), 49–55.

21. Norris's critique of conventional morality and delineation of its sometimes harmful effects are examined by Joseph R. McElrath, Jr., "Frank Norris's *Vandover and the Brute:* Narrative Technique and the Socio-Critical Viewpoint," *Studies in American Fiction*, 4 (1976), 27–43.

22. "Frank Norris," *The World's Work*, 5 (April 1903), 3276. Dolores Dereszewska of St. George's Church provided the information on Rainsford and Norris's relationship with St. George's. Donald Pizer, when examining Franklin Walker's interview notes, found that Norris met Rainsford in early 1898 after his move from San Francisco to New York City. He notes that Norris attempted to help Rainsford in regard to publication and that he gave him some assistance in his social work. Pizer focuses on Rainsford as an evolutionary theist and proponent of muscular Christianity: "Rainsford's strongly positive evolutionary view of man's relationship to nature and to God contained little that Norris had not found in Le Conte, but Rainsford's vibrant personality probably helped to revivify this aspect of Le Conte's thought in Norris's mind." That Norris established a relationship with Reverend Rainsford so soon after his arrival in New York tends to counter the possible argument that Norris became a parishioner solely for the purpose of facilitating the 1900 marriage at St. George's. Moreover, it seems improbable that Norris became a parishioner simply to please an evolutionary theist whose company he enjoyed.

23. "Frank Norris's *The Octopus*: Some Observations on Vanamee, Shelgrim and St. Paul," *Literature and Ideas in America: Essays in Memory of Harry Hayden Clark*, ed. Robert Falk (Columbus: Ohio State U Press, 1975), pp. 182–203.

24. Marcosson, "Some Recollections of Frank Norris," Louisville *Times* (27 October, 1902), p. 4; Clift, "The Artist in Frank Norris," *Pacific Monthly*, 17 (March, 1907), 313–322.

25. "Some Younger California Writers," *The University of California Magazine*, 3 (November, 1897), 80–82.

26. The first two quotations are derived from articles cited above. The Millard quotation comes from the San Francisco *Examiner* piece, also cited above.

27. "A Lesson from Frank Norris," *Overland Monthly*, 60 (December, 1912), 533–534.

28. Joseph Katz has significantly expanded the list of Norris titles in "The Shorter Publications of Frank Norris: A Checklist," *Proof* 3 (1973), 155–220. Recent, as yet unpublished work by Robert Morace, however, will result in an even larger list.

29. "Frank Norris," *North American Review*, 175 (December, 1902), 769–778.

30. "A Significant Literary Life."

31. Quoted in "With Some Authors We Have Known," Atlanta *Constitution* (4 January, 1903), p. 8, "The Sunny South" supplement.

32. Walker reports (pp. 305–306) that Norris decided, by September 1902, to go only to the South Seas rather than around the world. What that trip would have to do with the subject matter of *The Wolf* is moot. Perhaps Norris scrapped his plans for field research on *The Wolf* and chose to enjoy a much-earned vacation with Jeannette.

33. *Frank Norris: A Biography*, pp. 306–307.

34. "The Manuscript and the Man," *The Bellman*, 20 (27 May, 1916), 602–603.

REVIEWS

A California Novel

Geraldine Bonner[*]

One evening last winter, in New York, I was looking over the *Evening Sun,* when I came upon a chapter of *Moran of the Lady Letty.* It was chapter six toward the second half of the story, and I had read nothing that came before it, yet it held my attention with its brusque and almost defiant sharpness of phrase and the lurid picturesqueness of its setting.

"Good for California!" I thought; "I must see the rest of this."

But fate willed otherwise. For several subsequent evenings I was reft from the *Evening Sun* by engagements, and when these were over the *Evening Sun* was reft from me by other members of the family who got it first. When I finally did get hold of it, *Moran of the Lady Letty* had run its course, and the mystery of what caused the *Bertha Millner* to rise up and tremble as she lay moored to the kelp in Magdalena Bay remained a genuine mystery to me.

At intervals since then I have speculated about, and once, hearing two girls at a lunch discussing the book, I eagerly asked for a solution of the unusual performances of the *Bertha Millner,* and strange as it may seem, though they both had read it through, they neither of them could remember this particular point. The other day I got the book myself and read it from cover to cover, and then I knew why two up-to-date and intelligent young women had overlooked what seemed to me, in my ignorance, to have been the main point of the story.

It is a curious thing that one of the chief faults of the California writers should be a lack of sincerity. This is curious, because the Californians themselves, "in their habits as they live," are remarkably sincere. In fact, I think I should put this attribute as at once their best and their strongest. A sincerity sometimes defiant, sometimes indifferent, sometimes carelessly self-reliant, marks the race. Californians are, as a rule, true to themselves, whether they are serenely apathetic, or cheerfully nonchalant, or violently and aggressively unconventional. They do things because they like to do them, and that sums up their entire creed.

[*]Reprinted from *The Argonaut,* 43 (November 21, 1898), 7.

3

That the works of their writers should be marked by a peculiar, meretricious extravagance I think rises from the fact that most Californians, and certainly all Californian writers, have it on their consciences that they have got to live up to the reputation of the State as a place where astonishing, lurid, and tremendous things have always happened. Outside California the Californians of the gentlest and quietest species have been forced by public expectation into the most surprising and embarrassing pranks. It is like the Americans in Paris. No one will believe in them until they begin to indulge in the strange, wild antics that the French novelists ascribe to them.

So the Californian writers feel that nothing ordinary or humdrum must come from the land of suns and snows. Mrs. Atherton, viewing her distant home through English spectacles, writes of heroines who must not disappoint her English readers—girls who never get out of the superlative degree; whose lovers, if they were ranged in line, would stretch from Lotta's Fountain to the ferry; whose riches are past the dreams of avarice; and who in behavior mingle the childish barbarity of M'liss with the sophisticated fascinations of Mrs. Skaggs.

Mr. Norris's muse has had little to do with the devious ways of society. He is a romanticist of the savage type. Belles and ball-rooms have had no attractions for him. He likes the darkling by-ways of the Barbary Coast. The lean-bodied, slinking grisette of the local Latin Quarter, furtively stealing along by the walls, with shawled head and side-glancing black eyes, has more attractions for his pen than the scented, corseted, silk-lined siren of his own world. He writes fierce, dark tales of the lawless beings who dwell in tenements that hang by the eyelids on the ledges of Telegraph Hill. The haunted, inner chambers of China-town, thick with opium smoke and dim with mystery, appeal to his sense of the horrible. The water-front, with the great ships sticking their noses over the wharves; the swarthy sailor-men, with their brown faces and their strange, clear eyes; the alluring scents and the thousand voices of the sea—exert over him their exultant and uplifting charm.

But his work has always shown the effort of attempting to give reality to the unusual. It has lacked the power of convincing, and, like Mrs. Atherton's—with brilliancy and cleverness—has missed the sincerity which impresses the reader. I have not read all, but have read a good many of Mr. Norris's stories, and in almost all of them have felt the absence of the imaginative force which compels us to accept and receive these wild tales of strange people.

But in *Moran of the Lady Letty* Mr. Norris at last got real control of his story, and for the first half was the master of it. I suppose every writer has felt that buoyant sensation of mastery which comes with the knowledge that he has control of his work; that the tale is following his lead; that it is docile to his command, and under his guidance is sweeping forward, steadily and confidently, toward its climax. And I also suppose that no honest writer living—from the impatient amateur who has never yet been published to the great master who has his disciples and his imitators—has not known the misery of feeling his story quietly slip through his fingers without a moment of warning, break away from him, shake off his guiding and controlling hand, and dash forward on its once wavering course, shattering itself as it plunges onward.

This is what *Moran of the Lady Letty* did. For the first half the author had his idea completely under his control, and it moved forward with strength, firmness, and an exultant force and sincerity. Then, suddenly, just about in the middle of the story, he lost command of it and never regained it to the end. I think that it was the introduction of the Eternal Feminine, as represented by Moran—the massive and monumental heroine—that broke up the harmonious relations between the author and his work. Mr. Norris knew whereof he dealt when he wrote of the little schooner nosing her way through the crisp, green seas; of the humming of the wind in the strained cordage; of the miracle of gold-leaf sunrises and flaming sunsets; of the silent, oily calms, and star-strewn midnights on the breast of the still and tremendous Pacific.

Up to the finding of the derelict the book is alive, full of vitality, and vigor, and truth. The chill, wild breath of the trades sweeps through it, the rustling rush of seas crushed under the *Bertha Millner's* bows sounds from page to page. We feel the still heats of noonday, the enormous quietude of evening. The few figures that move against this canvas, blazing with the colors of the vast ocean floor and the vast sky dome, are natural and simple with the elemental simplicity of those who go down to the sea in ships. We follow the narrative, caught and carried away by its swinging, onward rush, with quick, curious sympathy. The fascination of the Pacific is there, the sense of mystery that blows across it from the strange and wonderful East—the mysterious East whence so many things that are weird, and evil, and beautiful, and terrifying, come.

If Mr. Norris could write a whole book, and keep it on the key as he has kept *Moran of the Lady Letty* up to, say, the fifth chapter, he would be one of those writers who are to reveal the genius of the West to the incredulity of the East. We are proud of him as it is, and I, for one, offer him my congratulations and prophesy for him a success that will be all round, not go half way and then stop, as it has done in the case of *Moran*.

For *Moran* grows into a disappointment. After the introduction of the heroine the story ceases to move forward. It becomes a series of adventures, more or less episodical and unnatural. Mr. Norris's descriptive talent, which is simple, strong, and vivid, stands him in good stead in these hurried chapters, where improbable incident crowds on incident, and where the tale suddenly appears to have quitted this part of the globe entirely, and to be taking place in some wild and distant land at some remote period of the world's development. There is no progression in the characters at all. They step on and they step off the stage; they do astounding things; battle, murder, and sudden death rage about them, and they remain as wooden as figure-heads on ships. The charm, the air of an elastic and buoyant life that marked the earlier chapters entirely disappears. Toward the end the feeling that the author was conscious of the falseness of his work, and grew tired of it, and hurried it up, struck me at least very strongly. Mr. Norris is too clever not to have felt what a mess he had got his people into when he tried to introduce a Valkyrie from German mythology to a little San Francisco *debutante* in white canvas shoes and a pink shirt-waist.

The sincerity of the story was lost when Moran took the stage. Moran, as an idea, is very fine. A sea-story, wild and free as the foam-crested billows, with a heroine, untamed, unconquered, fierce in her splendid independence as the winds that tore her hair, honest as the sun that tanned her cheek, was an original and harmonious conception. But Mr. Norris would not let well enough alone, and in order to draw her in the few, firm lines that befit the primitive type, made her appear as a sort of gigantic, mythological figure—a Titanic demi-goddess built on the scale of a huge statue. In order to bring her off her pedestal and make her fit into the background of an evil-smelling, dirty, begrimed trading schooner, he makes her drink whiskey, wear men's clothes, and when talking stand with her thumbs in her belt.

But the most unconvincing thing about Moran is her hair. I am an expert on hair, and I declare, over my signature, that Moran's hair is the most improbable of the many improbable things in the book. It is "rye-colored," and she has two braids of it as thick as a man's arm. Now, there are men's arms and men's arms. There is Sandow's arm and the arm of the living skeleton at the circus. If Moran had two braids that fell to her knees, each as thick as an arm of Sandow, she would have had some difficulty in carrying them around. As she is the strongest and most energetic of women, we will have to suppose the arm referred to was that of the living skeleton at the circus.

Moran, in her sou'wester and blue jeans, wears her hair in two braids, sometimes hanging forward over her shoulders. In the high moments of storm and tempest the braids lash out on the elements, at others they fall peacefully over her shoulders to her boot-tops. Once Mr. Norris gives us a glimpse of her while performing her morning toilet, and after braiding her rye-colored tresses, she knotted them. I have seen braids of hair tied up with little blue ribbons, like Christmas presents, and I have seen them turned up and fiercely bound around with what is technically known as "combings"; but to knot them I Never. It can't be done.

New York Letter

John D. Barry[*]

The Doubleday & McClure Company has lately brought out in *McTeague: A Story of San Francisco,* a volume which seems to me worthy to rank among the few great novels produced in this country. Before reading the story I had heard it well spoken of; but I was astounded by its profound insight into character; its shrewd humor; its brilliant massing of significant detail, and by its dramatic force. Many readers would consider the subject too unpleasant to be treated in fiction; but for those who do not go to fiction merely to be amused and diverted, and who believe that fiction may profitably be made an expression of life, *McTeague* will be a revelation. An authoritative reviewer recently spoke of it as a study of people who were on the verge of the criminal class. This statement, apparently made as a reproach, was hardly fair. But even if it were absolutely true, why should the author be blamed? People on the verge of the criminal classes, themselves, offer excellent material for serious study in fiction. "I can't understand," said a novelist the other day, "why reviewers are always blaming writers for making their disagreeable characters true, instead of praising them for making the characters express their evil meaning as they do in life." Mr. Frank Norris has been blamed and will unquestionably be blamed again and again for choosing the theme of *McTeague*; but it is only just to him to say that he has handled his material fearlessly; that he has steadfastly followed out his premises to the end. His characters are all common, and they make a picture of the common life in the San Francisco of today that, for clearness and vigor, leaves very little for criticism. Every figure is perfectly realized; every episode has its significance. The main theme, the relations between McTeague and the little German-American girl who becomes his wife, are indicated with extraordinary fidelity, the man's natural brutality, brought out through misfortune, being thrown into play with the woman's instinctive economy, stimulated into wild avarice by the chance that has won for her a five thousand dollar prize in a lottery. The description of the wedding feast of these

[*]Reprinted from *Literary World*, 30 (March 18, 1899), 88–89.

8

two people is one of the strongest pieces of writing that I have ever read. It is the kind of writing that, in its vivid presentation of the comic and the pathetic, makes the reader feel like laughing and crying at the same time. The subordinate interests are very skillfully woven into the work of the narrative. Perhaps the strange love affair between little Miss Baker, the retired dressmaker, and old Grannis, conducted in silence on either side of the partition that separates their rooms, has a little of the unreality of romance; and the marriage between the drudge, Maria Macapa, and Zerkow, the miser, founded on the story told by Maria of a wonderful gold service of one hundred pieces, contains a curious suggestion of the more extravagant fancies of Dickens. But both these motives are made absorbingly interesting, and many readers will find in the love of the two old people an exquisite poetry and pathos. The book deserves a great success, and it ought to place Mr. Norris in the first rank among our writers, beside Mary Wilkins, and Howells, and Stephen Crane. Indeed, *McTeague* is in treatment not unlike Stephen Crane's work, though without the least suggestion of imitation and without, too, the least suggestion of that striving for effect that Crane's writing shows. The style is wholly free from trickiness, and is simple and virile, evidently the natural expression of the author's thought. It is by no means, however, a mature and finished style, and in this regard Mr. Norris is sure to develop. Now and then the reader sees the author pulling the strings, so to speak, standing off and explaining the characters in a way that suggests superiority. This is a fault to which I have already referred in these columns, in connection with the work of nearly all our writers of fiction. Mr. Norris would have gained in power if he had not only projected his characters and allowed them to explain themselves as much as possible, but also used, whenever he spoke in his capacity as author, language wholly in harmony with theirs.

After reading *McTeague* I remembered that the name of Frank Norris had been connected with a volume published several months before, so I soon looked it up. It astonished me too, because it was so unlike the other book and yet so good. *Moran of the Lady Betty* [sic] is an adventure story that Stevenson might not have been ashamed to sign. It is capitally written, it moves swiftly, it has several nice sketches of character, and it tells a fine and thoroughly original tale of the sea. A man who could write both those books certainly has a rare versatility. In the last number of *McClure's*, too, Mr. Norris has a short story, "This Animal of a Buldy Jones," in still another vein, telling of an adventure in the art student life of Paris.

Since reading these stories I have learned something about Mr. Norris himself. He was born in Chicago ("but of course he couldn't

help that," he writes of "Buldy Jones," who was born in the same place),
and, as a young boy, he went with his family to live in San Francisco.
Ten years ago, when about eighteen, he went to Paris and studied for
a year at Julian's. This explains the "Buldy Jones" story. He gave up
the idea of becoming a painter, however, and he studied for a time at
the University of California, and for one year at Harvard, entering with
the class of '95. It was at Harvard that he began *McTeague*, writing it,
oddly enough, as a short theme in the composition course conducted by
Professor Gates, to whom the book is dedicated. Two years ago, after
his return to San Francisco, and after a period of service on the *Chronicle*
there, he decided to make a book of the sketch, and he joined a friend
who was working a mine in the mountains, where he could write in solitude. After three months the novel was completed. *Moran of the Lady
Letty*, though published first, was written after *McTeague*. For a time
Mr. Norris served as one of the editors of the San Francisco *Wave*,
coming to New York about a year ago at the invitation of the Doubleday
& McClure Company to take a position on their staff. He has, I hear, two
new books ready for publication.

McTeague

Edward and Madeline Vaughn Abbot*

It is seldom that we have any opportunity to differ from our New York correspondent, but with his enthusiastic estimate of *McTeague* in the last number of the *Literary World* we must confess ourselves somewhat out of sympathy. At the time Mr. Barry's letter was received we had seen only the outside of Mr. Norris's book, and as soon as time permitted we turned to it with all our expectations roused in its favor by Mr. Barry's high recommendation. With much that Mr. Barry says we must agree; Mr. Norris is undeniably a powerful writer. He has drawn his characters with rare skill; he has told their stories in most graphic fashion; he has presented the actuality of their life in San Francisco or the wildernesses of California mountains with all its sordidness, its wretchedness, and crime. That huge, stupid animal, McTeague the dentist, his anaemic little wife Trina, the quaint old maid seamstress and the equally quaint old bachelor dog doctor, the repulsive Jew junk dealer, all stand out from the pages with the individuality of life, and the inevitable consequences of misused life follow in their tracks. With relentless truth we are made to follow the decay of McTeague's prosperity, and accompanying it the decay of his own manhood. Stupid he was always, but the one victory he won over his animal nature was the prelude to uninterrupted defeats and a final descent into the very depths of animal brutality. Even more terrible was Trina's wretched life, for she had something to start with in mind and spirit, and the slatternly figure, maimed already through her husband's cruelty—which the story leaves face downward in a pool of blood, battered to death by her husband's fists—was once as neat and trim a little woman as you could find, and the idol of her big husband's heart. One has not the consolation of saying that in real life it could not have happened so. Trina's sordid miserliness, which worked the mischief, was the natural outcome of unnecessary petty economy in a character like hers, and in McTeague's elemental nature hate was quickly stirred and brutally followed. No

*Reprinted from *Literary World*, 30 (April 1, 1899), 99.

stronger picture could be given of the evil that lies rooted in the love of money.

That Mr. Norris has written an exceptionally strong and powerful novel we do not wish to deny. Neither do we hold that an author may not choose harsh and brutal subjects. But we do believe that highest art is not merely a question of execution, and that the spirit with which the brutal or the beautiful is treated is the quality that redeems or damns. To our thinking, with all our genuine admiration for its exceptional qualities, *McTeague* cannot be classed among great novels, for the spirit that animates is false to the highest standards. We can pardon, accept even with intellectual pleasure, loathsome details that are necessary to the artistic progress of the story, but grossness for the sake of grossness is unpardonable. Mr. Norris has written pages for which there is absolutely no excuse, and his needless sins against good taste and delicacy are fatal spots upon his work. *McTeague* undoubtedly will be widely read—it is too remarkable to pass speedily into oblivion; but we pray that a kind fate may bring it only to those of vigorous mind and, shall we say it, strong stomach. Norris has reason to be proud of his work, but the world will not be proud of it in the distant tomorrow which irrevocably sets true value on books of today.

A Case in Point

William Dean Howells*

The question of expansion in American fiction lately agitated by a lady novelist of Chicago with more vehemence than power, and more courage than coherence, seems to me again palpitant in the case of a new book by a young writer, which I feel obliged at once to recognise as altogether a remarkable book. Whether we shall abandon the old-fashioned American ideal of a novel as something which may be read by all ages and sexes, for the European notion of it as something fit only for age and experience, and for men rather than women; whether we shall keep to the bounds of the provincial proprieties, or shall include within the imperial territory of our fiction the passions and the motives of the savage world which underlies as well as environs civilisation, are points which this book sums up and puts concretely; and it is for the reader, not for the author, to make answer. There is no denying the force with which he makes the demand, and there is no denying the hypocrisies which the old-fashioned ideal of the novel involved. But society, as we have it, is a tissue of hypocrisies, beginning with the clothes in which we hide our nakedness, and we have to ask ourselves how far we shall part with them at his demand. The hypocrisies are the proprieties, the decencies, the morals; they are by no means altogether bad; they are, perhaps, the beginning of civilisation; but whether they should be the end of it is another affair. That is what we are to consider in entering upon a career of imperial expansion in a region where the Monroe Doctrine was never valid. From the very first Europe invaded and controlled in our literary world. The time may have come at last when we are to invade and control Europe in literature. I do not say that it has come, but if it has we may have to employ European means and methods.

It ought not to be strange that the impulse in this direction should have come from California, where, as I am always affirming rather than proving, a continental American fiction began. I felt, or fancied I felt, the impulse in Mr. Frank Norris's *Moran of the Lady Letty*, and now in

*Reprinted from *Literature*, N.S., No. 11 (March 24, 1899), 241–242.

his *McTeague* I am so sure of it that I am tempted to claim the prophetic instinct of it. In the earlier book there were, at least, indications that forecast to any weather-wise eye a change from the romantic to the realistic temperature, and in the later we have it suddenly, and with the overwhelming effect of a blizzard. It is saying both too much and too little to say that Mr. Norris has built his book on Zolaesque lines, yet Zola is the master of whom he reminds you in a certain epical conception of life. He reminds you of Zola also in the lingering love of the romantic, which indulges itself at the end in an anti-climax worthy of Dickens. He ignores as simply and sublimely as Zola any sort of nature or character beyond or above those of Polk Street in San Francisco, but within the ascertained limits he convinces you, two-thirds of the time, of his absolute truth to them. He does not, of course, go to Zola's lengths, breadths, and depths; but he goes far enough to difference his work from the old–fashioned American novel.

Polite readers of the sort who do not like to meet in fiction people of the sort they never meet in society will not have a good time in *McTeague,* for there is really not a society person in the book. They might, indeed, console themselves a little with an elderly pair of lovers on whom Mr. Norris wreaks all the sentimentality he denies himself in the rest of the story; and as readers of that sort do not mind murders as much as vulgarity, they may like to find three of them, not much varying in atrocity. Another sort of readers will not mind the hero's being a massive blond animal, not necessarily bad, though brutal, who has just wit enough to pick up a practical knowledge of dentistry and to follow it as a trade; or the heroine's being a little, pretty, delicate daughter of German-Swiss emigrants, perfectly common in her experiences and ideals, but devotedly industrious, patient, and loyal. In the chemistry of their marriage McTeague becomes a prepotent ruffian, with always a base of bestial innocence; and Trina becomes a pitiless miser without altogether losing her housewifely virtues or ceasing to feel a woman's rapture in giving up everything but her money to the man who maltreats her more and more, and, finally, murders her.

This is rendering in coarse outline the shape of a story realised with a fulness which the outline imparts no sense of. It abounds in touches of character at once fine and free, in little miracles of observation, in vivid insight, in simple and subtle expression. Its strong movement carries with it a multiplicity of detail which never clogs it; the subordinate persons are never shabbed or faked; in the equality of their treatment their dramatic inferiority is lost; their number is great enough to give the feeling of a world revolving round the central figures without distracting the interest from these. Among the minor persons, Maria Macapa, the Mexican chorewoman, whose fable of a treasure of gold turns the head of the Polish Jew Zerkow, is done with rare imaginative force. But all these lesser people are well done; and there are passages throughout the book that live strongly in the memory, as only masterly work can live. The one folly is the insistence on the love-making of those silly elders, which is apparently introduced as an offset to the misery of the other love-making; the anti-climax is Mc-Teague's abandonment in the alkali desert, handcuffed to the dead body of his enemy.

Mr. Norris has, in fact, learned his lesson well, but he has not learned it all. His true picture of life is not true, because it leaves beauty out. Life is squalid and cruel and vile and hateful, but it is noble and tender and pure and lovely, too. By and by he will put these traits in, and then his powerful scene will be a reflection of reality; and by and by he will achieve something of the impartial fidelity of the photograph. In the mean time he has done a picture of life which has form, which has texture, which has color, which has what great original power and ardent study of Zola can give, but which lacks the spiritual light and air, the consecration which the larger art of Tolstoy gives. It is a little inhuman, and it is distinctly not for the walls of living-rooms, where the ladies of the family sit and the children go in and out. This may not be a penalty, but it is the inevitable consequence of expansion in fiction.

A California Novelist

Anonymous*

Within the past year the reading world has been made aware that there is a new American novelist in sight, and that he "comes out of the West." Since Bret Harte and the Forty-niner no one has written of California life with the vigor and accuracy of Mr. Frank Norris; and the best of it is that he is not in the least like Bret Harte, or very much like anyone but himself. His *McTeague*, following close on his tentative adventure story *Moran of the Lady Letty*, settled his right to a place in American literature; and he has now presented a third novel, *Blix*, which is in some respects the finest and likely to be the most popular of the three.

The noticeable thing about these three books—the thing which strikes the reader at sight—is their wide difference from each other. It is an unprecedented thing in literature. Here is an author, practically unknown, who makes something of a reputation by a story of adventure dealing with types absolutely new in fiction; the heroine a woman Viking, the hero a nineteenth century college man, the incident one wild turmoil of moving events by sea and land, and the atmosphere realistic to the last degree. His next work is a powerful character study of San Francisco types which are yet the types of almost any large American city; a gruesome, half-disgusting, but perfectly accurate analysis of a semi-barbarous modern man, done with the realism of Zola and the idealism of Balzac all steeped in an atmosphere which can be nothing but American. Now we find this author turning from adventure and slum study to picture an exquisite, tender, yet humorous love-idyl of the City of the Golden Gate. The only thing which these novels have in common is their fidelity to nature. No one can prophesy what Mr. Norris's next venture will be; but it is safe to say that it will be good. There is one quality which is his in full measure, which is seldom possessed by either the saga man or the analyst; and that is the power to comprehend a woman. Wherever he touches feminine character he does it with as

*Reprinted from *Washington Times* (October 15, 1899), p. 8, part 2.

16

sure and confident a hand as in dealing with men; and his intuition rarely is at fault.

"Blix" is the nickname given by her lover to Travis Bessemer, a California maiden, serene, happy, beautiful and full of strength—the American girl at her best. She is a blossom of San Francisco gardens, but she might have grown in Chicago, Boston, New Orleans or New York and varied but slightly from the type. There is nothing phenomenal or abnormal about her. Her traits are possessed in some degree by thousands of charming girls all over this land; and yet she is an individual; one could never mistake her for anyone else. The same is true of Condy Rivers, the other character in the book—for to all intents and purposes there are but two. He is the writer-man; in certain peculiarities of dress, manner and temperament he is the Western type, but in him half the newspaper men and novelists of the country will recognize salient qualities of their own.

It would be spoiling the feast in store for the reader if one were to sketch the plot of this charming little love story, for it is in the unexpected turns and doublings of this plot, as well as in the character-drawing, that the interest of the book lies. It is thoroughly original and as thoroughly natural, from the first page to the last; and not for two minutes at a time can the reader say what is going to happen next, or what the two people most concerned will take it into their heads to remark. The comedy is odd and bright and rippling; the pathos—what there is of it—is delicately reserved; and the whole movement of the story is free, joyous, and confident. If Mr. Norris can write as careful and powerful novels of Eastern as of Western life, he may yet turn out to be that long-looked-for man, the man whom, perhaps, we lost too early in Harold Frederic—the man who will write the great American novel.

Blix gives the impression of having been written swiftly and rather easily, with great enjoyment. There is a hint of the author's own experience in novel writing here and there, and one gets an inkling of the methods by which *Moran* was accomplished. It may be for this reason that one or two unaccountable slips from accuracy occur in this book, for nothing of the sort is to be found in *McTeague*. Curiously enough they occur in the author's dealing with Kipling, for whom he has evidently a great admiration, almost a passion. He describes an afternoon in a Chinese restaurant where Condy read to Blix some marvelous tales, and she "fell under the charm of the little spectacled colonial, to whose song we all must listen and to whose pipe we all must dance," and he causes these tales to be read from "a paper-covered volume" entitled *Life's Handicap*. In this collection he finds "The Strange Ride of Morrowbie Jukes," and "The Return of Imri." Now, it may be that a special California edition of this work was published; but there was no other edition of it which appeared in paper, and the one generally circulated does not contain the "Morrowbie Jukes" story. Moreover, "The Return of Imray"—which Mr. Norris misspells—is hardly the sort of story which even Condy Rivers would select to read to a girl at luncheon-time in a restaurant. It is a perfectly proper tale, but the snakes and ghosts and corpses are rather too numerous to make it agreeable as an appetizer. Perhaps there was a reason for Mr. Norris' doing these things, but it is not apparent. It is a small matter, but the rest of the book is so finished in its realism that this tiny false touch jars on one.

Blix will be a revelation to those who have not read between the lines of the author's earlier works. It is fresh and simple and wholesome, full of ideality and high thought, without being sentimental or metaphysical, and the vein of drollery which runs through it gives life, vivacity and a certain careless strength and abandon to the whole. Perhaps Mr. Norris's next undertaking will be to give us something purely humorous. He could do it, and it would be worth doing; and it is one of the things which he has not yet done. Or he may turn his attention to the political novel; and there his opportunities would be simply unparalleled. Whatever he does next, he has already done so much that the curiosity of the public is piqued, and it desires to see more of him.

"Books and Magazines"

[Willa Cather*]

Last winter that brilliant young Californian, Mr. Norris, published a remarkable and gloomy novel, *McTeague*, a book deep in insight, rich in promise and splendid in execution, but entirely without charm and as disagreeable as only a great piece of work can be. And now this gentleman, who is not yet 30, turns around and gives us an idyll that sings through one's brain like a summer wind and makes one feel young enough to commit all manner of indiscretions. It may be that Mr. Norris is desirous of showing his versatility and that he can follow any suit, or it may have been a process of reaction. I believe it was after M. Zola had completed one of his greatest and darkest novels of Parisian life that he went down to the seaside and wrote *La Reve*, a book that every girl should read when she is 18, and then again when she is 80. Powerful and solidly built as *McTeague* is, one felt that method was carried almost too far, that Mr. Norris was too consciously influenced by his French masters. But *Blix* belongs to no school whatever, and there is not one shadow of pedantry or pride of craft in it from cover to cover. Blix herself is the method, the motive and the aim of the book. The story is an exhalation of youth and spring; it is the work of a man who breaks loose and forgets himself. Mr. Norris was married only last summer, and the march from *Lohengrin* is simply sticking all over *Blix*. It is the story of a San Francisco newspaper man and a girl. The newspaper man "came out" in fiction, so to speak, in the drawing room of Mr. Richard Harding Davis, and has languished under that gentleman's chaperonage until he has come to be regarded as a fellow careful of nothing but his toilet and his dinner. Mr. Davis's reporters all bathed regularly and all ate nice things, but beyond that their tastes were rather colorless. I am glad to see one red-blooded newspaper man, in the person of Condy Rivers, of San Francisco, break into fiction; a real live reporter, with no sentimental loyalty for his "paper," and no Byronic poses about his vices, and no astonishing taste about his clothes, and no money whatsoever, which is the natural and normal condition of all

*Reprinted from *Pittsburgh Leader* (November 4, 1899), p. 5.

19

reporters. Blix herself was just a society girl, and Condy took her to
theaters and parties and tried to make himself believe that he was in
love with her. But it wouldn't work, for Condy couldn't love a society
girl, not though she were as beautiful as the morning and terrible as
an army with banners, and had "round full arms," and "the skin of
her face was white and clean, except where it flushed into a most charming pink upon her smooth, cool cheeks." For while Condy Rivers was at
college he had been seized with the penchant for writing short stories,
and had worshiped at the shrines of Maupassant and Kipling, and when
a man is craft-mad enough to worship Maupassant truly and known him
well, when he has that tingling for technique in his fingers, not Aphrodite
herself, new risen from the waves, could tempt him into any world
where craft was not lord and king. So it happened that their real love
affair never began until one morning when Condy had to go down to the
wharf to write up a whaleback and Blix went along, and an old sailor
told them a story and Blix recognized the literary possibilities of it,
and they had lunch in a Chinese restaurant, and Condy, because he was
a newspaper man and it was the end of the week, didn't have any
change about his clothes, and Blix had to pay the bill. And it was in that
queer old tea house that Condy read Blix one of his favorite yarns by
Kipling, and she, in a calm, offhanded way, recognized one of the fine
technical points in it and Condy almost went to pieces for joy at her
doing it. That scene in the Chinese restaurant is one of the prettiest bits
of color you'll find to rest your eyes upon, and mighty good writing it is.
I wonder, though, if when Mr. Norris adroitly mentioned the "clack and
snarl" of the banjo Condy played, he remembered the "silver snarling
trumpets" of Keats? After that, things went on as such things will, and
Blix quit the society racket and went to queer places with Condy, and
got interested in his work, and she broke him of wearing red neckties
and playing poker, and she made him work, she did, for she grew to
realize how much that meant to him, and she jacked him up when he
didn't work, and she suggested an ending for one of his stories that was
better than his own; just this big splendid girl who had never gone to
college to learn how to write novels. And so how, in the name of goodness, could he help loving her? So one morning, down by the Pacific
with Blix and The Seven Seas, it all came over Condy, that "living
was better than reading, and life was better than literature." And so it
is; once, and only once, for each of us; and that is the tune that sings
and sings through one's head when one puts the books away.

Frank Norris's *A Man's Woman*

Anonymous*

Frank Norris has taken one of the much-discussed questions of the day, the attitude to be taken by husband and wife each toward the career the other has chosen, for the central theme of his latest novel, *A Man's Woman*. The husband is an Arctic explorer, and the woman a trained nurse—neither of which vocations is compatible with uninterrupted domesticity—and Mr. Norris's solution of the question is the same that has been found most acceptable since Adam delved and Eve spun: the woman gives up her own career and yet sends the husband out on his frigid search for fame.

Lloyd Searight, the woman, has endowed a home for trained nurses, and enrolled herself on its staff. Ward Bennett, the man she loves, and Dick Ferriss, his dearest friend, return from a polar expedition, and, Ferriss contracting typhoid fever, Lloyd is sent to nurse him. The case is a most malignant one and two nurses have succumbed to the infection. At a critical stage of the disease Bennett learns that Lloyd is the nurse, and, in spite of urgent calls from the servant momentarily at the sick bed, forcibly prevents her from attending the patient. Through this negligence Ferriss dies. Lloyd's love for Bennett is stunned—she thinks it dead—and Bennett himself sinks with the fever, and Lloyd nurses him. He tries to drive her from his bedside, as he had from his friend's, but she is the stronger, and nurses him back to life. They marry, and in time she helps him to another expedition to the pole.

The pictures of the explorers' sufferings and struggles in the frozen north, with which the book opens, are extraordinarily vivid, and equally lifelike are the scenes in which Lloyd is shown in her duties as a trained nurse. Mr. Norris has evidently collected his data with the painstaking care of another Zola. But the strain of this painstaking is apparent in every page, and there is not a passage in the book that it is a pleasure to read. As to the mental battles through which Lloyd struggles when Bennett breaks her career and when she forces herself to return to the nurses' house and state the facts to her companions—there are pages

*Reprinted from *The Argonaut*, 46 (March 12, 1900), 8.

21

and pages of these semi-delirious ramblings that are wearisome. Mr. Norris has got it all in, undoubtedly. What he should have done is to leave in only the salient points.

One can not but take exception, too, to Mr. Norris's title, *A Man's Woman*. Brute force is not the modern concept of true manliness, and Ward Bennett is, by his primitive directness of thought as well as by his simian features and physique, little better than a human gorilla, and it is an insult to the race to apply to a female whose love for a male, evoked solely by his force, survives what was in intent the murder of his friend, the high title of "a man's woman."

Mr. Norris's Ultra Realism

Anonymous*

Conan Doyle once said: "We talk so much about art, that we tend to forget what this art was ever invented for. It was to amuse mankind— to help the sick and the dull and the weary." The majority of our novelists must emphatically dissent from this, for one and all—with a few shining exceptions—seem to have taken for their motto the blood-curdling announcement of the Fat Boy in *Pickwick*, "I wants to make your flesh creep."

Mr. Norris's hero is an arctic explorer, his heroine a trained nurse, and he avails himself to the utmost of these opportunities to make our "flesh creep." The experiences in the arctic are a skillful mosaic of the worst sufferings of various expeditions. We have portrayed the extremes of cold and hunger, limbs amputated, dying and imploring companions deserted on the ice—terrible pictures of suffering and brutality. We turn for relief to the trained nurse, and we are made almost literally to assist at a fearful operation, every preparation, every detail, every movement of the surgeon and the nurse being given with a minuteness that is simply sickening. That removal of the child's hip joint is as

> "Photographically lined
> On the tablets of our mind"

as if we had been the nurse herself. After all this, it is, perhaps, a mere trifle to see a horse brained with a hammer, and to go through two cases of typhoid fever with almost as much attention to minutiae as was given to the operation.

We respectfully submit, Is this art?

But, steadying our nerves with restoratives, or handing the instruments to somebody else while we take a quiet little faint, let us accept Mr. Norris's canons of art and turn from the horrors to the romance.

Strong and original the book undoubtedly is, holding the reader's interest to the end. Nevertheless, it fairly bristles with faults. The hero

*Reprinted from *New York Times: Saturday Review of Books and Art*, 49 (February 10, 1900), 82.

is not only ugly—but let Mr. Norris describe him: "His lower jaw was huge almost to deformity, like that of the bull-dog; the chin was salient, the mouth close gripped, with great lips, indomitable, brutal. The fore-head was contracted and small—the forehead of men of single ideas—and the eyes, too, were small and twinkling, one of them marred by a sharply defined cast." Beyond force and endurance, Capt. Ward Ben-nett possesses no qualities to atone for this villainous physiognomy. The scene in which he consigns his best friend to certain death in order to snatch the nurse from a contagion already fully risked is brutal beyond belief. That nurse, the "man's woman," is the opposite of the type commonly supposed to be a man's woman. Her characteristics, many of them fine, are distinctively masculine. The author seems to be resolved that we shall not admire what appear to be self-sacrifice and generosity in his heroine, for he takes pains to tell us that she was not inspired by philanthropy nor a great love of humanity, but she wanted "to count in the general economy of things." Ferriss, whom his creator rather care-lessly casts aside, is the one really noble character of the story. It is singular that at first much is made of his unselfish falsehood, and that it is afterward wholly ignored and dropped, as if Mr. Norris had changed his mind as regards the working out of his plot.

There are some fine scenes in the book, notably, the one in which Lloyd drives into the pole of the arctic chart the worn banner of the former expedition. But why persistently call the Stars and Stripes "the stars and bars," the name which was borne by the flag of the short-lived Confederacy?

As we close the story, we cannot help wondering whether it was not written to see how much ultra-realism in what is painful and repulsive a long-suffering public intends to endure. It is a pity that a strong and capable pen should do these things. A novel is neither a chamber of horrors nor a surgical journal.

Norris *The Octopus*

Wallace Rice*

Frank Norris has written a novel, as fascinating, as repellent, as multifarious, as misshapen as the marine monster from which it gains its name of *The Octopus* (Doubleday, Page & Co.). Sufficiently absorbing to hold the reader with something of the Wedding Guest's insistence, once it is taken up, it leaves him with precisely the opposite impression with which Coleridge's masterpiece is laid down. It is wonderfully clever, and only where the author permits himself vain repetitions does its interest flag; but its philosophy is hideous, and the book is as certainly at war with itself as its characters are with one another. To its composition every crime lends its bad interest—rape, murder, train robbing, bribery, corruption in politics, prostitution, inordinate greed, lust for gold and lust for blood. In his characters, for the most part, vice is rebuked and morality upheld. To those who depart from the accepted standard, romantic justice, as unusual in life as it becomes customary here, is meted out with fine particularity. The bad man is killed with a rifle shot, the train robber is sentenced for life, the briber goes down into the darkness of insanity, the corruption-monger is strangled in his own accumulating wealth. Everywhere Mr. Norris shows himself to be animated by high principle in his treatment of his characters. But in the underlying principles which he demonstrates at the end, the babyish plea of elemental force and destiny is entered for the arch-devil of them all, and the other lessons go for naught.

The Octopus, like Mr. Norris's other well-known books, is a work of realism. Its foundation facts are derived from the history of the Southern Pacific Railroad, and almost all the story revolves around the machinations of the officials of that great monopoly. In this the author becomes a public benefactor—at least in intention. How difficult it will be for him to persuade Americans of the substantial truth of his indictment against such a corporation may be known to him, yet the fate which befell Messrs. Merwin and Webster's *The Short-Line War* two years ago will be interesting in this connection. The two authors came upon an

*Reprinted from *Chicago American Literary and Art Review* (April 6, 1901), 5–6.

attempt on the part of Jay Gould to grab one of the feeders of the Erie Railway, an independent company, as it appeared in the records of one of the courts in New York State. Finding the account more fascinating than anything they could plan for themselves, they made a careful investigation, and in writing the romance held themselves closely to the demonstrable facts.

The book was read by one of the leading officials of the Burlington Road at my instance, and he told me afterward that he himself had been through precisely such an experience in the West, identical with the narrative to such an extent that he knew every move of the warring factions in the corporation before he reached them. In the face of this, in spite of the double occurrence of just such depredations as the book disclosed, the New York Evening Post dismissed the story as incredible —the New York Evening Post at that time being controlled by the Villard interests. Mr. Norris makes a far more serious indictment against the Southern Pacific than this. He quotes actual documents to prove the wickedness of the position taken by its officials in ousting the men whom it induced to settle on its lands by what turned out to be the falsest of false pretenses; but he does not stop there. The Octopus has as many branches as its namesake. It controls the Railway Commission, it controls the Legislature, it controls the courts. In drawing his indictment against it in the earlier part of the book Mr. Norris does unconsciously the thing he represents the commissioners as doing corruptly; he raises his rate so high that it is certain to be rejected at the bar of public opinion. If his novel be one with a purpose, and that the exposure of infinitely corrupt corporation methods, it is self-defeated on the instant. He himself seems unaware of this later in the book, for his most intimate character says: "Tell the people five years from now the story of the fight between the League of San Joaquin and the railroad and it will not be believed."

This is the chief fault to be found with the construction of the book—and a book with a self-defeated purpose can hardly be called a book at all, even though, as here, it abounds in vivid descriptions, insistent characterizations and abounding interest. There are other faults, more noticeable in a book serving so realistic a purpose than in any other. Priests of the Roman Church do not quote the Protestant translations of the Scriptures, for example, as Father Sarria does here. The episode of Vanamee and Angele Varian, poetic and engrossing though it be, has no possible relevance in this work, nor is it in any way bound up in the rest of it. The sandwiching of the account of the dinner in the house of a millionaire and of the starving of a mother in the street is felt to be a trick, a tour de force, rather than literature—the literature that Mr. Norris affects to despise in more than one place in his pages, as though his book could have illiterary vitality.

But, as was intimated before, the philosophy of the book is its weakest point. After all the sin and suffering and death of its earlier pages, the whole question of personal responsibility for crime is dismissed by the archfiend of them all in these words: "Try to believe this—to begin with—that railroads build themselves. Where there is demand, sooner or later there will be a supply. Mr. Derrick, does he grow his wheat? The wheat grows itself. What does he count for? Does he supply the force? What do I count for? Do I build the railroad? You are dealing with forces, young man, when you speak of wheat and the railroad, not with men. There is the wheat, the supply. It must be carried to feed the people. There is the demand. The wheat is one force, the railroad another, and there is the law that governs them—supply and demand. Men have only little to do in the whole business. Complications may arise, conditions that bear hard on the individual—crush him maybe—but the wheat will be carried to feed the people as inevitably as it will grow. Blame conditions, not men."

It need not be pointed out that this hideous doctrine, the doctrine that would justify a Nero and damn an Antonine, can be urged in favor of any crime that ever was hatched in warped and brutal brains. It is the doctrine of personal irresponsibility, of a conscienceless world, of a godless universe. It is the plea of organized greed and unrestrained lust in all ages. Most unfortunately it is the plea which Mr. Norris represents as wholly converting the most intelligent character in his book, the character with which he asserts the greatest degree of personal intimacy and for which he makes the greatest appeal for the reader's sympathy.

Frank Norris's *The Octopus*

Frederick T. Cooper*

There is a character at the outset of Mr. Norris's new volume, the poet Presley, who is haunted by the dream of writing an epic of the West. His ambition is to paint life frankly as he sees it; yet, incongruously enough, he wishes to see everything through a rose-tinted mist—a mist that will tone down all the harsh outlines and crude colours. He is searching for true romance, and, instead, finds himself continually brought up against railway tracks and grain rates and unjust freight tariffs. All this is quite interesting, not because Presley is an especially important or convincing character, but because it is so obviously only another way of stating Mr. Norris's favourite creed: that realism and romanticism are, after all, convertible terms; that the epic theme for which Presley was vainly groping lay all the time close at hand if he could but have seen it, not merely in the primeval life of mountain and desert, and the shimmering purple of a sunset, but in the limitless stretch of steel rails, in the thunder of passing trains, in the whole vast, intricate mechanism of an organised monopoly.

No one is likely to quarrel seriously with this position. There certainly is a sort of epic vastness and power in many phases of our complicated modern life when treated in a broad, sweeping Zolaesque fashion—in the railroad, the stock exchange, the department stores when they are set before us like so many vast symbols, titanic organisms, with an entity and a purpose of their own. It is only when we come down to details, the petty, sordid details of individual lives, that realism and romance part company. Yet no one knows better than Mr. Norris that it is these very details which give to every picture of life its true value and colour, and he himself has often given them to us with pitiless fidelity. There are few writers of to-day who could cope with him in giving the physiognomy of some mean little side-street in San Francisco, of painting with a few telling strokes a living picture of some odd little Chinese restaurant, of making us breathe the very atmosphere of McTeague's tawdry, disordered, creosote-laden dental parlour, or the foul,

*Reprinted from *Bookman*, 13 (May, 1901), 245–47.

reeking interior of Bennett's tent on the ice fields of the far North. It is a trifle exasperating to find a man who can do work like this deliberately choosing every now and then, after the fashion of his poet Presley, to look at life through rose coloured glasses, instead of adhering fearlessly to the crude colours and the harsh outlines. It was this tendency which betrayed him into the melodramatic ending of *McTeague*; in real life the big, dull-witted dentist would probably have perished miserably in a gutter or a garret, if he had succeeded in evading the hangman; but it suited Mr. Norris's purpose better to apotheosise him, to drive him out into the midst of the alkali desert, forming, as it were, the one human note in a sort of vast symphony of nature. In the present work there is nothing quite so glaring, yet we detect the same underlying spirit. It is felt not alone in the vein of mysticism which runs through the book, the whole episode of Vanamee, the lonely, half-distraught shepherd invoking the spirit of his lost bride across the wide expanse of prairie. It is felt still more in the lack of vivid character drawing in *The Octopus,* in a certain blurring of the outlines, that suggests a composite photograph, in the substitution of types for individuals. In more than one way Mr. Norris is farther away from real life in *The Octopus* than he was in *A Man's Woman,* just as in that novel he was farther away than in *McTeague.*

The truth is that *The Octopus* is a sort of vast allegory, an example of symbolism pushed to the extreme limit, rather than a picture of life. Mr. Norris has always had a fondness for big themes; they are better suited to the special qualities of his style, the sonority of his sentences, the insistent force of accumulated noun and adjective. This time he has conceived the ambitious idea of writing a trilogy of novels which, taken together, shall symbolise American life, not merely the life of some small corner of a single State, but American life as a whole, with all its hopes and aspirations and its tendencies, throughout the length and breadth of the continent. And for the central symbol he has taken wheat, as being quite literally and truly the staff of this life, the ultimate source of American power and prosperity. This first volume, *The Octopus,* dealing with the production of wheat, shows us a corner of California, the San Joaquin Valley, where a handful of ranchmen are engaged in irrigating and ploughing, planting, reaping and harvesting, performing all the slow, arduous toil of cultivation, and at the same time carrying on a continuous warfare against the persistent encroachment of the railroad, whose steel arms are reaching out, octopus-like, to grasp, encircle and crush one after another all those who venture to oppose it. It is quite likely that Mr. Norris has been careful of his facts, that he has some basis for his presentment of the railway's acts of aggression, the unjust increase of freight tariffs, the regrading of land values, the violent evictions—in short, that his novel is well documented. From the symbolic side, however, the literal truth is unimportant. The novel typifies on a small scale the struggle continuously going on between capital and labour, the growth of centralised power, the aggression of the corporation and the trust. But back of the individual, back of the corporation, is the spirit of the nation, typified in the wheat, unchanged, indomitable, rising, spreading, gathering force, rolling in a great golden wave from West to East, across the continent, across the ocean, and carrying with it health and strength and hope and sustenance to other nations—emblem of the progressive, indomitable spirit of the American people. Such, at least, seems to be Mr. Norris's underlying thought, and he has developed it in a way which compels admiration, even from those who find *The Octopus* as a story rather disappointing. Especially deserving of cordial praise is the manner in which the two underlying thoughts of his theme are kept before the reader, like the constantly recurring *leitmotivs* of a Wagnerian opera. First, there is the *motiv* of the railroad, insistent, aggressive, refusing to be forgotten, making its presence felt on every page of the book—in the shrill scream of a distant engine, in the heavy rumble of a passing freight train, in the substantial presence of S. Behrman, the local agent, whose name greets us at the outset of the story in large flaring letters of a painted sign on a water-tank, "S. Behrman has something to say to *you*," and whose corpulent, imperturbable, grasping personality obtrudes itself continually, placid, unyielding, invincible. Now and then we have a clear-cut picture of the road itself, as in the graphic, ghastly episode of an engine, ploughing its way through a flock of sheep, which had somehow made their way through the barbed-wire fence and wandered upon the track. . . .

Such, in brief, are the purposes of Mr. Norris's book. It is full of enthusiasm and poetry and conscious strength. One can hardly read it without a responsive thrill of sympathy for the earnestness, the breadth of purpose, the verbal power of the man. But as a study of character, a picture of real life, of flesh and blood, it must be frankly owned that *The Octopus* is disappointing. A few of the characters are good, they promise at first to win our sympathies—characters like the slow, tenacious German, Hooven; the tall, commanding figure of Magnus Derrick, the "governor," to whom life was one huge gamble; the coarse-fibred, combative young farmer, Annixter, with his scorn of "feemales" and his morbid concern over the vagaries of a stomach which would persist in "getting out of whack." But, taken as a whole, the characters do not wear well; they come and go, love and suffer and die, and their joy and their misery fail to wake a responsive thrill. An exception, however, must be made in the case of S. Behrman. He, at least, is consistently developed and consistently hated. From first to last he has appeared invincible, out of reach of law, of powder and shot, of dynamite. And the final episode, where he is struck down at the very summit of his ambition, caught in a trap by his own wheat, and pictured writhing, struggling, choking to death miserably in the dark hold of the ship, beaten down and lashed by the pitiless hail of grain as it pours with a metallic roar from the iron chute, is a chapter tense with dramatic power —a scene for which a parallel must be sought in the closing pages of *Germinal* or the episode of the man-hunt in *Paris*. Whatever shortcomings *The Octopus* may possess, this one chapter goes far toward atoning for them. It gives a glimpse of Mr. Norris at his best, and holds out a hopeful promise for the future volumes of the trilogy.

The Pit: A Dispassionate Examination of Frank Norris's Posthumous Novel

Anonymous[*]

Just how much American literature lost by the death of Frank Norris is a difficult question, to which there will be many answers, none conclusive. That the work he had already done contained much of promise and something of achievement will probably be admitted by all. Opinions will differ widely as to the extent of the achievement, and achievement is, after all, the only safe basis of judgment, while recognition of a young author as "promising" is criticism not the less severe because in kindly form.

Clearly as Mr. Norris had proved himself to be a story teller with stories to tell, he had not revealed either the inerrant taste of genius or the patient industry of enlightened talent. He was in a hurry to do great things, and, conscious of strength, did not take the pains to acquire the technical skill upon which perfection of detail depends. His books, in consequence, were remarkable rather than admirable, or, at least, more remarkable than admirable, and one sometimes gets from them the impression of reading a first draft manuscript instead of the printed page. They evidence what it is customary to call fatal facility and seem to be written at high speed and left uncorrected.

If this seeming is deceptive, and Mr. Norris did in reality give his books the careful revision without which the conscientious artist is never content, then there is a chance that his work would have been "promising" to the end of a long life, as it was to the end of one pathetically short. For there was not much difference between *McTeague* and *The Octopus*, so far as literary finish went, and now comes *The Pit*, with all of the small faults as well as all of the large virtues of its predecessors. Nature made Mr. Norris a marvelously accurate observer of the life around him, and to this gift added the creative imagination, but she did not endow

*Reprinted from *New York Times: Saturday Review of Books and Art*, (January 31, 1903), 66.

him with an instinctive knowledge that the right word is worth a long search, and he had not discovered it for himself. He appreciated only too well the colossal effects produced by Zola, and imitated that master's devices only too successfully, for in imitating the devices he often missed the effects. Perhaps he had read both too much and too little; if he had read less his style would have been original, because he would not have thought anything about style, and if he had read more he would have been able consciously to make a style of his own—which comes to the same thing.

But Mr. Norris was what he was, and there is small profit in regretting, and less in resenting, that he was not something else. He followed a happy inspiration when he planned "the epic of the wheat," and, as *The Octopus*, which dealt with the growing and the growers of what means more to humanity than any other product of the soil, was no common book, so *The Pit*, which shows the fierce excitements of speculation in the staff of life, is something more than merely a piece of picturesque and vigorous writing. That it is an absolutely accurate picture of the Chicago Board of Trade and the men who contend therein is likely to be questioned by those with much personal knowledge of both, but that matters little to the rest of us, for grain brokers and their clients, or patrons, or customers, or whatever it is that grain brokers have, are at least as interesting as Mr. Norris saw them as they are in reality, and the novelist, even the realistic novelist, has the best of rights to leave history and statistics to the historians and the statisticians, and to consult only his own conscience—and needs—in regard to the amount of exaggerating and emphasizing he should do. He would not have claimed that Curtis Jadwin, his hero, is the ordinary speculator in wheat, or that every, or even any, attempt to "corner" that useful staple has passed through precisely the phases he records; but certain as it is that there are not many Jadwins, there is no obvious reason why there should not be one of them, and, given the one, the recorded "corner" would follow naturally enough.

Business has its adventures as well as its adventurers, nowadays, and the growing tendency of novelists to substitute the comedy and tragedy of business for those of war, hunting, and other similarly antiquated forms of activity is proof of great wisdom on their part, especially as "heart interest" combines as logically and inevitably with business as with the other occupations.

It does so in *The Pit*, which includes among its numerous personages several entirely comprehensible women—every one of whom, for a wonder, could safely submit her "past" to the inspection and commentary of publics even more censorious than that of Chicago is supposed to be.

The reader hardly sees, perhaps, why so many men fell in love with Laura Dearborn, or why the well-matured Jadwin thought himself so lucky to win her away from his less wealthy rivals; but real life is full of mysteries of that sort, and surely the realistic novelist is under no obligation to ignore the fact that unexpected results are often reached by the solution of personal equations. Laura made quite as good a wife as the somewhat priggish grain gambler deserved. Among the minor characters—Board of Trade men of various ranks and ages, the inevitable pair of youthful lovers, a maiden aunt bewildered by millions, and the like—are several that were carefully conceived and projected, and not the less sympathetic because they are the immemorial "types" of fiction and the stage, newly costumed, each serving the familiar purpose. Indeed, if one looks below the surface of *The Pit*, one soon realizes that not much more than its properties is new.

The Octopus seemed to be for the most part the product of actual experience, and the wheat was an essential feature of the story, but the second book of the "epic" reveals the use of second-hand information as to the methods and language of the grain speculators. The author's material was well studied up, not unconsciously acquired and thoroughly possessed. Had the third volume of the proposed series been written, the deterioration from the first would probably have been still more marked, for Mr. Norris was able to acquire a closer knowledge of Chicago than he would have obtained in regard to a European village stricken with famine, which was to have been the scene of a book called *The Wolf*, and dealing with the consumption of the wheat raised in California and made the object of a ruthless gamble beside Lake Michigan.

While on his own ground and voicing the wrongs of his own people, Mr. Norris won easier pardon for his verbal infelicities than when he wandered into new fields and imagined emotions instead of feeling them. The war between the wheat growers and the Pacific railways was something worth getting excited over; as much can hardly be said of a laborious demonstration that speculation in the necessities of life, when conducted on a large scale, is an immoral practice, and very wearing on the nerves of the speculator. The demonstration at best is not entirely convincing, and so far as it does convince it was unnecessary. Mr. Norris would have gone much further in the time alloted him if he had taken himself a little less, and his chosen profession a little more, seriously. He was a preacher turned novelist—a preacher, that is, of elementary sociology and economics, and his magnificent powers of observation and description were allowed to run wild in order that he might hasten to tell the world some true things that were not new and some new things that were not true.

Frank Norris, *Vandover and the Brute*: Some Notes on His Later Works

John Macy*

Frank Norris was the most important American novelist of his generation. He accomplished much and he promised more. In the twelve years since his death only one man has given us books which equal his in sincerity and depth of purpose—Mr. Theodore Dreiser. When Doubleday, Page & Co. announced that an unpublished manuscript of Norris's had been recovered and that it was his first completed novel, one waited for it with mingled hope and misgiving. He had not found time or impulse to revise it and it was the work of a young man just out of college. One would read *Vandover and the Brute* because Norris wrote it, and because the first steps of a man who finally arrived are interesting to trace. Never was moderate expectation more agreeably disappointed. The case-hardened professional reader, who, like the surgeon, cannot permit his nerves to be affected by his daily task, lay awake all night impelled to the end of the book.

If Norris had failed in *Vandover* he might have contemplated the failure with satisfaction; for the theme he chose is so great that to have conceived it in youth is honor enough, and not to have worked it out completely is no disgrace.

The book has faults; counsel would advise it to plead guilty on several counts. The nice girl of the story is drawn with uncertain strokes. There are signs of effort in the exposition of Vandover's character. No author under 35 or 40 could know enough to make all the steps of Vandover's descent self-evident. But the defects of the book are those of a large intention not quite realized. It is not the defects that would have insured the rejection of the book by any American publisher to whom Norris might have submitted it. It is the merits of the book that would probably have rendered it "unavailable" in the nineties. There is no way of proving it, but one can be fairly sure that if Norris had sent

*Reprinted from *Boston Herald*, 135 (May 9, 1914), 4.

this book to publishers twenty years ago, he would have wasted his postage stamps.

For he dares to be a disciple of Zola. He sends a man to the dogs with more regard to character and circumstance than to the allurements of a happy ending. He makes an innocent man victim of a dread disease —fifteen years before any of us heard of Brieux. His conception of "love interest" excludes the merry wedding bells; indeed, in his earnest pursuit of an idea, he forgot his nice young girl and let her disappear from the story, as if it were not his business to know what became of her. If the seriousness of his work, his lofty idea of the duty and pleasure of a novelist, his tragic sense of life were inharmonious with the prevalent spirit in American literature at the close of the nineteenth century, he revealed in *McTeague* and allowed to lie buried in *Vandover* some qualities which even American readers must respect. In the first place he has the gift of sustaining and increasing the power of a story, the art of crescendo. I remember no work of his which falls off after a good beginning. *Vandover* gets better and better as it proceeds. If Norris knew this to be true, he might have felt sure of his calling, for when a tyro lacks real power, he almost invariably puts what stuff he has in the first part of his book and weakens toward the end.

Another power which Norris disclosed in this early novel is objectivity in the management of character. The young writer, who knows little except himself, is likely to make his people think as he thinks, so that they are but variously labelled packages of his opinions. From the first Norris's imagination was strong enough to endow his personages with individual temperaments, motives, habits of thought and modes of speech; they lead their own lives; they seem to be out of control. And that is the most difficult, the most wonderful illusion that a creator of fiction can produce.

A third virtue which he was to exhibit to a greater degree in the later books marks *Vandover* as the work of a born novelist, the sensory reality of the scene. Whether he learned the trick from Zola or whether his experience as an art student taught him how to visualize things, he knew how to present persons as if they had air on all sides of them, streets as if they could be walked upon, even an entire city, San Francisco, as an organism with a life and visage peculiarly its own. He is never guilty of the young writer's vice of seeming to "do a description." He uses his eyes and is perhaps youthfully conscious that he sees life in an individual way and is not a victim of other people's trite observations. A minor example of his resolution to see things as they are, to penetrate sham and hypocrisy and convention, is his description of the entrance of a factory. "In front on either side of the main entrance were white stone medallions upon which were chiselled the head of a workman wearing the square paper cap that the workman never wears, and a bent-up forearm, the biceps enormous, the fist gripping the short hammer that the workman never uses."

The author of *Vandover and the Brute* is a stern young moralist who portrays the struggle in the individual between good and evil. In *The Octopus* and *The Pit* Norris became a student of the social structure, of the contests between forces, economic and natural, in which the individual is ruined or succeeds, finds his hour of happiness and meets his hour of death. To say that these books are an epic of Daily Bread is not to misuse a large word. The story of wheat is the history of an empire, of vast migrations, conquests, and disasters, controlled, as all national movements and private destinies have been controlled, by the mute motive of hunger. Wheat is a fact and a symbol. It drowns the individual Behrman, who for the moment is the personal representative of the great impersonal system, the esurient Octopus; it inundates the grain market and makes havoc of Jadwin's fortunes. Viewed singly these deaths and failures are but accidents of the game; perhaps Behrman's death is too obviously accidental. But seen more deeply they are typical, inevitable, poetically just.

The last page of *The Octopus*, conceived upon a plane of eloquence from which a fall would be easy, has a Whitmanian breadth of vision. "The WHEAT remained. Untouched, unassailable, undefined, that mighty world force, that nourisher of nations, wrapped in Nirvanic calm, indifferent to the human swarm, gigantic, resistless, moved onward in its appointed grooves. Through the welter of blood at the irrigation ditch, through the sham charity and shallow philanthropy of famine relief committees, the great harvest of Los Muertos rolled like a flood from the Sierras to the Himalayas to feed thousands of starving scarecrows on the barren plains of India."

From Bret Harte to Jack London many writers of unquestionable talent have sent us stories of the great West, its ranches, deserts and mines. If a general fault may be charged, subject to many exceptions, it is that they seem to have their eyes upon a New York or Boston publisher rather than upon their subject; they have packed their goods for the eastern market and have adulterated life with spurious romance. Three men above all others have looked at some aspects of the West with honest and perspicacious vision; two were humorists; Mark Twain and O. Henry and the other was Norris, who had little humor except of the kind that does not make one laugh. There is no legitimate ground for quarrel with any piece of good writing, whatever the author's mood or general view of life. It will always be a pleasure to read Bret Harte;

he was an artist in his kind, but of a tradition that has passed in every country except America. It is still a pleasure to read Mr. Jack London, and one has faith that he has not wholly capitulated to the many-headed god of popularity. But if fiction is to be taken seriously and held accountable as a record of life as well as an entertainment, we shall, in our old age, look back for a glimpse of the true West to the wise jokers, Mark Twain and O. Henry, who, each in his generation, laughed foolish romance out of countenance; and we shall look back to the sombre realism of Norris. He was the one trained American novelist (trained of course in France) who happened to live in California and to write of the life he knew. His ranchers, bad men, Mexicans, train robbers seem to be drawn from life.

The frontispiece of an English edition of *The Octopus* is a picture of a duel between a man on horseback and a man on foot. If one saw that picture in a magazine one would carefully avoid reading the story. But the episode in Norris's text which the picture illustrates is different. It is different in one supremely important respect; it is not merely an exciting scene narrated for its own sake, it is deeply rooted in the social soil from which it springs and it invites the eye to look past it to a broad human landscape.

The Work of Frank Norris

Hamlin Garland*

The three books on which the fame of Frank Norris already rests are these—*McTeague, The Octopus,* and *The Pit. McTeague,* as its name implies, is an exhaustive study of two or three persons—one of which is a profound characterization. *The Octopus* is a presentation of sociologic conditions in California and *The Pit* is a social and sociologic study of Chicago.

I began my acquaintance with Norris over the pages of *McTeague*. The amazing particularity and unfailing interest of this grim story led me to a belief that its author could do anything—even write a "Trilogy of Wheat." Once a very wise and gentle man listened to a plan which involved several volumes—and at the end said quietly—very quietly: "Admirable—only be sure you don't lose interest in your plan." I thought of this when Norris outlined his scheme for the trilogy. It is to be forever incomplete, not because the author lost interest in its final volume, but because he is dead, and his master, Zola, is dead, and *The Wolf* remains only a title in Norris's last preface.

In the place of this third volume we may set *McTeague*—or rather it should come first, and *The Octopus* and *The Pit* be moved up the line—for there is no need of apology in dealing with *McTeague*. In it is some of the best work Norris ever did, and as a whole it stands as a sort of preparation work—a superb thesis on the individual, leading to a consideration of the sociologic—the epic.

It is the study of a poor, badly equipped young man who painfully gains a certain place in society and struggling blindly and brutishly, fails to maintain it—a lonely, harmless creature, dull, gross, and good-tempered, to whom law is a menace and poverty a never-absent, hell-ward-sloping gulf just at his feet. He has few helpers and no brethren, but has many enemies. He is at once tragic and comic. His history is of a kind with Daudet's *Jack* and Flaubert's *Madame Bovary*. It is inexorable in its unrelenting lifelikeness. It is one of the most masterly studies in our literature, but the reader is forced at the end to ask "Of

*Reprinted from *The Critic*, 42 (March 1903), 216–218.

what avail this study of sad lives?" for it does not even lead to a notion of social betterment. It is gray, gray and cold, in tone. It ends in a desert, with two of its chief characters locked in death-grapple.

Norris's interest was not that of the ethical teacher, the reformer who turns on the light. He rejoiced in McTeague and Trina as terms in a literary theorem. Their sufferings lead to no conclusions. They are in the book because they appealed to his dramatic sense, his love for character. This book is without direct prototype. You may say it reminds you of Flaubert in treatment, or of Zola in theme, but in reality it is without fellow. Its originality is unquestionable. There are flaws in it, but they do not seriously detract from its essential greatness. It is vital and compelling on every page.

In *The Octopus* the intention is frankly sociologic. A map prefaces the story, a cast of characters is thrown upon a screen. The author is in the country and concerned with wide horizons rippling with vast wheatfields; he is dealing not with a few persons huddled into a flat, but with proud landowners in combination against a giant corporation. McTeague was a blind fighter but the farmers in *The Octopus* are immense landlords, oppressors in their own right, banding together for purely mercenary reasons; had they all been really fighting for life, as was the poor engineer turned tiller of the soil, the book would have been heart-wringing. In every chapter *wheat* is taken for the motive, the ever-recurring refrain. The impersonal is uppermost; individuals are subordinated, inexorably crushed, or senselessly exalted as in life by blind forces.

At times the attempt to apply the methods of Zola is too apparent. We weary of adjectives which seem to have been taken directly from *La Terre*. The motive is too insistent, the impersonal ceases at times to interest. The use of the refrain is Wagnerian, but it loses in effect at times. Perhaps it is not a trick, but it certainly is an artifice and legitimate enough. Reference to Trina and McTeague was often made in words to the same effect—in *The Octopus* the dead bride Vanamee, Hilma Tree, Annixter, Behrman are announced by almost exactly the same phrases— wonderfully good phrases too—precisely as Wotan and Siegfried are announced by the same trumpet flares, varied to the flow of the orchestral score. This gives unity to the structure of the novel and produces a most vivid and powerful impression on the mind of the reader, but it also adds formality and fixedness—restricting free development. In the case of Magnus Derrick the artifice proved not merely ineffectual but practically impossible, for his was a dynamic characterization. He grew. Even Annixter (one of the most individual of all Norris's characters) breaks away from his old self. The phrase departs so widely from the original that it ceases to be recognized.

I do not know that I object to this repetition, but I do consider the constant use of adjectives in the style of Hugo and Zola a disfigurement. Their use was a survival of his boyish idolatry of the two men who labored to make the French language something more than the mincing periphrasis of court intriguers. *McTeague* may be said to partake of the method of Balzac. *The Octopus* certainly was founded upon *Germinal* and *La Terre*. But there his indebtedness ceased—for McTeague, and Annixter and Trina and Derrick—for the throngs of marvellously realized characters in each of these books we are indebted to the keen eyes, the abounding insight, and the swift imagination of a born novelist. Norris studied life or rather he absorbed it, without effort and without conscious design. *McTeague* is a mine of inexhaustible riches of observation. A second or third reading gives increasing wonder as to how the boy acquired so much knowledge and so much discernment.

It is not necessary to apologize at any point for Norris. It is not necessary in criticising some mistakes of judgment in *The Octopus* to say "He will become a great novelist." He was a great novelist. *The Octopus* is a bitter and sweeping arraignment of impersonal conditions—a sort of inexorable clash of forces, and while it rose higher on some sides than *McTeague*, it fell below it on others—but it showed Norris's power in another way. It demonstrated his ability to transfer his scene as well as his characters. He was not bound to the slums of San Francisco. As he knew Polk Street, so he seems to present the San Joaquin Valley and its life, and this knowledge stood him in full hand. His first novel was worthy of his great plan. It is fairly tremendous.

He now permitted himself a greater display of power. He laid the scene of the second number of his Epic of the wheat in Chicago. But here again he knew his ground. His boyhood had been spent in the great city of the Wheat Pit. He knew certain phases of it as the keen-eyed youth saw it, and he studied it later with definite purpose, with the eyes of the novelist, in preparation for his last book *The Pit*. I saw a great deal of Norris during the time when this story was forming in his brain, and I confess I was more uneasy than he. He smoked his pipe and made merry and discussed everything else under the sun—and appeared quite at ease. He said he knew that it was, in a way, the most important test of his powers, and yet he seemed not to be taking pains. He appeared almost too confident of his powers.

But *The Pit* is a worthy successor to *The Octopus*. It is sunnier and more hopeful than *McTeague*, and less cumbrous and set of form and phrase than *The Octopus*. It is, in fact, a superb study of Chicago on certain well-defined sides. *The wheat* is there, of course, by design, and is to my mind too much insisted upon, but the impersonal does not submerge and dissolve the characterization. It is there as a sound, a wind in the trees, a reminder, but the characters move to and fro, acting and reacting on each other, quite freely, quite naturally. The great speculator, Jadwin, is a most admirably drawn type of Western business man—worthy to be put beside *Silas Lapham*. Laura Dearborn, if she has not the subtlety of emotional experience of Mr. Howells's Marcia Gaylord, is quite as vital. She does not convince at all points, but as a whole she is Norris's most important study of a woman.

The Pit does not pretend to be a society story of Chicago—and it is unduly bleak on that side—but as a presentation of the strong forces finding expression in its business centres it is thus far unrivalled. Henry Fuller's *Cliff Dwellers* is its worthiest companion-piece. The projected final volume, *The Wolf*, would have been a more difficult problem than either of those preceding it, for it not merely prospectively dealt with foreign material, but it involved a succession of incidents rather than a dramatic clashing of interests. Norris would have written it had he lived, but its working-out offered peculiar dangers, it seems to me.

Thus far the reader will get only the grim side of Norris, but in *Blix*, fortunately, is the author as his intimate friends knew him, boyish, fun-loving. He was the best company in the world. His eyes glowed with humor. His face shone with roguery and good cheer. His antic manner was never coarse, and his jocular phrases were framed in unexpected ways. He was always and constantly interesting, and to be in his company was to find the world better worth while.

Youth makes a savage realist, for youth has boundless hope and exultation in itself. When a man begins to doubt his ability to reform, to change by challenge, he softens, he allows himself to pity. Norris in *The Pit* is more genial, that is to say, more mature, than in *McTeague* and *The Octopus*. He was thirty-two and successful. He was entering on a less inexorable period. He was not written out, as perhaps Stephen Crane was; on the contrary, his mind was glowing with imagery. His ideals were fine, his life without strain, and his small shelf of books will stand high in the library of American fiction.

ARTICLES AND ESSAYS

The Masculine-Feminine Ethic
in Frank Norris's Popular Novels

Donald Pizer*

Quite correctly, the emphasis in Norris criticism has been on *Vandover and the Brute, McTeague, The Octopus,* and *The Pit.* The first two works are among our earliest naturalistic novels, and the two completed parts of the trilogy of the wheat reveal Norris's mind and art at their most mature and complex. The three novels which come toward the middle of his brief career have been either ignored or casually dismissed because of their obvious defects. Unlike his experimental or unconventional major works, these three narratives—*Moran of the Lady Letty* (1898), *Blix* (1899), and *A Man's Woman* (1900)— were written within popular formulas. All appeared originally in newspapers or magazines, and all are love stories within the conventional molds of the novel of adventure, of courtship, and of exploration.

But despite the lesser importance and obvious weaknesses of these works they deserve closer study than they have received. I will attempt to show that the three novels are a kind of trilogy, in that they deal with a similar theme. There are several reasons why it is helpful to think of the three works in this way. First, the theme itself—that of the correct sexual roles for man and woman—is developed clearly and forcefully in these novels, and therefore an understanding of it will throw light on its frequent appearance elsewhere in Norris's fiction. Moreover, this theme is closely related to Norris's beliefs concerning the ethical nature of man, and his treatment of it in these three novels marks one stage in his progressive exploration and dramatization of his ethical beliefs. Lastly, to conceive of the novels as unified by one theme despite their distinct plots, settings, and characters is to suggest the trial or apprentice role of this trilogy in relation to the similar though more successful trilogy which was to follow.

*Reprinted from *Texas Studies in Literature and Language*, 6, No. 1 (Spring 1964), 84–91, with permission of the University of Texas Press and the author. © 1964, University of Texas Press.

I

As his titles suggest, Norris's focus in each of the novels was on its chief female character, and more particularly, on her role in aiding the central male character achieve a correct masculinity. Within this process the woman also changes, though Norris above all emphasizes her function in the transformation of the male.

In *Moran of the Lady Letty* Ross Wilbur is initially an attender of teas and yachting parties, a man whose male force and gravity have been dulled by the feminine world of social convention and affectation. After being shanghaied, he is forced to rely on his strength and wits, until finally—with the fight against the Chinese pirates at Magdalena Bay—he has completely adapted to an eighth-century world of primitive barbarism in which strength, brutality, and treachery are required to survive. Moran herself is the most striking symbol of this world and its values, and her function in the rationale of the novel is to inspire Wilbur by her actions and her ideas to develop a masculine strength and courage. In short, the novel begins with Wilbur in a feminine role, Moran in a masculine one. (Clothes are important here. Wilbur is "reborn," Norris tells us, when he sheds his gentlemanly dress for rough sailor clothing, and Moran is at first mistaken for a man because of her male clothing.) It is only when Wilbur conquers Moran by sheer physical strength that he acquires a full masculinity, in which he assumes from Moran the masculine qualities of leadership and of strength of purpose. Moran, on the other hand, not only surrenders her earlier masculinity when she is conquered, but also achieves femininity for the first time. She is "just a woman now," she tells Wilbur, and having lost her former masculine strength and independence of mind, she relies upon him for protection and centers her attention on aiding him, whatever his goals. Wilbur, with his newly gained seriousness, rejects the effete San Franscisco world for the man's work of filibustering in Cuba.[1]

With all its absurdity and contrivance, then, the novel embodies a coherent masculine-feminine ethic. Man's correct role is that of "a man's man"—a man whose strength of mind and body aids him in "doing things," in participating in vigorous activity of any kind, as long as the product of that activity is in some way vaguely beneficial. Woman's correct function is that of "a man's woman"—to encourage man to affirm his masculinity by herself representing its qualities. But once the man achieves his full masculinity, the woman surrenders to his now superior strength. By her surrender, however, she not only gains love and sexuality (Norris carefully stresses the asexuality of Moran before Wilbur conquers her), but also a protector and a new role of "backing up" her mate in his endeavors and interests. With her surrender, the dynamic of the ethic is complete, since both partners now have static and permanent roles.

Blix clarifies Norris's masculine-feminine ethic by normalizing the plot and characters in which it appears and by dealing more fully with the relationship between masculinity and moral force. In *Moran*, though Wilbur "felt a sudden quadrupling of all his strength, moral and physical,"[2] after his transformation to masculinity, his moral growth is unconvincing because it takes the form of physical brutality and conquest. In *Blix*, however, Condy Rivers' weakness early in the novel is not only a lack of purpose and seriousness, but also an explicit moral laxity in his gambling, a vice which Norris uses here and elsewhere as symbolic of a general moral flabbiness. Blix's role is similar to Moran's. First, she leads Condy back to the "natural" world of sincerity and away from the conventional social world of parties and flirtations. Their unaffected relationship, and their fishing trips and long walks in the Presidio and explorations of San Franscisco, are the thematic equivalents—within a courtship novel—of the blunt, open relationship between Moran and Wilbur and of their adventures at Magdalena Bay. Gradually, Blix inspires Condy, by her masculine force of character and purpose and by her interest in his improvement, to become strong enough both to fight his desire to gamble and to pursue his career with energy and perseverance. Blix is "the kind of girl that are the making of men," (III, 105) Condy tells her at one point. As a result of her influence, the novel ends with "all the fine, virile, masculine energy of him . . . aroused and rampant." (III, 171) He has conquered his vice and has seriously undertaken his life's work as a writer. At this point, as in *Moran*, the man's newly acquired masculinity is accompanied by the woman's discovery of her love and of her sexuality and by her transformation to a dependent femininity. Condy and Blix prepare to leave the "garden" of their courtship for marriage and the trials of life, "and as they stood there, facing the gray and darkening Eastern sky, their backs forever turned to the sunset, Blix drew closer to him, putting her hand in his, looking a little timidly into his eyes. But his arm was around her, and the strong young force that looked into her eyes from his gave her courage." (III, 174)

Moran and *Blix* are therefore thematically similar. In both novels man is reborn to masculinity with the aid of "a man's woman" who then herself achieves a true femininity.[3] In *Blix*, however, Norris more clearly establishes the connection between "a man's woman" and moral development. Blix aids the moral growth of Condy in two ways. First, her purity and goodness cause Condy to recognize more fully his own moral potential. By knowing and responding to her goodness, he "felt his nobler side rousing up and the awakening of the desire to be his better self." (III, 129) But Blix emphasizes to Condy that the key to the development of his "nobler side" is strength. "'What's a good man if he's weak?'" she asks him—"'if his goodness is better than he is himself? It's the good man who is strong—as strong as his goodness and who can make his goodness count—who is the right kind of man.'" (III, 56) Norris's ideal "man's woman" (and Blix represents that ideal more than does Moran) thus embodies both halves of a correct ethical balance—a feminine spiritual purity or moral awareness and a masculine strength—and encourages man in the development of a similar balance in his own moral character.

If *Moran* introduces Norris's basic masculine-feminine ethic, and *Blix* amplifies it, *A Man's Woman* corrects a possible major misunderstanding of it. At the opening of this novel Ward Bennett and Lloyd Searight appear to have already achieved their proper roles—indeed, she is called "a man's woman," he "a man's man." (VI, 16, 34) A courageous and iron-willed Arctic explorer, he is strikingly masculine, while she, having disdained affectation and petty interests, is aiding the world's work as a nurse. But Norris desired in this novel not only to glorify these roles, but also to point out the dangers inherent in them. Most of all, he demonstrates that a Bennett can become the victim of his iron resolve, that a fixed resolution can embody a bestial selfishness and blindness as well as a praiseworthy purposefulness. Bennett's career in the Arctic had conditioned him to respond to all opposition as forces to be subdued, since the ice and the immense distances of the Arctic are insensate obstacles which must be overcome if he is to survive. Lloyd also has fought against an unreasoning opponent—in her case disease rather than ice—and also has developed a firm will. Her error is to mistake strength for independence, to center herself too exclusively on her own career and her own work. Like Bennett, she has allowed strength to narrow into pride and selfishness.

In the central scene of the novel these two powerful and fiercely independent wills clash when Bennett attempts to force Lloyd to leave a patient dangerously ill with an infectious disease. As in *Moran*, the man conquers, though now by strength of will rather than by physical power. Lloyd for the first time begins to realize the "intended natural weakness of the woman." (VI, 120) As she surrenders, her love emerges clearly. But with her love and capitulation, Bennett must now assume the role of responsibility for her well-being. It is on this basis that Lloyd appeals to Bennett to reconsider his demand that she leave—that his obligations include her spiritual as well as physical welfare, and that to leave would violate her "code of life." She tells him:

> "I am all different now. I am not the woman I was a half-hour ago. You must be brave for me now, and you must be strong for me and help me to do my duty. We must live up to the best that is in us and do what we think is right, no matter what risks we run, no matter what the consequences are. I would not have asked you to help me before—before what has happened —but now I need your help." (VI, 129)

Bennett, however, rejects the full responsibility of his new role, and almost destroys Lloyd's love for him by forcing her to do something which she knows is wrong.

With this scene, Lloyd has discovered her correct feminine role, though her pride is not completely chastened until she goes through a humiliating confession to her fellow nurses that she had left a patient. Bennett, meanwhile, gradually realizes that he might have been mistaken in his demand, and that his monomaniacal intensity not only conquered Lloyd but also broke and violated her spirit by forcing her to be false to her sense of duty. For the first time in his life he faces the possibility that force is not enough, that human beings are not objects to be blindly subjected to his will. Like Lloyd, he is shaken in his pride and his supreme self-confidence, and like her he undergoes humiliating confessions of his error to others. In short, the bulk of the novel is devoted to the process by which a strong-willed woman learns submission and a strong-willed man learns to temper strength with understanding. Or, put in another way, the novel affirms that selfishness and pride—characteristics that are often disguised as firmness of will—must be overcome if love is to flourish. "Was not the struggle with one's self the greatest fight of all," Lloyd concludes after her confession to her fellow nurses, "greater, far greater, than had been the conflict between Bennett's will and her own." (VI, 182)

In both characters, then, Norris amends some of the implications of his earlier dramatizations of masculinity and femininity as he stresses that masculinity is not simply brute force and that femininity is not a New Woman indifference to domesticity or a preoccupation with one's own career rather than the husband's. (Significantly, Lloyd gives up her profession when she marries Bennett.) It is only when Lloyd and Bennett have shed the excesses of their strength that the novel takes on the pattern of *Moran* and *Blix*. The last quarter of *A Man's Woman* contains the familiar business of Lloyd encouraging the now weak Bennett (weakened by illness and by the blow to his self-assurance) to again assert his masculinity, to return to his career as an explorer. The novel thus closes as do *Moran* and *Blix*—the man about to begin a man's work, the woman, having achieved love and sexuality, fully occupied in the career of the man.

II

The three novels explore what I have called a masculine-feminine ethic, in which men achieve a correct masculinity with the aid of women who themselves move from masculinity to femininity. Norris's heroines thus have masculine names (Travis is Blix's first name) and are tall and full-bodied not simply because Norris was fascinated by Viking types. Rather, their masculine names and physiques symbolize their masculine force—that they are women who want to "do things" rather than devote themselves to trivialities, and, most of all, that they have a strength and seriousness of character which it is their function to encourage in man. The fact that all three heroines affirm a life of action rather than of thought[4] suggests, too, that Norris associated masculinity with the primitive, the felt, the "natural" rather than with either civilization or intellect— in other words, with an atavistic physical force which man first developed in fighting nature or his enemies but which he must continue to draw upon if he is to progress materially and morally. As I have pointed out, however, *A Man's Woman* imposes limitations on unreasoned atavistic strength, and thus modifies and completes the ethic.

In all three novels woman is the prime mover in man's transformation—without "a man's woman" Wilbur would be a San Francisco playboy, Condy Rivers a vice-ridden hack, and Bennett (after his illness) a "professor" rather than a "doer." Within this theme Norris shifted his emphasis from woman's role in encouraging strength to her part in directing the use of that strength. In *Moran* he celebrated the emergence of the "half-brute" in Wilbur in order to dramatize sensationally the theme of masculinity. In *Blix* and *A Man's Woman*, however, he stressed that man is not simply a creature of conquest and strong-willed gratification—that strength plays a major role in resisting temptation and that it must not be used cruelly or selfishly. Lloyd has a "larger better nature" than Bennett, even after his self-abnegation, and like Blix, her function is "not only to call back his strength, but to guide it and direct it into its appointed channels." (VI, 209–210)

The three novels are weak not only because of their conventional and superficial plots of adventure and romantic fulfillment, but because of the inherent inadequacy of Norris's masculine-feminine ethic as a representation of the complex world of sexual relations. His themes of man as primitivistic conqueror and woman as reservoir of moral purity and strength take on much of their coloration from nineteenth-century social beliefs, particularly those which allotted unequal portions of the animal and spirit to man and woman. There is much in Norris of that nineteenth-century tendency to substitute woman for Christ as the hope and salvation of fallen man. Whatever the sources of these themes, however, Norris dramatizes them programmatically. His masculine-feminine ethic is moral in the narrow sense of the term—it tells us not so much about human beings as about conventions of social expectation, that this is the way men and women are supposed to act. Although such conventions interest the social historian, they limit the viability of the novel dominated by them. The novels occasionally rise above their weaknesses when Norris either creates compelling sensational symbols of various aspects of his ethic (Moran, the Arctic) or neglects the ethic entirely for the intrinsic appeal of scene and event (a good deal of *Blix* is successful on this level). The novels fail most obviously when Norris attempts to give the ethic a depth of analysis it cannot bear.

Yet, as I indicated earlier, a recognition of the thematic unity of the three novels is helpful for several reasons. First, Norris's full presentation of his masculine-feminine ethic clarifies fragments of this ethic in his other works. For example, such details elsewhere, as the Vandover-Turner Ravis relationship in *Vandover and the Brute*, the emergence of Trina's sexuality in *McTeague*, and the near-failure of the marriage between Laura and Jadwin in *The Pit*, appear in sharper focus within Norris's overall masculine-feminine ethic. Moreover, this ethic is closely related to Norris's fundamental evolutionary ethical dualism, in which man must draw upon his animal past for strength, but must be guided primarily by his higher and more distinctive attribute, the human spirit.[5] In *Vandover* and *McTeague* Norris had dramatized the fall of men who succumb to bestiality. These works derive much of their power and interest from Norris's awareness of the tragic potential of this theme and from the directness of his attempt to render this aspect of human experience. In his "middle trilogy" of popular novels, Norris went on to develop a theme implicit in *Vandover* and *McTeague*, the ability of man to exploit for good his dual nature rather than be a victim of it—to use brute force, with the aid of "a man's woman," to invigorate moral strength and strength of purpose. In his last two novels, and particularly in *The Octopus*, Norris attempted to deal with man's ability to perceive the cosmic laws of nature and to ally himself with those laws. In other words, Norris's "middle trilogy" represents an important stage in his intellectual history, as he moved from the tragic to the beneficial possibilities of man's relationship to his natural world. Lastly, Norris's realization of the weaknesses of his "middle trilogy"[6] no doubt was one of the factors which led him to aim higher in his trilogy of the wheat—to attempt in it a greater complexity of both theme and form. In all, *Moran, Blix,* and *A Man's Woman* do not deserve "rediscovery," but they do deserve re-examination by the historian of American sexual myths and by the literary critic concerned with the total configuration of Norris's mind and work.

Notes

1. Here and below I disregard Moran's death at the end of the novel. Her murder was primarily Norris's solution of his plot dilemma—what to do with Moran, who couldn't be kept permanently afloat in the eighth century and who couldn't convincingly be expected to adapt to the nineteenth. Her death contributes in a minor way to the novel's theme, since the closing scene in which her body rides out to sea symbolizes her return to the raw, untamed natural world which formed her. But Norris's masculine-feminine ethic is independent of her fate.

2. *Complete Edition of Frank Norris* (Garden City, New York: Doubleday, Doran & Company, 1928), III, 290. Citations from Norris's novels are from this edition, and will appear hereafter in the text.

3. Blix is explicitly designated "a man's woman" (III, 144). Norris first used the term, I believe, in a review of drawings by Charles Dana Gibson, "A Question of Ideals," San Francisco *Wave,* 15 (December 26, 1896), 7. He wrote of the Gibson girl that "somehow you feel that she is a 'man's woman' and would stand by a fellow and back him up if things should happen."

4. See particularly III, 234, and VI, 49.

5. See my "Evolutionary Ethical Dualism in Frank Norris's *Vandover and the Brute* and *McTeague,*" *PMLA,* 76 (December, 1961), 552–560.

6. See Norris's disparaging references to these novels in *The Letters of Frank Norris,* ed. Franklin D. Walker (San Francisco: The Book Club of California, 1956), pp. 7, 22, 48.

The Writer and His Middle Class Audience: Frank Norris, A Case in Point

Robert A. Morace°

What an author writes is in large measure shaped by the nature of the audience he writes for and the extent to which he is aware of that audience.[1] For the American Realist, the author's problem of defining his audience was necessarily difficult. One part of the problem derives from the broad democratic thrust of the Realist movement itself,[2] and another stems from the incredible expansion and changing character of the American reading public during the late Nineteenth Century caused in part by various advances in printing technology and in the distribution of printed matter.[3] There were more literate Americans buying more books, magazines, and newspapers than ever before. For the Realist this meant a larger market, but too it often meant having to write for an audience that was either dangerously vague, as is evident in DeForest's *Miss Ravenel's Conversion,* or unfortunately reductive, as Boyesen's "Iron Madonna" and Howells's "Young Girl" make all too clear. However, there was one way in which some of the Realists were able to avoid these extremes; at least this is what the career of Frank Norris suggests. In 1896 and 1897 Norris served as a staff writer and then the assistant editor of the San Francisco weekly, *The Wave. The Wave's* readership was small and homogeneous. It was one which Norris knew intimately and to which he quickly learned to adapt his writings. Moreover, after he left *The Wave* and began to write for a national audience, he continued to write with a specific type of reader in mind—a type that was usually, though not always, identical with his earlier *Wave* audience.

The Wave was founded in 1888 by Ben C. Truman, a member of the publicity staff of the Southern Pacific Railroad.[4] The Del Monte *Wave,* as it was then called, served as the advertising organ for the Southern Pacific's new resort, the Hotel Del Monte, located just outside Monterey, California. In 1890 *The Wave* was moved north to San Fran-

*Reprinted from *Journal of American Culture*, 3 (Spring 1980), by permission of *Journal of American Culture* and the author.

cisco where it was purchased by two enterprising local journalists, Hugh Hume and John O'Hara Cosgrave. Although Hume soon lost interest in the venture, *The Wave* steadily developed under Cosgrave's direction into a magazine of considerable, if entirely local significance. By mid-1895 the sub-title, "A Weekly for Those in the Swim," was no longer appropriate to its new character as "A Society, Literary, and Political Journal" and so was dropped. Although its character had changed from advertising organ and society sheet, one aspect of *The Wave* remained the same: it continued to direct itself to the same upper middle class readers who frequented resorts such as the Hotel Del Monte. It made no attempt to appeal to the entire range of middle class readers as, for example, Hearst's newspaper the San Francisco *Examiner* did. Nor did it make any pretense about being the journal of the city's upper crust whose activities were reported in gossipy paragraphs in the "Things and People" section rather than the regular society column which was re-served for its own class of readers, such as Norris's mother, founder of the city's Browning Society. During its twelve-year life, *The Wave* never did become "the *Collier's* or *Harper's Weekly* of the Pacific Coast" as Cosgrave hoped it would, nor did it ever become financially stable for more than very brief periods. It did, however, publish the early work of such notable American writers as Gelett Burgess, Will Irwin, Jack London, and Frank Norris. Moreover, it served its own class of readers rather well—so well in fact that it even had a small circulation among vacationing and expatriated San Franciscans in Chicago, Washington, New York and Paris.

The relationship which existed between Norris and his *Wave* audience consists of four distinct aspects. One is generic. *The Wave* was a weekly magazine, not, as some have thought, a newspaper.[5] As a result, its writers could not simply fill up the sixteen pages of each issue with news stories, these having been already covered by the city's numerous dailies. Weekly journalism forced the writer to find new material or, if he did choose to cover week-old news, to find some new angle that would interest his readers. Norris recognized that magazinists faced other difficulties too. Since the modern magazine had to cover a wide variety of subjects, space was often in short supply. The writer, especially the short story writer, had to resort to use of various literary "tricks" which seasoned magazine readers learned to recognize and even look for. Then there was also the problem of taste to be considered. As Norris pointed out, the standard of taste varied according to the magazine and the audience it served. *Scribner's, Harper's,* and *The Century* were governed by the tastes of the "Young Girl." *McClure's,* on the other hand, was noticeably less restrained, and *The Wave* had an even less priggish editorial policy as a result of its audience's demand for a more truthful presentation of life, or so Norris believed.

Another aspect of the relationship between Norris and his audience is its having been a relationship in time. However obvious this point may seem, the specific historical context of Norris's *Wave* writings has usually been entirely overlooked. Consider the case of the rather slight story, "The Puppets and the Puppy." One critic called it Norris's "most cynical work,"[6] and another thought it his most complete denial of the will.[7] Norris's readers, however, would have seen it in a far different light. They would have known that the story's sub-title, "Disrespect-fully Dedicated to Annie Besant," linked the story to the lecture by Mrs. Besant, a Theosophist leader, at San Francisco's Metropolitan Hall on May 9—just thirteen days before the story appeared in *The Wave*; as a result, they would have read the story for what it was and is—a satirical take-off on Mrs. Besant's lecture on reincarnation. One of these same critics made the same kind of mistake with another story, " 'Boom,' " seeing in it evidence of what he called Norris's "almost hysterical hatred of a decadent civilization."[8] Given this critic's overall interpretation of Norris as a transcendental populist, the reading is plausible, but that interpretation has nothing to do with the story's actual historical context. *The Wave's* readers would have known that the story's setting, the city of San Diego, was, as Norris described it, the victim of real estate speculation, and, moreover, they would have read " 'Boom' " chiefly as a warning to San Franciscans then being caught up in the excitement and reckless speculation of the Alaskan gold rush.

This brings us to the geographical aspect of the relationship, for Norris was specifically and consciously addressing a San Francisco audience. His readers understood that a parenthetical mention of "private rooms" in an article about the California oyster industry was an allusion to improprieties in certain San Francisco saloons.[9] And they would have known the three beggars who figure prominently in the story "The Associated Un-Charities" not just as fictional characters but as three of the city's most familiar street people. Norris also shared with his readers certain biases, such as the sense of urban superiority which lies behind his ridicule of Monterey's flag-raising ceremony and a Santa Cruz Venetian Carnival. This division between city and country Norris put to a more serious use on several occasions, as in his article "Man-Hunting" where he was able to effectively jar his readers' sense of security simply by pointing out the proximity of an outlaw refuge to their own city homes.

But as I noted earlier, Norris's audience can be defined even more closely. Specifically they were members of Norris's own social sphere, the upper middle class. When, for example, he mentioned "a summer resort down the coast," he was drawing on a personal experience that he knew was also a class-wide experience shared by his readers. Knowing that there existed a common store of experiences and a common background, he could be reasonably sure that what struck him as new and unusual would strike his readers in the same way. Thus he was often able to clarify his point by citing a shared experience and then contrasting it with whatever new experience he had just had.

Just how fully aware Norris was of the specific character of his audience is evident in his report on the funeral of the notorious "Little Pete," a Chinese shoe manufacturer who had been murdered on January 23, 1897. Both the murder and the funeral had been amply covered in the newspapers during the week before Norris's article appeared on January 30. That meant that Norris had to find a new angle, and the one he chose was to point out the incredible vulgarity of the white mob of onlookers who eventually plundered the funeral altar. This aspect had been barely mentioned—when it had been mentioned at all—by the city's newspapers. Given the anti-Chinese sentiment then so pervasive among San Franciscans in general—among, that is, the newspapers' general readership—the reticence is understandable. Norris and the readers of The Wave were not as a class any less prejudiced and, of course, were in fact part of that same general readership. Yet Norris could make copy out of something the newspapers were reluctant to even mention because he knew that his readers stood as far removed from the vulgar white mob as they were from the city's Chinese population, and that an attack on one or on both would not have challenged their own sense of superiority.

This finding of a unique angle of vision parallels the chief point in Norris's literary creed: the writer must break through the surface realism of middle-class respectability in order to expose the naturalistic truth below. In his novels and in much of the short fiction published in The Wave, he accomplished this goal by limiting the action to periods of crisis. Most of his contributions to The Wave were non-fiction, however, and for these he had to devise a new method. The one he chose seems simple enough: he would present some value, idea, or viewpoint common to his readers and then contrast it with another based on first-hand observation rather than mere convention. The problem with this method is that to use it on a weekly basis, and in Norris's case often in more than one article each week, is to risk alienating the readers whose views are being repeatedly deflated. In order to obviate the risk, Norris developed a repertoire of three narrative poses, each of which differs from the other two both in tone and in character.

In one Norris cast himself in the role of discoverer. This pose was

adopted chiefly for reports about places he had visited and was often
signalled by means of a formulaic opening sentence, such as this one
from an article about a trip to a nearby navy yard:

> To fit out a cruiser for sea service implies an amount of
> labor and expense that the lay landsman can have but little
> idea of until he has visited the docks (dry and otherwise) of
> Mare Island and seen the great war engines laid up there for
> repairs.

Norris employed the discoverer pose in a more imaginative way and for
a more critical purpose in a number of other *Wave* writings. In "How
it Strikes an Observer," for example, he used it to prick the bubble of
middle-class respectability within which his readers had enclosed themselves a few nights earlier while attending a fashionable horse show.
The women who were, as Norris says, "rigidly decorous and reserved"
at the show, had "shouted [themselves] hoarse and split their gloves in
their excitement" at a recent football game. And the men who had suppressed "all emotion" at the horse show were "not decorous, nor reserved,
nor choice in their language" at a boxing match just one week before.
And at the end of his article "Latin Quarter Christmas," he made a similar
point by means of a fine use of second and third person pronouns. After
having described some children gaping at a gimcrack nativity scene at
one of the city's poorest churches, Norris wrote:

> Can't you imagine the effect of positive awe upon some of the
> little Italian children of the quarter—some of those, for in-
> stance, who have never seen Kearny Street? Looking at it,
> with the tiny red lamps burning about it, there can be but
> little doubt that they feel much the same as you do—at mo-
> ments—for instance, the other day when Mr. Eddy was playing
> the "Twelfth Mass" on the great organ of St. Ignatius. You
> who "have seen Kearny Street" and "the world outside" must
> have a sixty thousand dollar organ and the greatest organist
> between the oceans before you can rise to the sensation. But
> a few cheap toys, the manikins of statuette vendors, and
> crumpled cloth suffice for those little Italians of Dupont and
> Filbert streets.
> And after all, is there so much difference between you?

In his second pose Norris acts the part of a bumbling naif. As the
discoverer his tone is serious and his reader is asked to personally involve
himself in the act of discovery. Here, however, the tone is comic, and
the reader is allowed to remain detached; he is able to learn Norris's
point without having to undergo the same indignities suffered by the

narrator. This pose Norris adopted most often in his pieces about the theater, especially his interviews with actresses and vaudeville performers. The naif stumbles around backstage, or is struck dumb by the beauty or volubility of some visiting starlet, or nearly suffers nervous prostration while interviewing a professional actor "waiting for his cue," all to show the reader the reality that lies behind the scenes.

At the opposite pole from the naif is the third pose, the authority. Although related to the discoverer in that both confront the reader directly with the errors of his views, the two differ in tone: the authority is hypercritical and even condescending rather than explanatory. Here the risk of alienating the reader is greatest, and not surprisingly, Norris was quite sparing in its use, reserving it for just a few editorials, some of his literary criticsm, and, most conspicuously, the series of football reports he wrote in the fall of 1896. Throughout these reports Norris repeatedly criticized the local teams for what he considered inferior and uninspired play and reproved the spectators who he felt did not perceive these faults and therefore failed to demand more of their teams. Since football matches were as much society functions as athletic contests in the San Francisco of the 1890's, to attack the spectators as Norris did was also to attack a large portion of his *Wave* audience. By adopting his third pose Norris was able both to make his points and to make them seem just. He buttressed his position with a consistent and well-defined theory of football strategy and interlarded his reports with an imposing array of fact drawn from his careful observation of games he had witnessed as a student at Berkeley and Harvard. In addition Norris further strengthened his case by touching on various responsive chords in his readers. He based his appeal on the strenuous life philosophy then coming very much into vogue among the city's upper middle class, and he also mentioned the rivalry between the East and West Coasts that was certain to elicit a response from chauvinistic San Franciscans. Moreover, he focused his criticism on the University of California, his own alma mater and the favorite team among his local readers. And finally he appealed to one of the chief concerns of the middle classes—getting their money's worth. Apparently Norris thought this pose succeeded rather well. Each week his reports became more forceful and more critical. And at the end of the football season he used many of the same tactics in one of his best known pieces of literary criticism, his attack on " 'The English Courses' at the University of California."

Norris's intimate knowledge of his audience was the chief factor that affected the relationship between himself and his reader, but it was not the only one. Another was his changing attitude towards his position on *The Wave*.[10] When he first joined *The Wave* as a staff writer in April

1896, he apparently thought of himself as an author, not as a journalist. His position enabled him to at least partially free himself from his financial dependence on his mother and, while he slowly recovered from the fever he had caught in South Africa, to practice the craft of fiction. During the first three months he contributed mostly short stories and book reviews, and only rarely showed even the slightest awareness that he was addressing a clearly defined audience. Following a three-month break, Norris returned to *The Wave* in October and worked steadily and prolifically until March. He virtually abandoned the writing of fiction as he immersed himself in what he later called "the hammer and tongs work" of weekly journalism. The would-be novelist had transformed himself into the professional journalist, and his awareness of his audience became a significantly noticeable characteristic of his writing. During this same period Norris became a much more visible presence in San Francisco society, chiefly as a result of his starring role in a well publicized charity performance of the Tom Robertson play *Caste* in January. At the beginning of his third *Wave* period in May, Norris suddenly realized that the careers of journalist and fiction writer need not be incompatible, that the one could, in fact, be turned to the other's advantage. His excitement over this possibility is most enthusiastically expressed in his article "An Opening for Novelists: Great Opportunities for Fiction Writers in San Francisco." "The tales are here," he wrote. "The public is here. A hundred clashing presses are hungry for you, future young story-writer of San Francisco, whoever you may be. Strike but the right note, and strike it with all your might, strike it with iron instead of velvet, and the clang of it shall go the round of the nations. A qui le tour, who shall be our Kipling?"

The question was, of course, merely rhetorical, but in his excitement Norris had unfortunately mistaken his limited success on *The Wave* as a sure sign of imminent success among a larger local and even national audience. Despite his best efforts to become the California Kipling, he was not able to find a publisher for the short story collection he had just prepared, and as a result he began to see the limitations rather than the "great opportunities" for the writer working in San Francisco. Parallelling this disenchantment with his local chances for success was Norris's growing critical attitudes towards his own society that resulted from his courtship of Jeannette Black, a social non-conformist who had refused to "come out" in society. This attitude manifests itself in the sudden spate of social fiction written during this period, especially the Leander-Justin Sturgis dialogues that appeared in July and August. After spending several months away from San Francisco revising *McTeague*, he returned to *The Wave* with little interest in his *Wave* work and even less concern for his readers' pleasure. From late November through January he offered them perfunctory articles and reworkings of fiction he had written at Harvard three years earlier. Even his most important work of this period, the serialized *Moran of the Lady Letty,* was written not for the local readers but in hopes of attracting the attention of an Eastern publisher. It did, and in February, while in St. Louis visiting Jeannette Black on yet another of his breaks from *The Wave,* Norris accepted an offer from S.S. McClure to join his staff in New York.

What Norris learned on *The Wave* about the relationship between an author and his audience affected his career in several significant ways. For one thing, as he made clear in his essay "The Novel with a Purpose," he continued to think of his readers as members of the upper middle class. This definition of his audience may in turn have been at least partly responsible for his decision not to publish his earliest novel, *Vandover and the Brute*; perhaps he realized that his readers would have found its naturalistic portrayal of a well-to-do young man's degeneration both shocking (as they did find *McTeague*) and too close to home. Norris's revision of *McTeague,* it should be remembered, occurred at the end of his *Wave* tenure and involved the re-casting of his characters on a lower social plane than they had at first occupied in the original draft composed at Harvard in 1895. In his post-*Wave* literary criticism, too, there is clear evidence that Norris continued to write with a specific audience in mind.[11] The seventeen pieces he wrote for the Chicago *American* from May to August 1901 have a breezy style and are often anecdotal—just the right combination for this Hearst newspaper. His contributions to a much more staid newspaper, the *Boston Evening Transcript,* are much more formal in tone and in structure. At the same time he was writing these pieces for the *Transcript,* he was also writing essays for syndication.[12] Although the subjects for both are frequently identical, again there are important differences: the tone and style of the syndicated pieces are less constrained and more like the earlier weekly letters published in the Chicago *American*; furthermore, in the syndicated essays he twice made disparaging remarks about New England's contributions to American literature that were not included in his *Transcript* essays. Perhaps more interesting are the articles he wrote for *World's Work,* an offshoot of Doubleday, Page & Company, Norris's publisher and the firm for which he was then working as a reader. The twin ideals of the success ethic and beneficent capitalism emphasized in *World's Work* were also prominent themes in Norris's essays for this magazine—specifically, he stressed the moral responsibilities of the novelist and the formula for literary success. Norris's last—and longest—literary essays appeared in *The Critic.* Founded in

1881 by Jeannette and Joseph Gilder as a high-toned literary review, *The Critic* became less elitist after it was purchased by the Putnams in 1898. Although most of what Norris said in his "Salt and Sincerity" column was a rehash of points he had developed earlier, one new element was his espousal of a Whitmanic faith in the American public—a reading public that he was talking *about*, not *to*; a reading public that formed his subject, not his audience.

In summary, we can say that among the several benefits Norris received as a result of his tenure on the San Francisco *Wave* was the opportunity to write for a clearly defined audience and to learn to adapt his writing so as to accommodate his own artistic purposes as well as the values of his readers. Late in his career, Norris defiantly claimed that he had "never truckled"; he didn't mention that he had, however, rewritten passages in two novels—*McTeague* and *A Man's Woman*—that reviewers of the earliest printings had found objectionable. This is not to say that Norris did indeed truckle, merely that he didn't really have to. His relationship with his readers was not antagonistic, as, for example, Stephen Crane's seems to have been at the beginning of his career; nor was it one of compromise, as Hamlin Garland's certainly was at the end of his. Rather, it was one of accommodation that derives chiefly from his *Wave* experience. In an age in which the reading public was expanding and the author was in danger of thinking of his reader—if at all—as an amorphous archetype of the American middle classes, Norris, and perhaps other Realists who shared a similar experience, was able to adapt to the possibilities of a growing mass market audience without losing sight of the specific character of his "Dear Reader."

Notes

1. Although the theory of the author-audience relationship is itself of great significance, most of the subtle distinctions that have been made concerning it apply chiefly to contemporary writers like Barth (and to a lesser extent earlier writers, especially Poe) but very little to the Realists (Henry James excepted) for what seem to me to be obvious philosophical implications of Realism. The theory has been variously discussed, in books by Wayne C. Booth and Norman Holland for example, and in three especially important articles: Walker Gibson, "Authors, Speakers, Readers, and Mock Readers," *College English*, 11 (February, 1950), 265–69; Walter J. Ong, S.J., "The Writer's Audience Is Always a Fiction," *PMLA*, 90, no. 1 (January, 1975), 9–21; Peter J. Rabinowitz, "Truth in Fiction: A Reexamination of Audiences," *Critical Inquiry*, 4 (Autumn 1977), 121–41. For a provocative, though often far-fetched, discussion of how the knowledge of one's audience can be used for manipulative purposes, see Wilson Bryan Key, *Media Sexploitation* (1976; rpt. New York: New American Library, 1977).

2. See especially the first chapter of Edwin H. Cady, *The Light of Common Day: Realism in American Fiction* (Bloomington: University of Indiana Press, 1971).

3. Joseph Katz, "Bibliography and the Rise of American Literary Realism," *Studies in American Fiction*, 2 (Spring 1974), 75–88.

4. The following sketch of *The Wave* is drawn from Robert A. Morace, "A Critical and Textual Study of Frank Norris's Writings from the San Francisco *Wave*," Diss. University of South Carolina, 1976.

5. Joseph J. Kwiat, "The Newspaper Experience: Crane, Norris, and Dreiser," *Nineteenth-Century Fiction*, 8 (September, 1953), 99–117; Joseph J. Kwiat, "Stephen Crane and Frank Norris: The Magazine and the 'Revolt' in American Literature in the 1890's," *Western Humanities Review*, 30 (Winter 1976), 309–22. For a rebuttal see Joseph Katz, "Frank Norris and 'The Newspaper Experience,'" *American Literary Realism*, 4 (Winter 1971), 73–77.

6. Warren French, *Frank Norris* (New Haven: College and University Press, 1962), pp. 26, 121.

7. Arnold L. Goldsmith, "Charles and Frank Norris," *Western American Literature*, 2 (Spring 1967), p. 45.

8. French, p. 122.

9. See Norris's description of the Imperial in *Vandover and the Brute*.

10. The bibliographical history of Norris's *Wave* tenure can be found in Morace, "A Critical and Textual Study of Frank Norris's Writings from the San Francisco *Wave*"; a corrected bibliography, Joseph Katz and Robert A. Morace, *Frank Norris: A Bibliographical Checklist* (Columbia, S.C.: J. Faust & Co.), is forthcoming.

11. I am indebted to Paul Werstein for first pointing out to me the relationship between Norris's later literary criticisms and the newspapers and magazines in which they appeared.

12. These syndicated pieces were published in early 1902, not 1903 (as was reported in *The Responsibilities of the Novelist*); see Joseph Katz, "The Elusive Criticisms Syndicated by Frank Norris," *Proof* 3 (Columbia, S.C.: University of South Carolina Press, 1973), pp. 221–51.

[The Genesis of *McTeague*]

Donald Pizer*

The initial inspiration for *McTeague* was probably a San Francisco murder in late 1893, when Norris was in his senior year at Berkeley and was deeply immersed in Zola's novels. A laborer named Collins, separated from his wife, stabbed her to death in the cloakroom of a kindergarten, for which she was the charwoman, when she refused him money.[1] Norris was no doubt intrigued by two aspects of the crime. First, the unusual setting for the murder, a kindergarten, was closely related to his mother's philanthropic activities. It was the custom for wealthy San Francisco society women to endow kindergartens, and Mrs. Norris had founded and continued to support the Lester Norris Memorial Kindergarten.[2] In *McTeague* Norris shifted the scene of the murder from Second and Folsom, where it had occurred, to Pacific Street, the location of the Lester Norris Kindergarten. He also introduced a number of "grand ladies of the Kindergarten Board" who are decorating the kindergarten for a children's festival.[3] His playfulness, however—which led him to describe himself in a scene at the Big Dipper Mine and to have Trina's dental appointments coincide with the meeting time of English 22[4]—did not extend to a portrayal of Mrs. Norris herself.

Besides the piquancy of the setting, Norris was attracted by the similarity of the murder to themes and incidents he was encountering in Zola. The newspaper accounts of Collins stressed that he was a drunken brute; "whenever he got drunk he beat [his wife] and if she did not give him money he knocked her down."[5] Indeed, "brute" was the key word in the reports of Collins, an interpretation encouraged by the viciousness of the crime ("Twenty-Nine Fatal Wounds" ran one head-line),[6] by Collins's dull-witted, inept attempts to conceal it, and by his lack of remorse. "Collins has the face of a brute," the *Examiner* noted, while the *Chronicle* stated that "Collins continues to bear himself with a stolid, brutish indifference that marks him as a type of all that is low

*Reprinted from *The Novels of Frank Norris* by Donald Pizer (Bloomington: Indiana University Press, 1966), pp. 52–63, by permission of Indiana University Press and the author.

in humanity."[7] In short, here was a vicious crime in a low-class setting involving drunkenness, poverty and brutality—a combination characteristic of such Zola novels as *L'Assommoir, La Bête humaine, Thérèse Raquin,* and *Germinal.* "Terrible things must happen to the characters of the naturalistic tale," Norris wrote in June, 1896, referring to Zola's work at a time when *McTeague* was still incomplete. "They must be twisted from the ordinary, wrenched out from the quiet, uneventful round of every-day life, and flung into the throes of a vast and terrible drama that works itself out in unleased passions, in blood and in sudden death."[8]

When Norris began writing *McTeague* at Harvard, he stressed those sensational elements common to both the Collins murder and Zola's novels. His Harvard themes on *McTeague,* eight in all, from January 7 to March 8, 1895, are primarily on McTeague's drunkenness, his brutal mistreatment of Trina, and his murder of her in the kindergarten. Norris's last theme, on March 8, is a plot summary:

> McTeague who is a third class dentist in an uptown business street marries Trina a kindergarten teacher. Their misfortunes begin after a few years. McTeague, having no diploma, is forbidden to practice and begins to drink heavily. For a long time Trina supports the two, until she finally loses her place and in short while the household falls into great poverty and misery. McTeague goes from bad to worse and finally ends by killing his wife. He manages to escape and goes back to the mines where the first part of his life had been spent. The facts concerning him come to light here and he is obliged to run for it. His way is across an arm of an Arizona desert. Here he is ridden down by a deputy sheriff. The two are sixty miles from the nearest human being and McTeague determines to fight, he kills the sheriff and is about to go on when he discovers that even in the fight the sheriff has managed to handcuff their wrists together. He is chained to the body sixty miles from help.[9]

Some details of the finished novel, such as McTeague's lack of a diploma and the fight in the desert, are in this early summary. One detail now present—that Trina is a kindergarten teacher—was to be changed. Absent entirely from the summary are several major segments or themes in the novel: the lengthy account of the courtship and early married life of Trina and McTeague, the theme of Trina's avarice, and the two subplots.

Norris apparently continued to work on *McTeague* during the spring of 1895, despite the fact that none of his extant themes after March 8 deal with the novel. On March 19 he drew out from the Harvard Library a book on dentistry from which he derived the technical dental details used in the novel.[10] Moreover, his letter to Lewis E. Gates, as well as his dedication to him, suggests that by the time he left Harvard he had carried *McTeague* beyond isolated scenes and a cursory plot summary.

How much of the novel he wrote at Harvard, however, is difficult to say. In his later accounts of *McTeague*'s composition he said that though it was begun at Harvard, it was written in the fall of 1897, when he spent several months at the Placer County mine of his friend Seymour Waterhouse.[11] It is also uncertain whether he worked on *McTeague* between the late spring of 1895, after leaving Cambridge, and the fall of 1897. During this time he published three excerpts from *McTeague* in the *Wave*, but two of these appeared when he was rewriting the novel (October and November, 1897) and the third is a description of Mc-Teague's dental parlor which comes early in the work.[12] In any case, the extant pages of the manuscript of *McTeague* suggest that the novel was either completely revised or freshly composed in late 1897. This manuscript is primarily a clean copy, with some minor revisions, and served as printer's copy. It was undoubtedly the copy which Norris made just before or after he completed his stay in the Sierras, which he then submitted to Doubleday and McClure early in 1898, soon after he joined the firm.[13] The novel was "held up by Doubleday's hesitancy because of the realistic contents," one of the company's editors later recalled,[14] but it was finally published in February, 1899. There were some protests from readers and reviewers about the scene in the theatre in which "Owgooste" Sieppi suffers a physiological calamity not uncommon among young children, and the scene was revised in later issues. It does not appear in its original form in the *Complete Edition* republication of *McTeague*, but it was restored in a private press edition in 1941 and in most editions since then.

In the interval between early March, 1895, and October, 1897, *McTeague* continued to grow and take shape in Norris's mind, whether he worked extensively on it during this time or not. It emerged finally, in his revision of late 1897, as rather a different work from what is suggested by his 1895 plot summary. The major influences on the novel during this intervening period need to be traced, since they will help explain much in the finished work.

The Zola novels which had the greatest effect on the development of *McTeague* were *L'Assommoir* and *La Bête humaine*.[15] To the pivotal event of the Collins murder, Norris added much of the spirit and detail of *L'Assommoir*, including its love triangle, its plot movement of gradual decline after initial prosperity, and its detailed rendering of a middle- and lower-class milieu. It is possible to find traces of *L'Assommoir* throughout *McTeague*, from characterization (Lantier and Marcus, the initial suitors, are both intemperate radicals) to scene (a wedding feast) to plot (a crucial stroke of fate). But McTeague differs from the drunken Coupeau of *L'Assommoir* in two important ways—he commits a murder, and he himself is a brute of a man, huge, strong, dumb. In the characterization of McTeague, Norris appears to have been influenced primarily by the contemporary accounts of Collins and by Zola's portrait of an unrepentant vicious murderer in *La Bête humaine*. In that work Jacques Lantier, the victim of an inherited homicidal mania, stabs his mistress to death. What is particularly significant in the characterization of Lantier is that his mania is portrayed as an uncontrollable atavistic urge to kill any woman who arouses his sexual desire. The alcoholism and insanity of Lantier's forefathers have made him a "human beast," a man who exhibits psychological vestiges of the prehistoric savage. Moreover, though Lantier is neither stupid nor physically brutish, he does have a striking atavistic facial characteristic—a very prominent jaw.

Zola had dramatized the effects of inherited degeneracy throughout the Rougon-Macquart series, and his earlier *Thérèse Raquin* contains a brutish murderer. But in *La Bête humaine* he portrayed for the first time the instinctive homicidal criminal. In this portrait he was directly and acknowledgedly influenced by the late nineteenth-century school of criminal anthropology, and more particularly, by Cesare Lombroso, the founder and leader of the school.[16] Lombroso's central and most widely disseminated belief was that the criminal is characterized by atavism resulting from degeneration of the nervous system, with alcohol one of the chief causes of that degeneration.[17] He held that criminals were members of a biological subspecies which was at an earlier stage of evolution than normal man, and he popularized the term "born criminal" to describe the lawbreaker who inherited his criminal tendencies either from criminal parents or from parents who had undergone a degenerative process. According to Lombroso, the born criminal exhibited physical and mental stigmata of his atavism. There were numerous stigmata, and they differed somewhat depending on the class of criminal (murderers, burglars, rapists, etc.), but among the most common were prognathism, square-headedness, and moral and physical insensitivity. ("Ne pas oublier les signes du criminel-né," Zola reminded himself in his notes for *La Bête*.)[18] Such characteristics, Lombroso believed, were the "outward and visible signs of a mysterious and complicated process of degeneration, which in the case of the criminal evokes evil impulses that are largely of atavistic origin."[19]

Lombroso's theories were popular in the late nineteenth century for several reasons. They not only confirmed superstitions about criminal physiognomy and about the effects of alcohol, but they also embodied an optimistic Darwinism in which the criminal was a reversion to an earlier epoch rather than a product of evolutionary progress. Moreover, they supported the traditional belief in the "sins of the fathers," but did so by exact physical measurements and descriptions and by elaborate statistical proof. Zola was attracted to Lombroso's ideas because the entire Rougon-Macquart edifice was built on the foundation of hereditary alcoholic degeneracy; Norris because the idea of criminal atavism was a sensational endorsement of his ideas about the importance of man's animal past.

It is doubtful that Norris was aware of Lombroso's theories at first hand when he began writing *McTeague* in early 1895, despite the wide-spread knowledge of criminal anthropology at that time among both criminologists and laymen. Rather, the early influences in the novel appear to have been the Collins murder, *L'Assommoir*, and the characterization of Lantier in *La Bête humaine*. But by the time Norris completed *McTeague* in the fall of 1897, he had acquired and exhibited an acquaintance with Lombroso's ideas, though he had apparently still not read Lombroso at first hand. The most obvious source for this increase in knowledge is Max Nordau's *Degeneration*, which was published in March, 1895, and which by June had become the most discussed book of the year.[20] Nordau's study was dedicated to Lombroso and was an attempt to use the idea of the stigmata of degeneracy in an attack on the major artists and art movements of the day. Nordau not only mentioned Lombroso throughout his work, but also defined degeneracy in Lombrosian terms. "The degenerate organism," he wrote, "has not the power to mount to the height of evolution already attained by the species, but stops on the way."[21] Norris's story "A Case for Lombroso," which appeared in the *Wave* on September 11, 1897, reveals that he associated Lombroso with Nordau. He subtitled his clipping of the story, "A Subject for Max Nordau,"[22] and its theme is related to Nordau's depiction of egomania and morbidity among degenerative artists.

Norris may also have learned of Lombroso's ideas from his friend Dr. Lawlor, who from mid-1895 to mid-1898 was prison doctor at San Quentin.[23] Norris wrote two articles on San Quentin for the *Wave*, and in one of them, "New Year's at San Quentin" (January 9, 1897), he both accepted the idea of inherited homicidal mania and mentioned Dr. Lawlor by name.[24] Dr. Lawlor, as a prison doctor, would probably have known of Lombroso's theories, particularly at San Quentin where the prison chaplain, August Drähms, was a confirmed Lombrosian, whose book *The Criminal* (1900) contained a commendatory preface by the master.[25]

That Norris during 1896–1897 was responding to the complex of ideas involving degeneracy and inherited criminality is revealed by a number of articles and stories which he wrote for the *Wave* during this period. One of his earliest *Wave* sketches, "Man Proposes—No. 2" (May 30, 1896), is about a coal heaver whose mother had "drunk herself into an asylum." He is a huge brute of a man, dull-witted and slow, with "his lower jaw immense, probably like the jaws of the carnivora."[26] (There is much in this sketch which is also in *McTeague*, but it is impossible to tell whether it draws upon the novel or vice versa.) In "A Reversion to Type" (August 14, 1897), a seemingly docile department store floor-walker suddenly reverts to the criminality of his father. "Little Dramas of the Curbstone" (June 26, 1897) combines the themes of alcoholic atavism and criminal reversion. The "dramas" are accounts of parental degeneracy which has resulted in children who are idiots, cripples, and criminals. Of one of the children, "a creature far below the brute," a medical student says, "Heredity . . . , father a degenerate, exhausted race, drank himself into a sanitarium." Norris concluded the sketch with the comment that "the chief actors [the fathers] in these three Little Dramas of the Curbstone had been somehow left out of the programme."[27]

These stories and sketches reveal Norris's preoccupation with the theme of atavism and reversion (the two terms were used interchangeably in his day), and particularly with the role of heredity in causing either an obvious physical or mental devolution or a return to an earlier family condition. Norris had dealt with the theme of reversion as early as 1891 in his story "The Son of a Sheik." It is a theme found frequently in Kipling, and indeed it appeared in much post-Darwinian literature once some of the implications of evolution were revealed. ("Evolution ever climbing after some ideal good," Tennyson wrote, "and Reversion ever dragging evolution in the mud.") But in Norris's *Wave* pieces of 1896–1897, the theme appears in the context of alcoholism and criminality, which relates it significantly to Lombroso and *McTeague* rather than to Kipling.

Thus Norris's initial impulse to develop McTeague in terms of a brutish criminality caused by alcoholism was no doubt sharpened during the composition of the novel by the popularity of Nordau's and Lombroso's theories of degeneracy.[28] The result of this variety of influences impinging on the conception of McTeague is that though he is not a literal portrait of a Lombrosian born criminal, he does have sufficient characteristics of that type to indicate that Norris was loosely drawing upon contemporary ideas involving degeneracy and atavistic criminality. McTeague lacks many of the explicit stigmata listed by Lombroso, such as epilepsy and tattooing. McTeague's characteristics are rather those which indicate Norris's imaginative response to the dramatic possibilities inherent in the idea of alcoholic degeneracy resulting in atavistic criminality, particularly those characteristics which immediately suggest atavism, such as physical size and strength and mental slowness. So McTeague's father has died of acute alcoholism, and McTeague himself is huge, strong, stupid, and crude. Moreover, he has the protruding jaw,[29] square head, and alcoholic intolerance of the Lombrosian criminal.

McTeague is dull and slow except when roused to anger or desire, at which time the beast within him—"the brute that in McTeague lay so close to the surface" (VIII, 200)[30]—prompts him to seize or destroy with uncontrollable violence. Early in the novel he is a potential criminal when he kisses the anesthetized Trina and when he breaks Marcus's arm while wrestling. Later, under the influence of alcohol, which stimulates the release of a vicious brutality in him, he tortures and then murders Trina. After the murder, McTeague displays one of the outstanding characteristics of the atavistic criminal—lack of remorse for his crime. On his return to the Placer County mining area, he feels an instinctive kinship with the primeval landscape. Finally, in fleeing his pursuers, his persistence in traveling with his canary causes him to be easily followed, yet he possesses an animalistic sixth sense which warns him of approaching danger.

Responsive to the dramatic possibilities of the atavistic criminal and encouraged by Zola's many animal-like characters, Norris exaggerated McTeague into a gross brute of a man, just as he had exaggerated Vandover's sensuality into lycanthropic hallucinations. Not that the struggle between flesh and spirit does not occur within McTeague. As he views the anesthetized Trina,

> Suddenly the animal in the man stirred and woke; the evil instincts that in him were so close to the surface leaped to life, shouting and clamouring.
> . . . Within him, a certain second self, another bettter McTeague rose with the brute; both were strong, with the huge crude strength of the man himself. . . . It was the old battle, old as the world, wide as the world—the sudden panther leap of the animal, lips drawn, fangs aflash, hideous, monstrous, not to be resisted, and the simultaneous arousing of the other man, the better self that cries, "Down, down," without knowing why; that grips the monster; that fights to strangle it, to thrust it down and back (VIII, 26).

In this first encounter with the "monster," however, McTeague succumbs immediately, as he crudely kisses Trina. Norris then asks the reason for this fall, and quickly answers his question:

> Why could he not always love her purely, cleanly? What was
> this perverse, vicious thing that lived within him, knitted to
> his flesh?
>   Below the fine fabric of all that was good in him ran the
> foul stream of hereditary evil, like a sewer. The vices and
> sins of his father and of his father's father, to the third and
> fourth and five hundredth generation, tainted him. The evil
> of an entire race flowed in his veins. Why should it be? He
> did not desire it. Was he to blame? (VIII, 27)

No wonder that Norris asks "Was he to blame?," for the implication is
that, given McTeague's hereditary disposition toward atavism, the
victory of the brute is beyond his control, though that victory—as all
such victories—is to be deplored.

    This notorious passage, blatant as it is, involves a more complex
idea of McTeague's atavism than appears at first glance. For Norris's
analysis of McTeague's "evil instincts" combines the limited theme of
criminal atavism ("the vices and sins of his father") with the more
generic theme of racial atavism—that is, the Le Contean theme of man's
animal sensuality going back to the "five hundredth generation." Norris
further develops this larger theme—or rather suggests more firmly its
earlier presence—when he writes in the next paragraph that the pull of
sexual desire had at last faced McTeague "as sooner or later it faces
every child of man." His use of the term "race" in the passage also implies a dual atavistic theme. The term embodies both the common
meaning of "mankind as a whole" and the more specialized sense of
"family heritage." Norris had used it in this second sense in "Little
Dramas of the Curbstone" and "A Case for Lombroso."[31] The passage
is confusing because it rather muddily combines these two sources of
McTeague's "foul stream of hereditary evil." But it is out of this complexity, here fuzzy but elsewhere clearer, that the main theme of the
novel emerges. McTeague's fall is the product of both special circumstance as an atavistic criminal and his general sensual fallibility as a man.
Both flaws stress man's atavistic nature, that he is frequently controlled
by unanalyzable instincts which derive from his family and racial past.

    Norris, therefore, seems to have begun *McTeague* as a story of
alcoholic degeneracy, closely related to this theme in Zola. He then
saw the possibility of heightening his portrait of McTeague by intro-
ducing some of Lombroso's ideas on criminal atavism. But as he filled
out and rewrote the novel, he probably realized that the theme of atavism
involved more than an explanation of the criminal, that it also embodied
other central human characteristics which absorbed him, that most of all
it was related to the source and nature of man's sexual desires. Under

the impact of this larger conception of atavism, Norris expanded and developed the novel in directions either absent or barely implied in his original plan. He now gave more attention to the courtship and marriage of Trina and McTeague than to Trina's murder or McTeague's capture; he introduced two additional love subplots; and he made Trina's avarice a parallel atavistic theme to McTeague's criminality. And it is this expansion of the atavistic theme, until it transcends Norris's source of it in the Collins murder and in Zola and Lombroso, which almost succeeds in turning the novel into that mythical creature of literature, a naturalistic tragedy.

Notes

1. The murder was fully reported in the San Francisco newspapers on October 10, 1893, and for several days thereafter. This source was first noted by Charles Kaplan in his "Frank Norris and the Craft of Fiction" (Ph. D. diss., Northwestern University, 1952).

2. Eleanor Davenport, in a letter to Franklin Walker, October 5, 1930 (Franklin Walker Collection, Bancroft Library).

3. *McTeague* in *The Complete Edition of Frank Norris* (Garden City, N. Y.: Doubleday, Doran & Co., 1928), VIII, 315. Hereafter, citations from *McTeague* are from this edition and will be included parenthetically in the text.

4. Trina's appointments are at 2:00 P.M., Tuesday, Thursday, and Saturday; English 22 met at 1:30 P.M. on those days.

5. San Francisco *Examiner,* October 10, 1893, p. 12.

6. San Francisco *Examiner,* October 10, 1893, p. 12.

7. San Francisco *Examiner,* October 11, 1893, p. 4 and San Francisco *Chronicle,* October 12, 1893, p. 4. Collins was eventually found guilty of murder and was executed.

8. Norris, "Zola as a Romantic Writer," *Wave,* 15 (June 27, 1896), 3.

9. Frank Norris Collection, Bancroft Library. I am indebted to Professor James D. Hart for permission to publish this theme prior to his forthcoming edition of Norris's Harvard themes.

10. Willard E. Martin, Jr., "Frank Norris's Reading at Harvard College," *American Literature,* 7 (May, 1935), 203–204 and Charles Kaplan, "Fact Into Fiction in *McTeague,*" *Harvard Library Bulletin,* 8 (Autumn 1954), 381–385.

11. See, for example, Norris to Charles F. Lummis, April 9, 1900; published by Donald Pizer, "Ten Letters by Frank Norris," *Quarterly News-letter* of the Book Club of California, 27 (Summer 1962). See p. xliii.

12. Norris, "Suggestions. IV. The Dental Parlors," 16 (March 13, 1897), 7; "Judy's Service of Gold Plate," 16 (October 16, 1897), 6; and "Fantaisie Printaniere," 16 (November 6, 1897), 7.

13. About seventy manuscript pages have been recovered (from what was a manuscript of over 300 pages) and are now in the Frank Norris Collection.

14. John S. Phillips, in a letter to Franklin Walker, April 18, 1932 (Franklin Walker Collection).

15. Zola's influence on Norris is one of the most thoroughly investigated fields in Norris criticism. The two standard studies are Marius Biencourt, *Une Influence du naturalisme français en Amerique: Frank Norris* (Paris: Marcel Giard, 1933) and Lars Ahnebrink, *The Beginnings of Naturalism in American Fiction* (Cambridge, Mass.: Harvard University Press, 1950). I rely on these two studies throughout, but will not cite them hereafter.

16. The fullest study of Lombroso's influence on Zola's conception of Jacques is by Martin Kanes, *Zola's "La Bete humaine": A Study in Literary Creation* (Berkeley and Los Angeles: University of California Press, 1962), pp. 35–36, 60–61. Lombroso himself critically examined Zola's dramatizations of his theories in "Illustrative Studies in Criminal Anthropology. I. 'La Bete Humaine' and Criminal Anthropology," *Monist*, 1 (January, 1891), 177–185.

17. Lombroso's major work, *L'Uomo delinquente* (Milan: Fratelli Bocca, 1876; 5th rev. ed., 1896) was translated as *L'Homme criminel* (Paris: F. Alean, 1887). An English version, adapted by Gina Lombroso-Ferrero, did not appear until the publication of *Criminal Man, According to the Classification of Cesare Lombroso* (New York and London: G. P. Putnam's & Sons, 1911). Lombroso's ideas, however, were well known in England and America by the late 1880's. Havelock Ellis's *The Criminal* (London: W. Scott, 1892) and Arthur MacDonald's *Criminology* (New York: Funk & Wagnalls Company, 1893) were heavily Lombrosian, and Lombroso's translated articles appeared in such journals as the *Forum, Century,* and *Contemporary Review*. See also Arthur E. Fink, *Causes of Crime: Biological Theories in the United States, 1800–1915* (Philadelphia: University of Pennsylvania Press, 1938), pp. 99–150.

18. Kanes, *Zola's "La Bete humaine,"* p. 61.

19. Lombroso-Ferrero, *Criminal Man*, p. 24.

20. See Grant C. Knight, *The Critical Period in American Literature* (Chapel Hill, N. C.: The University of North Carolina Press, 1951), pp. 70–76.

21. Max Nordau, *Degeneration* (New York: D. Appleton and Company, 1895), p. 556.

22. Frank Norris Collection.

23. See the *Biennial Report of the State Board of Prison Directors of the State of California* for the years 1895–1898.

24. The second article was "A 'Lag's' Release," 16 (March 27, 1897), 4.

25. See also Kenneth Lamott, *Chronicles of San Quentin: The Biography of a Prison* (New York: D. McKay Co., 1961), p. 128.

26. *Wave*, 15, p. 7.

27. *Wave*, 16, p. 9.

28. Eugene S. Talbot, in *Degeneracy: Its Causes, Signs, and Results* (London and New York: W. Scott; Charles Scribner's 1899), p. vii, noted that the topic of degeneracy received its "popular apotheosis under Lombroso and Nordau."

29. Many of Norris's characters have prominent jaws and yet are not criminals. Norris used prognathism as a crude symbol of the primitive strength which breaks down all barriers in its drive toward a goal or possession. He distinguished between criminal and non-criminal primitivism in terms of ends, not means. A prognathous Ward Bennett, for example, uses his strength beneficially, according to Norris, when he drives his men across the ice to safety in *A Man's Woman*, even though he commits inhuman acts in achieving that goal.

30. Norris also indicated on pp. 26, 155, and 362 (in almost the exact words) the unusual volatility of McTeague's animal nature.

31. Norris, "Little Dramas of the Curbstone," *Wave*, 16 (June 26, 1897), 9, and "A Case for Lombroso," *Wave*, 16 (September 11, 1897), 6.

Art in *McTeague*

Don Graham°

Frank Norris's *McTeague* (1899) is typically seen as a straight Naturalistic novel embodying such standard assumptions as sexual determinism, atavistic degeneracy, the influence of sordid milieu, and the operation of chance.[1] There is no question that quasi-scientific theorizing is one side of *McTeague*. Like Dreiser and London, Norris often chose to ground his fiction in the presumably authoritative scientific opinion of the day. (The difference between this faith and a present-day novelist's reliance upon post-existential assumptions is slight.) Still, there is no reason to believe that Norris and the other Naturalists were preoccupied with Content and Truth to the point of not caring about the art of fiction. Norris in fact produced a fair amount of practical criticism himself and was capable of ideologically neutral statements: "After all in fiction, the main thing is fiction."[2]

Praised for its exposition of Naturalistic ideas, *McTeague* seldom receives favorable mention of its art. Warren French, for example, would seem to speak for a whole generation of critics when he observes, "as art *McTeague* leaves much to be desired. The novel is not likely to excite much enthusiasm among critics who cherish formal perfection. . . ."[3] Warner Berthoff's summary indictment of Norris's formal crudities is worth quoting too: "All in all, composition in Norris's novels seems to be reckoned exclusively in calculations of decibels and gross tonnage."[4] *Gross tonnage* may be a successful impressionistic rendering of the feeling aroused by a book like *McTeague,* whose hero is ostensibly a brute, but it is not an accurate description of Norris's art in this novel. The word that Ellen Moers has applied to Dreiser's artistry in *Sister Carrie* is needed to describe Norris's efforts in *McTeague*: "finesse."[5]

It is the ending of *McTeague*, those last three chapters detailing the hero's flight from the city, that has come in most often for derogation.

°Reprinted from *Studies in American Fiction*, (1975), 143–155, by permission of *Studies in American Fiction*. An expanded version of this essay appears in *The Fiction of Frank Norris: The Aesthetic Context* (Columbia: University of Missouri Press, 1978).

Any defense of the art of *McTeague* has to account for the ending. From the first reviews on, the desert material has provoked controversy. In an otherwise very favorable review, William Dean Howells faulted only the desert flight, which he saw as a lapse into melodrama.[6] Interestingly, another novelist has found the ending worthy of high praise. In an essay on Stephen Crane, Edward Dahlberg says grandly, "Death Valley is what makes Frank Norris."[7] Norris wrote Howells a thank-you note for that kind review with one demurrer: "I agree in every one of your criticisms, always excepting the anti-climax, the 'death in the desert' business. I am sure it has its place."[8] He is right. Thematically and structurally the ending of *McTeague* is justified; far from being anti-climactic, it climaxes the evaluation of landscapes, of interior and exterior space, that forms a central and controlling tension in the novel.

Norris's management of background material in *McTeague*, whether interior decor or external landscape, constitutes a kind of internal non-discursive rhetoric of object and symbol. Long descriptive catalogues of a room's contents are never purely documentary in purpose, never merely the recorded habits of a photographic realist. The interior of the Big Dipper Mining Office, for example, is a highly symbolic rendering of the novel's issues. This setting occurs in Chapter 20, which marks the break with the urban environment. After murdering his wife Trina, McTeague has fled San Francisco and has returned to the landscape of his childhood. Looking about, he observes certain changes that have taken place over the years:

> There was a telephone on the wall. In one corner he also observed a stack of surveyor's instruments; a big drawing-board straddled on spindle legs across one end of the room, a mechanical drawing of some kind, no doubt the plan of the mine, unrolled upon it; a chromo representing a couple of peasants in a ploughed field (Millet's "Angelus") was nailed unframed upon the wall, and hanging from the same wire nail that secured one of its corners in place was a bullion bag and a cartridge belt with a loaded revolver in the pouch.[9]

Putting the chromo's title in parentheses indicates the care with which Norris records McTeague's consciousness. Millet is outside the experience of McTeague, who recognizes neither the artist nor the cultural context of the painting.[10] But the "Angelus" does a great deal more than reflect McTeague's lowbrowness: it projects a pastoral and traditional world, a peasant culture unavailable to McTeague, a peasant himself. The figures in the painting are a man and a woman, apparently husband and wife, paused in their work, struck still by the sounding of the Angelus bell from a steeple dimly visible in the background. They are emblems of a rude life of toil and reverence. Their society is stable; the church bell commands their respect and orders their days. The "Angelus" is a painting which dramatizes the "time-tested verities of work, companionship, and the guidance of Providence."[11] It therefore has obvious ironic parallels with the lives of the McTeagues who through the loss of meaningful work, the death of companionship by routine and attrition, and the absolute lack of Providence or any external model of belief, have destroyed each other. In the world of McTeague and Trina there is no Angelus, no ploughed field. That is part of their tragedy.

Three details in the Big Dipper Mining Office symbolize the reasons for its distance from Millet's world. One is the telephone, which has penetrated even to this primitive mining territory. Product of an industrial civilization, the telephone is one of those machines that define city life, that create the kind of complexity before which McTeague is largely helpless. McTeague understands neither urban communication nor transportation. Buying theater tickets confounds him; government regulations concerning the licensing of dentists precipitate his ruin. A second symbolic detail is the bullion bag, one of the countless versions of the gold motif in the novel. The central impulse of McTeague's world, whether city or Placer County, is to get gold. The third point is the revolver in the pouch, emblem of the frontier ethic, one of the echoes of recurring violence in the novel. (A calendar advertising rifles hangs in McTeague's dental parlors.) Telephone, gold, and gun cancel the pastoral quietude evoked by the Millet painting: they make such a world impossible.

The decor of the Big Dipper Mining Office is the last of many interiors described in the novel. Together with the first interior, McTeague's dental parlors, it frames the social world of the novel. This framing consists of the bottom and top levels of pastoral hierarchy, peasantry, and aristocracy. The Mining Office alludes to the first; McTeague's dental parlors to the second. The objects in McTeague's parlors range from high culture to the commonplace and low:

> Three chairs, a bargain at the second-hand store, ranged themselves against the wall with military precision underneath a steel engraving of the court of Lorenzo de' Medici, which he had bought because there were a great many figures in it for the money. Over the bed-lounge hung a rifle manufacturer's advertisement calendar which he never used. The other ornaments were a small marble-topped centre-table covered with back numbers of "The American System of Dentistry," a stone pug dog sitting before the little stove, and a thermometer. A stand of shelves occupied one corner, filled with the seven vol-

umes of "Allen's Practical Dentist." On the top shelf McTeague kept his concertina and a bag of bird seed for the canary. The whole place exhaled a mingled odor of bedding, creosote, and ether (pp. 3–4).

The court of Lorenzo de' Medici is notably above McTeague. Like the "Angelus" this engraving projects an ordered, traditional, and stable society. The "Angelus" presents the peasant sphere, a suitable but unavailable world for McTeague; Lorenzo's court, with its patronage of art, its manners, gives the other level of the pastoral mode, the courtly and aristocratic.[12] This is, of course, a sphere remote from McTeague and one which he can at best only grotesquely mime. The steel engraving and the chromo encompass an ideal social world of the past: they gauge the extent of McTeague's estrangement from tradition and tranquillity. Outside the ideal are the actual urban life of the McTeagues and the desert, Death Valley.

The symbolic exploitation of the "Angelus" painting is a reliable guide to Norris's method. Everywhere in *McTeague* aesthetic objects function as an index of character value and as keys to the evaluation of interior and exterior landscapes. The single most famous art object in *McTeague*—though never perceived by critics as such[13]—is the golden tooth which operates in just this symbolic fashion. Trina gives McTeague for his birthday a huge golden tooth, something he has dreamed of for a long time as "gorgeous and attractive" (p. 4). To possess it is to own all of beauty and self-esteem. Indeed the tooth alters the perspective of the other objects in McTeague's quarters:

> The whole room took on a different aspect because of it. The stone pug dog before the little stove reflected it in his protruding eyes; the canary woke and chittered feebly at this new gilt, so much brighter than the bars of its little prison. Lorenzo de' Medici, in the steel engraving, sitting in the heart of his court, seemed to ogle the thing out of the corner of one eye, while the brilliant colours of the unused rifle manufacturer's calendar seemed to fade and pale in the brilliance of this greater glory (pp. 128–29).

The golden tooth that McTeague has imagined as "beautiful, beautiful" (p. 72) here fulfills that fancy. It whimsically makes the patron of art envious and shames the calendar. It also stimulates the canary to sing. McTeague, one of whose epithets is "caged brute" (p. 259), is analogous to the canary in the cage, yearning for space, aesthetic immensity.[14] The imagery of entrapment closes the novel as well, McTeague in dumb agony handcuffed to the dead body of his city pursuer, Marcus Schouler.

The tooth looks backward to McTeague's childhood in the mining country and forward to his eventual return.

In an improper setting, the golden tooth loses its beauty, becomes an image of debased and confined aesthetic possibility. When McTeague loses his dental practice, the tooth is dismantled and kept in the McTeagues' new, smaller living quarters:

> It was not gay, that life. The room itself was not gay. The huge double bed sprawled over nearly a fourth of the available space; the angles of Trina's trunk and the washstand projected into the room from the walls, and barked shins and scraped elbows. Streaks and spots of the "non-poisonous" paint that Trina used were upon the walls and woodwork. However, in one corner of the room, next the window, monstrous, brilliant, shining with a light of its own, stood the dentist's sign, the enormous golden tooth, the tooth of a Brobdingnag (p. 245).

The only aesthetic object in the room, the tooth is "monstrous," grotesque. Like its owner, it needs space for the restoration of aesthetic harmony. It is still another image of the gigantic figure rendered ludicrous by a constrictive milieu. The tooth, the canary, and McTeague are all trapped.

The golden tooth undergoes a final debasement. In the last quarters inhabited by the McTeagues, formerly the miser Zerkow's apartment, the tooth is grotesquely abused:

> And the tooth, the gigantic golden molar of French gilt, enormous and ungainly, sprawled its branching prongs in one corner of the room by the footboard of the bed. The McTeagues had come to use it as a sort of substitute for a table. After breakfast and supper Trina piled the plates and greasy dishes upon it to have them out of the way (pp. 285–86).

The words describing the tooth are identical to those applied to McTeague throughout: gigantic, enormous, ungainly, sprawled. Its degradation mirrors his, the loss of space, the neglect of beauty.[15]

Since over three-quarters of the novel takes place in rooms, interior decor assumes imperative importance in Norris's rhetoric of aesthetic experience. Rooms, interior space, define the sensibilities of the two central characters and disclose the aesthetic premises of the novel. If McTeague's cardinal aesthetic principle is space, Trina's is constriction, the narrowness of rooms filled with little, crowded objects.[16] Her room at her father's house reflects her Lilliputian mode:

> It was an ordinary little room. A clean white matting was on the floor; gray paper, spotted with pink and white flowers,

covered the walls. In one corner, under a white netting, was
a little bed, the woodwork gayly painted with knots of bright
flowers. Near it, against the wall, was a black walnut bureau.
A work-table with spiral legs stood by the window, which was
hung with a green and gold window curtain. Opposite the
window the closet door stood ajar, while in the corner across
from the bed was a tiny wash-stand with two clean towels.
    And that was all (p. 67).

The emphasis upon smallness and Trina's pretensions toward gentility
define the dimensions of Trina's aesthetic. Under the stress of need, none
of Trina's aesthetic objects count for anything. McTeague in such a room
is, as he perceives, a colossal intruder; yet it is to rooms like these that
marriage to Trina brings him. Under her tutelage, he undergoes an
education in taste. He learns refinement. He begins to dress better,
washes more often, is courteous to women, smokes a higher-priced
cigar, drinks better beer, and reads the newspaper. These are all superficial matters of hygiene and appearance; they have nothing to do with
McTeague's deepest needs. At one point he even begins to dream of
owning a small house with "a grass plat in front and calla lillies" (p. 165).
This desire marks Trina's most complete domination of McTeague, the
usurpation of his aesthetic by hers.

    It is generally assumed that Trina's taste is superior to McTeague's,
and that his life with her marks an improvement in his condition, at least
for the placid first three years of their marriage.[17] The obvious vulgarity
of McTeague's cherishing a huge golden tooth can hardly be denied, but
in fact Trina's taste is qualitatively identical to McTeague's. At the
burlesque show which they attend during courtship, McTeague is
enraptured by a drunken skit and a rendition of "Nearer, My God, To
Thee" on beer bottles. But Trina splits her gloves applauding the Society
Contralto's sentimental songs and exclaims "Ain't it beautiful" in response to the scenes depicted on the stage curtain, of swans, roses, a
young man in a gondola (p. 85). Trina's taste is only the sentimental and
shabby-genteel reverse of McTeague's rib-poking barroom variety.

    But the major point to note is the meaning of aesthetic experience
for each. With McTeague, aesthetic perception is a constant and fundamental part of his being. It expresses a need and loyalty beyond Trina's
capacity for feeling. His playing the concertina, limited artistic skill
that it is, is directed towards pleasure and self-expression. Trina's artistic
skill, carving toy animals, is directed only towards money-making. Moreover, McTeague does not willingly relinquish a single aesthetic possession. Upon the occasion of Trina's decision to sell everything rather than
draw upon her lottery winnings, he tells her of his affection for certain

objects: "That steel engraving I bought in Sacramento one day when it was raining. I saw it in the window of a second-hand store, and a fellow *gave* me that stone pug dog" (p. 235). The canary, of course, he never forsakes, carrying it even into the desert.

With McTeague, aesthetic experience is a matter of sentiment; with Trina, of sentimentality. Thus she gladly yields up all the aesthetic ornaments in their first household, including their wedding photograph, and easily justifies the liquidation of their furnishings: "We've got to leave here—leave the flat where I've been—where *we've* been so happy, and sell all the pretty things; sell the pictures and the melodeon" (p. 227). The melodeon is her concertina. Significantly, a strong motivating factor in the murder of Trina is her pawning her husband's concertina.

Trina's constrictive aesthetic dominates McTeague's life from the moment he is ensnared by the mystery of sex until that aesthetic is pushed to its narrowest limits and McTeague makes a stunning Darwinian aesthetic judgment. From this point on, a counter, outward movement begins. The dynamics of constriction versus expansion are noted with barometric exactness in the extensive description of rooms and their furnishings. The married life of the McTeagues begins on the top-floor in a lower-middle class tenement house and ends in a sordid lower-depths apartment on the bottom floor.[18] The first place, decorated by Trina, bears all the marks of her tastes and values:

> Three pictures hung upon the walls. Two were companion pieces. One of these represented a little boy wearing huge spectacles and trying to smoke an enormous pipe. This was called "I'm Grandpa," the title being printed in large black letters; the companion picture was entitled "I'm Grandma," a little girl in cap and "specs," wearing mitts, and knitting. These pictures were hung on either side of the mantlepiece. The other picture was quite an affair, very large and striking. It was a coloured lithograph of two little golden-haired girls in their nightgowns. They were kneeling down and saying their prayers; their eyes—very large and very blue—rolled upward. This picture had for name, "Faith," and was bordered with a red plush mat and a frame of imitation beaten brass.

> A door hung with chenille portieres—a bargain at two dollars and a half—admitted one to the bedroom. The bedroom could boast a carpet, three-ply ingrain, the design being bunches of red and green flowers in yellow baskets on a white ground. The wall-paper was admirable—hundreds and hundreds of tiny Japanese mandarins, all identically alike, helping hundreds of almond-eyed ladies into hundreds of impos-

sible junks, while hundreds of long-legged storks trailed contemptuously away from the scene. This room was prolific in pictures. Most of them were framed coloured prints from Christmas editions of the London *Graphic* and *Illustrated News*, the subject of each picture inevitably involving very alert fox terriers and very pretty moonfaced little girls (pp. 136–37).

Such extensive description repays close attention. The Grandma-Grandpa pictures express perfectly the infantile, sentimental cast of Trina's mind. They echo a motif developed at length in the meeting and courtship of McTeague and Trina, the adolescent or child-like state of their sexual awareness. They also project an ironic future, McTeague and Trina as grandparents, who are never parents (though McTeague begins to dream of a son named Daniel). The third painting, all sentiment and innocence and religiosity crowned with a "frame of imitation beaten brass," derives from those "Ideal Heads" that Trina admired at the Mechanics' Fair. The bedroom wallpaper, with the *hundreds*, further suggests the bad taste that characterizes everything about the place. The concern with numbers is peculiarly Trina's, as is her delight in counting the gold pieces; McTeague's chief concern, of course, is size. The effect of the hundreds is a crowded, cramping atmosphere, the Lilliputian world of Trina. The prints from the London papers, though probably left here by the former occupant, a photographer, nevertheless fit Trina's overall conception well by repeating the sentimental motif of the innocent girl. The idealized dogs contrast with McTeague's aesthetic dog—the inscrutable pug dog—and with two sets of actual dogs, Marcus Schouler's, like its owner a noisy, cowardly sort, and the dog in the water-pump cage at the Sieppe house. All three are far removed from the stylized fox terriers.

The McTeagues' second dwelling, a small apartment in the rear of the same tenement building, results from Trina's unwillingness to draw upon her savings when McTeague loses his dental practice. In some respects this single room recalls the decor and atmosphere of Trina's bedroom in her father's house. Only here the effort at genteel prettiness has been dropped; everything is reducd to a grubby functionalism:

> The room was whitewashed. It contained a bed, three cane-seated chairs, and a wooden wash-stand with its washbowl and pitcher. From its single uncurtained window one looked down into the flat's dirty back yard and upon the roofs of the hovels that bordered the alley in the rear. There was a rag carpet on the floor. In place of a closet some dozen wooden pegs were affixed to the wall over the wash-stand. There was

a smell of cheap soap and of ancient hair-oil in the air
(p. 231).

Perhaps the most revealing detail here is the absence of a closet, a
notation which recalls McTeague's plunging himself into Trina's clothes
hanging in the closet of the Sieppe house. In the present room there is
no evidence of feeling, no sensuous apprehension at all. And with Trina's
increasing neglect of minimal household chores, the room grows quite
foul. It becomes "grimy" and takes on "an aspect of desolation and
cheerlessness lamentable beyond words" (p. 257). It is this degradation,
symbolized by the canary's feeble chittering, that leads McTeague to his
finest perception in the novel. He tells Trina that she likes living in a
"rat hole" (p. 254). Here the Darwinian and aesthetic insights are merged
in one compelling image. In Naturalism's bestiary, rats are bottom drawer.
If McTeague is a bit of a beast himself, he is a gigantic one who, as he is
fond of saying, cannot be made small of.

The second dwelling also foreshadows the last McTeague household,
a hovel visible from the top floor of the tenement house. In search of
cheaper quarters Trina seizes upon the first-storey apartment formerly
inhabited by Zerkow the miser. This place has a kind of negative grandeur
and measures how far the McTeagues have fallen:

> This bed, a couple of chairs, Trina's trunk, an ornament
> or two, the oil stove, and some plates and kitchen ware were
> all that they could call their own now; and this back room in
> that wretched house with its grisly memories, the one window
> looking out into a grimy maze of back yards and broken sheds,
> was what they now knew as their home (pp. 384–85).

> The one room grew abominably dirty, reeking with the
> odours of cooking and of "non-poisonous" paint. The bed was
> not made until late in the afternoon, sometimes not at all.
> Dirty, unwashed crockery, greasy knives, sodden fragments
> of yesterday's meals cluttered the table while in one corner
> was the heap of evil-smelling, dirty linen. Cockroaches ap-
> peared in the crevices of the wood-work, the wall-paper
> bulged from the damp walls and began to peel. Trina had
> long ago ceased to dust or to wipe the furniture with a bit of
> rag. The grime grew thick upon the window panes and in the
> corners of the room. All the filth of the alley invaded their
> quarters like a rising muddy tide.

> Between the windows, however, the faded photograph
> of the couple in their wedding finery looked down upon the
> wretchedness. Trina still holding her set bouquet straight be-

fore her, McTeague standing at her side, his left foot forward, in the attitude of a Secretary of State, while near by hung the canary, the one thing the dentist clung to obstinately, piping and chittering all day in its little gilt prison (pp. 285–86).

This room possesses one aesthetic memento from happier days, the wedding picture (Trina had tried to sell it too, but nobody wanted it), and one aesthetic object from McTeague's bachelor life, the canary. The room grotesquely mimics two backgrounds: the bulging wallpaper recalls their first home, and the "rising muddy tide" echoes their courtship by the sea. Trina is so contented here that she is unable to distinguish a much nicer place, the room over the kindergarten, from this hovel. She is completely indifferent to her surroundings.

But McTeague is not. As Trina's housekeeping continues declining into sheer filth, as the golden tooth is pressed into service for a dining table, McTeague begins to search for an alternate landscape. It will have to be out-of-doors, it will have to offer qualities that life in Trina's house does not, it will have to be spacious. The sea is ideal, the perfect symbolic opposite of the "rising tide" of trash that invades the apartment. By the sea McTeague is a figure restored to aesthetic harmony:

> He liked the solitude of the tremendous, tumbling ocean; the fresh, windy downs; he liked to feel the gusty Trades flogging his face, and he would remain for hours watching the roll and plunge of the breakers with the silent, unreasoned enjoyment of a child (p. 283).

This scene recalls an earlier one in McTeague's life, when he was courting Trina. The scene consummately blends elements of city-scape, aesthetic expression, and the impulse outward:

> The wind blew strong, carrying with it the mingled smell of salt, of tar, of dead seaweed, and of bilge. The sky hung low and brown; at long intervals a few drops of rain fell.

> Near the station Trina and McTeague sat on the roadbank of the tracks, at the edge of the mudbank, making the most of the landscape, enjoying the open air, the salt marshes, and the sight of the distant water. From time to time McTeague played his six mournful airs upon his concertina (p. 71).

In this terrain, a transitional stage between urban and natural landscapes, McTeague and Trina are "making the most out of the landscape," and McTeague is shaping an aesthetic response upon his concertina. Without Trina, the seascape would be even better, conferring thereby the additional solace of solitude. But the irony of McTeague's final situation is that in his flight towards space he gets the wrong kind; he gets Death Valley, which is neither ocean nor fertile land; it is the bed of "some prehistoric lake" (p. 353).

The evaluation of interior and exterior landscapes through the symbolism of aesthetic documentation is brought to a logical and climactic conclusion with the desert ending. Norris carefully registers the degree of delight which his inarticulate hero experiences upon breaking free of Trina and her cramped rooms, and returning to Placer County. There McTeague finds an immense backdrop commensurate with his size:

> The life pleased the dentist beyond words. The still, colossal mountains took him back again like a returning prodigal, and vaguely, without knowing why, he yielded to their influence—their enormous power, crude and blind, reflecting themselves in his own nature, huge, strong, brutal in its simplicity (p. 329).

With Trina's rat-hole world far behind, McTeague has again an appropriate landscape. Yet he cannot remain at the mine. City forces, the law, drive him away.

In flight from Placer County, he confronts another man dispossessed of his landscape. The Indian buck Big Jim, whom McTeague mutely encounters at a railroad watering hole, is his double.[19]

> An immense Indian buck blanketed to the ground approached McTeague as he stood on the roadbed stretching his legs, and without a word presented to him a filthy, crumpled letter. The letter was to the effect that the buck Big Jim was a good Indian and deserving of charity; the signature was illegible (p. 333).

Looking back, McTeague sees the Indian as a "forlorn and solitary point of red, lost in the immensity of the surrounding white blur of the desert" (p. 334). McTeague winds up in an identical position, lost in Death Valley. And he is a kind of Indian himself, a primitive with nowhere to live, harried by forces which he cannot understand.

In a desperate attempt to escape, McTeague enters Death Valley, the ultimate Darwinian landscape.[20] The desert is not without beauty:

> It seemed strange that such barrenness could exhibit this radiance of colour, but nothing could have been more beautiful than the deep red of the higher bluffs and ridges; seamed with purple shadows, standing sharply out against the pale-blue whiteness of the horizon (p. 355).

But its predominant note is terror, for Death Valley is the negation of life:

It was abominable, this hideous sink of alkali, this bed of some primeval lake lying so far below the level of the ocean. The great mountains of Placer County had been merely indifferent to man; but this awful sink of alkali was openly and unreservedly iniquitous and malignant (p. 360).

The Darwinian dimension cannot be missed. This lake is primeval and lies *below* the level of the ocean.[21] The alkali soil is the furtherest possible remove from Millet's ploughed ground.

For a novel which explores severely limited consciousnesses, *McTeague* contains a surprising amount of highbrow aesthetic reference, allusions to paintings, descriptions of decor, landscape portraiture. This kind of "solidity of specification" is reminiscent of such radically different books from *McTeague* as *The House of Mirth* or *The Spoils of Poynton* and would seem to be quite foreign to the interests of a seamy Naturalist.[22] What such material is doing in a lower-depths fiction is certainly not to signal Norris's distance from the depraved and shoddy tastes of the poor. In "Brute," a stark sketch often quoted as a paradigm of Norris's Naturalistic vision of animality, a gigantic steelworker puts a flower into his great jaws and chews it up. In his dimly flickering consciousness the brute has a perception of beauty. When Jimmie, in Crane's *Maggie, A Girl Of The Streets,* looks up at the sky and exclaims, "Deh moon looks like hell, don't it?" he means that the moon is lovely; he is moved by beauty. Naturalistic fiction is filled with such moments, from *McTeague* and his canary to Georgette and her recitation of "The Raven" (another bird) in *Last Exit To Brooklyn.*

Willa Cather hailed *McTeague* as "a new and a great book," and in one passage she tried to define the center of that greatness:

> There are many ways of handling environment—most of them bad. When a young author has very little to say and no story worth telling, he resorts to environment. It is frequently used to disguise a weakness of structure, as ladies who paint landscapes put their cows knee-deep in water to conceal the defective drawing of the legs. But such description as one meets throughout Mr. Norris's books is in itself convincing proof of power, imagination and literary skill. It is a positive and active force, stimulating the reader's imagination, giving him an actual command, a realizing sense of this world into which he is suddenly transplanted. It gives to the book perspective, atmosphere, effects of time and distance, creates the illusion of life.[23]

Perhaps what Norris learned from Zola was an aesthetic structure rather than a catalogue of arrant stinks.

Notes

1. For discussion of these themes, see Donald Pizer, *The Novels of Frank Norris* (Bloomington: Indiana University Press, 1966), pp. 63–79; William B. Dillingham, *Frank Norris: Instinct and Art* (Lincoln, Neb.: University of Nebraska Press, 1969), pp. 74–75, 83; Charles C. Walcutt, *American Literary Naturalism, A Divided Stream* (Minneapolis: University of Minnesota Press, 1956), pp. 132–138; and Ernest Marchand, *Frank Norris, A Study* (Palo Alto: Stanford University Press, 1942), pp. 56–64. Two readings that depart from the emphasis upon naturalism examine *McTeague* as a Populist romance pitting city against country: Richard Chase, *The American Novel and Its Tradition* (Garden City, N. Y.: Doubleday, 1957), pp. 198–202; and George W. Johnson, "The Frontier Behind Frank Norris's *McTeague*," *Huntington Library Quarterly,* 26 (1962), 91–104. Mention should also be made of Warren French's attempt to make *McTeague* relevant to the 1950's by applying S. I. Hayakawa's concept of the "thing-handler" to the characterization of McTeague: *Frank Norris* (New York: Twayne Publishers, Inc., 1962), pp. 72–75. For a useful corrective to the critical dogma that naturalistic fiction exists for the sake of idea hunting, see Donald Pizer's argument that ideas ought to be considered as fictional devices having "the same relationship to the theme and form of the novel as a particular action, character, or setting": "The Problem of Philosophy in the Novel," *Bucknell Review,* 18 (1970), 54.

2. "Frank Norris's Weekly Letter," *The Literary Criticism of Frank Norris,* ed. Donald Pizer (Austin: University of Texas Press, 1964), p. 55.

3. French, p. 68.

4. *The Ferment of Realism: American Literature, 1884–1919* (New York: Free Press, 1965), p. 225. A recent and welcome exception to the derogation of Norris's work is Suzy Bernstein Goldman's formalist analysis of the imagery in *McTeague*: "*McTeague*: The Imagistic Network," *Western American Literature,* 7 (1972), 83–99. She believes that "Norris was a far more conscious artist than we have yet realized" (p. 83). So do I.

5. "The Finesse of Dreiser," *American Scholar,* 33 (1964), 111.

6. "A Case in Point," *Literature,* 4 (April 8, 1899), 370.

7. "Stephen Crane: American Genius," in *The Leafless American,* ed. Harold Billings (Sausalito, Calif.: R. Beacham, 1967), p. 60.

8. Norris to Howells, March 1899 (?), *The Letters of Frank Norris,* ed. Franklin Walker (San Francisco: Book Club of California, 1956), p. 34.

9. *The Complete Edition of Frank Norris* (Garden City, N. Y.: Doubleday, Doran & Co., 1928), VIII, 325. Hereafter all citations to *McTeague* are from this edition and will be included in the text.

10. Millet's work was well known and highly acclaimed in the San Francisco area. Gertrude Stein, for instance, recalls having been taken to see Millet's *Man With A Hoe* in the 1880's: *Everybody's Autobiography* (New York: Random House, 1937), p. 255.

11. Amy Lee Turner, "Milton and Millet," *Studies By Members of SCMLA,* 30 (1970), 227.

12. The best discussion of the class-structure underlying pastoralism is to be found in William Empson's *Some Versions of Pastoral* (London: Chatto & Windus, 1935), especially the chapters "Proletarian Literature" and "They That Have Power."

13. Most critics see the golden tooth as merely another symbol of greed. Edward Dahlberg, however, sees it as a "gaudy phallus" (*Can These Bones Live?* [New York: New Directions, 1960], p. 68). Goldman comes closest to seeing it correctly, but falls short in not granting the tooth equal status with the canary and concertina as sacred objects expressing McTeague's artistic side (*"McTeague:* The Imagistic Network," p. 95).

14. Goldman emphasizes the bird's spiritual affinities and connects its song with a significant pattern of musical images in the novel (p. 95).

15. In stressing the positive aesthetic qualities of the golden tooth, especially its spatial relationships with other objects in the novel, I should not wish to overlook the inherent falsity of the tooth. It is constructed of French *gilt,* and in both the inorganic and superfluous effects suggested by these two terms, the essential gaudiness of McTeague's taste is evident. In this respect McTeague is very much a man of his time, the Gilded Age.

16. George W. Johnson observes in "Frank Norris and Romance," *American Literature,* 33 (1961), 58, "McTeague's world is one of expansion, his tastes gross, his measurements quantitative. Trina's experience, on the other hand, is constrictive, her tastes delicate, her standards qualitative." The expansive-constructive polarity is apparent, but Trina's taste is every bit as quantitative as McTeague's.

17. Johnson, p. 58.

18. A similar pattern of symbolic dwelling places occurs in Zola's *L'Assommoir,* frequently cited as one of the formative books in Norris's development.

19. Johnson relates the Indian to the vanished frontier; in his reading, McTeague is a frustrated mountain-man, a hunter, a mute Mike Fink ("The Frontier Behind Frank Norris's *McTeague,*" p. 104.)

20. As Charles S. Watson has demonstrated, this landscape has Dantean associations as well: "A Source for the Ending of *McTeague,*" *American Literary Realism,* 5 (1972), 173–174.

21. Goldman finds this aridity a perfect conclusion to the water imagery developed throughout the novel (pp. 98–99).

22. The term is James's, "The Art of Fiction," in *The Future of the Novel,* ed. Leon Edel (New York: Vintage Books, 1956), p. 14.

23. "Frank Norris's *McTeague,*" *Courier* (April 8, 1899), pp. 2–3; reprinted in *The World and The Parish: Willa Cather's Articles and Reviews, 1893–1902,* ed. William R. Curtin (Lincoln, Neb.: University of Nebraska Press, 1970), pp. 606–607.

The Structure of *McTeague*

George M. Spangler*

For most readers the first impression of Frank Norris's *McTeague* (1899) must surely be that it is a novel almost embarrassing in its obviousness—in its simple characterization, melodramatic plot, ponderous style, and jejune philosophizing. Yet *McTeague* is anything but obvious, and from the large number of very able critics who have written about the novel come appropriately diverse interpretative conclusions, even as they agree about its intensity and power.[1] What at first seemed simple begins to appear very complicated indeed as references to LeConte, Zola, Lombroso, and Freud, to Calvinism, the success ethic, the American Adam, and the genteel tradition, proliferate. Finally, however, what emerges from the commentary is neither simple nor bewildering, but two contradictory interpretative emphases, one that stresses McTeague and Trina as victims of sexual instinct and a second that attributes their destruction to materialistic values.[2] Clearly neither emphasis is adequate, no matter how handsomely the competing point of view is acknowledged, nor is a synthesis of the two logically convincing. Rather, contradiction is the formal and thematic essence of *McTeague* and only after its importance is fully granted can a definite rhythmic unity be discerned in the novel and its compelling force understood.[3]

Specifically, the novel is divided into two roughly equal parts, apparently different in thought and radically different in texture, the point of division being McTeague's inexplicable return to sexual dormancy after a few months of marriage to Trina. Each of the two parts, moreover, has an overt and a latent aspect which may be expressed in simple propositions that are logically inconsistent or unrelated. In the first part the overt idea is that man's instincts, especially his sexual desire, have great power to trap and degrade him. The quite contradictory, though equally commonplace, latent idea is that sexual love has great creative potential, that love ennobles the individual. In this first part the

*Reprinted from *English Studies,* 59 (February, 1978), 48–56, by permission of Swets Publishing Service and the author.

texture is pervasively realistic. In the second part, which is surrealistic
nightmare, the overt idea is that avarice destroys, a traditional moral
proposition which many readers have seen as the theme of the novel.
Far more decisive to the texture and feeling of the second part, however,
is the logically unrelated, latent 'idea' (fear, anxiety) that female
sexuality is threatening and finally destructive to men. Since this latent
'idea', which the psychoanalytic critic would no doubt call castration
fear and trace to repressed incestuous wishes, is unacceptable to the
consciousness of both author and audience, it must be disguised and expressed by the acceptable proposition that the love of money is the
root of all evil. Paradoxically, the conflicting overt and latent ideas of
part one are more closely, though not logically, related to the latent idea
of part two than to its overt theme, their conflict serving perhaps to
trigger the covert fear. Finally, when the crucial importance of the latent
element of the second part is perceived, the recognition provides an
explanation for the rhythmic alternation of stasis and disruption that
pervades the novel, including the flashback to McTeague's boyhood
and especially the often disparaged conclusion.

The contention that McTeague's loss of sexual interest in Trina
during the first year of their marriage is the dividing point between the
two parts of the novel, the muted signal that the realistic narrative is to
become surrealistic nightmare, requires some explanation. Not only
do two other events—Trina's winning $5000 in a lottery and especially
McTeague's losing his license to practice dentistry—have strong claims
as structural centers, but in addition Norris's treatment of McTeague's
regression is quite without emphasis. He reports that after about six
months of marriage McTeague takes 'great delight' in his wife's presence,
'But that tempest of passion, that overpowering desire that had suddenly
taken possession of him that day when he had given her ether, again
when he had caught her in his arms in the B Street station, and again
and again during the early days of their married life, rarely stirred him
now'. There is in fact 'no passion in the dentist's regard for his wife.'[4]
Despite this lack of emphasis, McTeague's retreat from sexuality is
striking because it is so completely improbable; indeed it is inexplicable
until seen from the perspective of the fear latent in the second part of
the novel. Contrary not only to all the reader knows of McTeague, who
has been repeatedly presented as a man whose deeply aroused sexual
desire leads him to marriage, but also simply to the reader's common
sense, McTeague's failure of passion even as Trina's desire intensifies
ironically foreshadows the latent sexual content of their subsequent
destructive antagonism. Of course early in the novel Norris endorses the
conventional notion that a man's respect for a woman decreases as their

intimacy grows. But this hint of explanation for McTeague's new attitude does not bear scrutiny, for the loss of romantic awe is a quite different matter from a return to sexual dormancy. In a word, McTeague overtly and casually suppresses what soon will be latently and terrifyingly threatened—his masculinity. Moreover, the more obvious turning points in the plot serve to enforce this point of view: the lottery money, which comes before McTeague's restored dormancy, means an access of power to Trina; and the loss of his profession, which comes after, represents a loss of power for McTeague. These events of course are crucial to the plot, but their full significance, as distinct from their immediate cause (chance and Marcus's hatred) and their overt function (the introduction of the economic theme of part two), may be less arbitrarily assigned if the teasingly improbable shift in sexual attitude that separates them is given its full due of attention.

Unlike this view of the actual point of division in the novel's essentially divided structure, the statement that a moralistic view of man's instinctual nature overtly dominates the first part of the novel hardly requires defense. Norris's beliefs and their sources have been written about extensively, and the author himself can be agonizingly explicit. The now almost notorious passage occurs just after McTeague's 'better self' has lost its struggle with the 'beast' in him, and McTeague has kissed the etherized Trina 'grossly, full on the mouth.' 'Below the fine fabric of all that was good in him ran the foul stream of hereditary evil, like a sewer. The vices and sins of his father and his father's father, to the third and fourth and five hundredth generation, tainted him. The evil of an entire race flowed in his veins' (p. 29). The reader also hears in the first part of the novel of other dangerous instinctual proclivities, but they are inconsequential compared to sexuality. The sporadic alcoholism of McTeague's father apparently underlies the son's use of whiskey once his degeneration begins, but drinking merely allows for rather than causes McTeague's brutal treatment of his wife. Similarly, Trina's instinctive thrift, which Norris attributes to a 'hardy and penurious mountain race,' is ludicrously inadequate as an explanation for her insane obsession with money in the second half. Sex is the chief villain in part one, and the failure to repress this base instinct represents the triumph of the beast lurking beneath the civilized, ethical surface of humanity.

Donald Pizer has shown that the immediate source of this ethical dualism was Norris's Berkeley professor Joseph LeConte, who attempted to reconcile traditional morality and post-Darwinian science. Yet such divisions of body and soul, flesh and spirit, are so common in human ethical and religious thought that Norris's immediate source seems much less important than the appalling intensity with which he endorses the separation.[5] Indeed the overt aspect of the first part is most notable perhaps as a haphazard compendium of received commonplace ideas about sexual relations. The reader hears, for example, that the sexes have an intuitive fear of each other, that women feel the need to be mastered, and that men lose respect for women once they are intimate. From the perspective of the horrors of the second part, this collection of moral and psychological clichés strongly suggests a man vainly trying for intellectual control of a deep anxiety rather than simply an inexperienced young novelist betraying a superficial mind. Moreover, what is latent in part one does not merely add to the feeling of tension and confusion, it makes for absolute contradiction.

To point out once more what Norris says about sex in part one is, though necessary, very much a matter of trusting the teller not the tale. For along with the overt structuring idea—in essence, that sex is evil—which the author expresses in his own voice, there is present a latent and contradictory idea, a positive view of sex, which is dramatized rather than stated and which Norris's critics have not noticed. In a word, what Norris says about the courtship of Trina and McTeague is often in contradiction to what he shows. The reader is told, for example, that McTeague's sexual awakening means the arousal of the beast, but what he sees in dramatized fact is that sexual love causes an unwonted tenderness in McTeague. As he begins to be attracted to the woman who is his patient, the thought of hurting her torments him. 'To hurt Trina was a positive anguish for McTeague, yet an anguish which he was obliged to endure at every hour of sitting. It was harrowing—he sweated under it—to be forced to torture her, of all women in the world; could anything be worse than that?' (p. 27). His love also leads him to attempt more complex dental work than he has ever tried in order not to 'disfigure such a pretty mouth.' 'It was the most difficult operation he had ever performed. He bungled it considerably, but in the end he succeeded passably well,' and the operation is just the beginning, for he gives much thought and many hours to filling in the gap attractively. The extracted tooth he keeps as a token. He also becomes newly articulate, able to work and talk at the same time. When she is present, he feels 'blindly happy,' and his 'first romance' makes his life 'delightful.'

Though Norris's tone is at first annoyingly patronizing, the creative effect of romantic love is nonetheless clear; and soon his treatment of the courtship achieves a sort of comic gaiety as the lovers go on family picnics, attend a vaudeville show, discuss their future. This positive treatment of sexual relations, so at odds with Norris's overt talk of the 'foul stream of hereditary evil,' is also present in the comic portrayal of Trina's family, the Sieppes. Again the tone is patronizing, but the humor is unmistakable and suggests that normal domestic life, like romance, is anything but evil. Thus it seems especially significant that the Sieppes drop out of the story immediately after the wedding, to be replaced by the perverted Zerkow and Maria and the desexualized Miss Baker and Old Grannis. After the marriage Norris notes that Trina improves her husband's appearance, manners, and tastes, but this is the last the reader hears of any positive results of the relationship, and at this same point in the text he learns that McTeague has lost sexual interest in Trina. What follows is all for the worse. The latent structuring idea of part one—that sexual love is creative—is of course just as much a commonplace as the overt rejection of sexual feeling, but the crucial point is that the two are in contradiction, a contradiction that Norris cannot consciously and rationally resolve. Instead the ambivalence of the first part, its tension of inconsistent commonplaces about sex, gives way to, in fact probably sets off, a nightmare of degeneration and death in part two in which a savage overt attack on greed allows for and gains intensity from the latent expression of profound unconscious fear of threatening female sexuality.

The overt aspect of the structure of the second part of the novel is based on yet another commonplace idea: the love of money is the root of all evil. Like the puritanical editorializing of part one, Norris's embodiment of the precept has received extensive critical attention, providing as it apparently does abundant evidence for those commentators who see the McTeagues as victims of American materialism. The obsessive lust for money pervades the second part, corrupting and destroying every human value and feeling. Ties of family, friendship, and marriage are violated, sex is perverted, productive work denied, nature raped. Trina refuses to send money to her needy family; Marcus, relentless in his envy, betrays his friend; Zerkow marries and murders Maria for gold that does not exist; the California mountains are torn apart for gold ore; even Old Grannis despairs (temporarily) when he sells his book binding apparatus. Gold becomes the malevolent deity of a violent, brutal world. Yet insistent and compelling as it is, Norris's sermonizing on greed presents serious critical problems, and an interpretation based on it raises as many questions as it answers.

Most obviously, the economic theme is virtually discontinous with the sexual concerns of part one. Though overt links between the parts do exist, they are most striking for their tenuousness. Moreover, the thematic discontinuity has a revealing analogue in a change in the novel's texture from realistic to surrealistic. Norris's careful descriptions of the San Francisco milieu, which so many readers have admired, are largely absent from the second part, so that concrete details of social and his-

torical context are most lacking precisely when the socially critical intention often attributed to Norris supposedly comes to the fore. Norris
of course can and does make his overt moral point, but it is at least worth
asking why, if his aim is social criticism, he chooses the method of *The
Pardoner's Tale* rather than *A Hazard of New Fortunes*, why indeed he
switches from the one to the other in the middle of his narrative.[6] This
change in technique is also evident in matters of character motivation. For
example, in the first part the sexual basis of the McTeagues' relationship
is clear; only Norris's evaluation of it is contradictory. But in the second
part the prime mover, Trina's avarice, does not begin to be accounted for.
Norris's passing references to her thrifty peasant ancestors and her miserly
instincts (pp. 107, 148), his only two gestures at explaining her psychotic
behavior, simply are not adequate. Similarly, Marcus's envious hatred of
McTeague, which lasts for years and which makes him risk and lose his
life, is highly implausible, as is the whole lurid sequence involving the
marriage, murder, and suicide of Zerkow and Maria.

Most important, however, first in making the reader ask and then in
allowing him to discover what lies beneath the overt concern with greed
is Norris's sexualization of Trina's hoard of gold pieces. In what are surely
among the most shocking passages in a novel pervaded in its second half
with perverse pleasure and violent death Norris portrays Trina in patently
erotic relationship with her money. Even before McTeague had deserted
her, she buries her face in a pile of gold pieces, delighting in their feel
and smell. 'She even put the smaller gold pieces in her mouth and jingled
them there' (p. 238). After her husband is gone and she is deprived of
the masochistic delights he sometimes provided, her passion for the
money intensifies. 'One evening she had even spread all the gold pieces
between the sheets, and had then gone to bed, stripping herself, and
had slept all night upon the money, taking a strange and ecstatic pleasure
in the touch of the smooth flat pieces the length of her entire body'
(p. 277). Such passages of course show yet again how the love of money
corrupts but they also establish an implicit identity between Trina's
sexuality and her avarice. That is, quite simply, gold comes to stand implicitly for female sexuality, and thus what is latent in part two becomes
clear. The economic theme, though certainly compelling in itself, is
also a way of expressing, through a moral commonplace acceptable to
the consciousness of both author and audience, a repressed fear of
castration. The McTeagues are not family victims of sexual instinct
in general, as part one states, nor of money lust, as part two insists.
Rather McTeague, who remains innocent about money and who quickly
withdraws from sex, is the victim of Norris's version of the fatal woman,
who, in a recurrent phrase in the novel, 'makes small' of him. And thus

the two parts of the novel have a certain continuity, though not a rational coherence: the contradictory evaluation of sexual love in part one leads to a disguised expression of terror at female sexuality in part two.[7]

That Trina is the villain of the piece, the destroyer, is an easy case to make, and a further look at her behavior and its contexts clarifies the sexual meaning of her degradation of her husband. When McTeague is no longer allowed to practice dentistry (the deprivation due to Marcus would obviously suggest the punishing father to the Freudian critic), Norris makes clear that Trina's economics are unnecessarily severe, that she welcomes an excuse to add to her hoard, even at the cost of a degraded way of life. Having encouraged him to dream of a house of their own, she first refuses their opportunity for one and then, after McTeague is forbidden to practice, she sells their household goods and moves them from their pleasant flat to a single room. Later on, after the death of Maria and Zerkow, she sees a chance to save and again insists on their moving: 'and the back room in that wretched house with its grisly memories, the one window looking out into a grimy maze of backyards and broken sheds, was what they now knew as their home' (p. 258). Of the other events through which Norris dramatizes Trina's continual humiliation of her husband, the most effective occurs the day McTeague loses his job with a dental supply firm. When he returns home, she demands that he immediately look for another job, and, despite the threat of rain, denies him a nickel for carfare. He does not find work, and he returns cold, wet, and enraged with Trina, aware that her hoarding degrades him: 'You can't make small of me *always*' (p. 230). For the first time he is brutal to her, but Trina's response is to wonder where he got money for the whiskey that contributes to his fury.

This conclusion to the episode is suggestive for it gives the reader further cause to excuse McTeague's physical brutality and place the burden of responsibility on Trina. Norris uses a similar tactic later on as McTeague becomes more and more savage with Trina: he must resort to cruelty as the only way to get a few pennies from the hoard his wife continues to accumulate at the cost of their basic human decency, whereas she soon begins to take masochistic pleasure in the pain he inflicts. Even the murder is presented in a way that shifts responsibility from murderer to victim. Having deserted her for several months, McTeague returns to beg for food and shelter, which she denies him, unable as she is to forgive his having taken $400 when he left. Soon after he discovers that she has sold his concertina, one of his two dearest possessions, sold it, Norris emphasizes, with great delight. The sight of the concertina reminds him of Trina, and he first demands money to buy it back, then all her money. Fully aware that it is now a question of her gold or her life, Trina futilely chooses to protect the gold and McTeague kills her. The murder is, as Norris puts it, 'abominable,' yet Norris quite skilfully manages to make the reader feel at least some sympathy for McTeague and none for Trina, a sympathy that increases as McTeague assumes the role of doomed fugitive in the final pages of the novel. Throughout the process of their degeneration then, Norris presents McTeague as Trina's victim.

Moreover, the latent sexual meaning of the victimization is repeatedly indicated in the almost embarrassing amount of sexually suggestive language Norris provides. In addition to the sexualization of the gold, most conspicuous are Trina's demand that McTeague 'love me big' even while she 'makes small' of him; the swelling chamois bag in which she hides her money, surely the ironic womb of the childless couple; the whittling knife Trina uses so industriously to make toy animals, a skill that suggests Circe, especially since she does not carve human figures; and the concertina, the sale of which leads directly to the murder. Even the huge gold tooth which Trina gives to McTeague as a wedding gift and which he uses to advertise his dental parlor takes on a sinister meaning in the second part of the novel, as does the characteristic act of the profession McTeague is forced to abandon.

The fear of the threatening woman in the second part is also conveyed through the two couples that Norris portrays in addition to the McTeagues. Led on by her fantastic tale of a lost set of gold dishes, Zerkow married the demented Maria. But after the marriage and the death of their child, Maria becomes sane and forgets all about the gold dishes. Deprived of his mad dream of getting possession of the dishes, Zerkow cuts Maria's throat and drowns himself. The conscious emphasis is of course on Zerkow's avarice as a moral parallel to Trina's, but again the gold, illusory this time, is associated with the woman and again it leads to debasement and death. In contrast, the one personal relation that does prosper in the second part is that between the Dickensian old couple, Old Grannis and Miss Baker. That the success of their relation depends on its asexual nature is an inescapable implication. Indeed they only overcome years of shyness when Miss Baker comforts Old Grannis after he sells the little book-binding machine he invented—another incident so implausible that it can only be read symbolically, for selling the design could not possibly prevent the old man from making another model and continuing his hobby. Only when the man is childlike in his age and incapacity can the woman be other than threatening. If he is not, as McTeague and Zerkow are not, she deceives, debases, and destroys, her destructive power symbolized in this novel by gold, whether real or imaginary.

Though often disparaged as extraneous melodrama, the final three chapters dealing with McTeague's hopeless flight after the murder function as a recapitulation of the essential structural tension of the second part of the novel. When McTeague gets work at a gold mine in his native region, his manhood is in effect briefly restored. The comparison between what he lost and what he regains is obvious even to McTeague himself. 'In the burly drill he saw a queer counterpart of his old-time dental engine ... It was the same work he had so often performed in his parlors, only magnified, made monstrous, distorted, and grotesqued, the caricature of dentistry' (p. 298). Here he is briefly happy again, but even before his 'strange sixth sense' warns him of pursuit and makes him flee, the situation, the close association with gold, is threatening. Norris presents the miners' penetration of the mountains as violent and destructive, '... now with hydraulic monitors, now with drill and dynamite, boring into the vitals of them, or tearing away great yellow gravelly scars in the flanks of them, sucking their blood, extracting gold' (p. 293). In turn, the men are endangered by the work, by 'the silent vast titanic force, mysterious and slow, that cracked the timbers supporting the roof of the tunnel and that gradually flattened the lagging till it was thin as paper' (p. 298).

The stark suggestiveness of the language makes clear that gold in the final chapters continues to have the double meaning it acquired in the second part of the novel; and when McTeague becomes aware of pursuit, the choice he has is between gold and life, much as it once was between remaining with Trina and preserving some measure of manhood, however diminished. These same alternatives, gold or survival, are presented to him two more times in the final chapters. The first time, after he and his new partner discover a rich vein of gold, the lure of riches is powerful, but McTeague again chooses survival and flees in obedience to his instinctive sense of danger. Finally, however, gold—Trina's gold—wins out. The implausible appearance of Marcus, who, as when he deprived McTeague of his dental practice, represents in Freudian terms the father who punishes for the incestuous wishes underlying castration anxiety, signals the inevitable end. Having shot the mule and lost the drinking water, they know that they have next to no chance of survival. Yet they quarrel absurdly over the gold McTeague took from Trina. Having killed Marcus, McTeague awaits sure death, appropriately enough in Death Valley, Norris's final symbolic expression of the destructive female principle.

The essential structure of *McTeague* is then most accurately described as a discontinuous, contradictory complex of thought and feeling, overt and latent. Though it emphasizes unresolved tension in the novel, this view of the structure, especially as it makes clear the latent fear of female sexuality in part two, also allows the reader to perceive in retrospect a rhythmic continuity in the novel which is its chief principle of unity. Specifically, from start to finish the character McTeague is presented continuously oscillating between repose and disturbance—the repose dependent on sexual dormancy and the disturbance on fear of the destructive female, though the fear is at first disguised as a rational consideration of sexual instinct in general and then as a grim parable of greed. As a boy at the mine McTeague is satisfied, but his mother's fierce ambition makes him a dentist. In San Francisco the advent of Trina destroys his simple, sensuous equilibrium. Briefly at peace in his marriage (and again sexually dormant), his wife's avarice soon threatens him. After leaving Trina he finds a job and apparently some stability, only to discover that she has sold his concertina, a discovery that leads directly to the murder. Returning to the mining country, he twice finds a resting place, first at the mine and then with his prospecting partner, but both times he is forced to move on. Finally, even he and Marcus, once they see their common danger, have a brief truce, only to fight minutes later over the gold for the last time. In sum, what Norris's novel lacks in structural coherence it supplies in rhythmic unity, but to discern rather than merely feel the rhythm and its meaning, the reader must recognize the incoherence.

Notes

1. The best commentary on *McTeague*, indeed on all of Norris's fiction, is in Donald Pizer, *The Novels of Frank Norris* (Bloomington: Indiana University Press, 1966), pp. 52–85. Pizer's book brings together the impressive quantity of material Pizer first published in journals over a period of ten years before the book appeared.

2. The view that McTeague and Trina are victims of a commercial, industrial environment is most clearly stated in Jay Martin, *Harvests of Change: American Literature 1864–1914* (Englewood Cliffs, N.J.: Prentice-Hall, 1967), p. 251. A similar interpretative emphasis may be found in Warren French, *Frank Norris* (New York: Twayne Publishers, Inc., 1962), pp. 62–75. The importance of instinct is stressed in Pizer and in William B. Dillingham, *Frank Norris: Instinct and Art* (Lincoln, Neb.: University of Nebraska Press, 1969), pp. 74, 89, *et passim*.

3. Larzer Ziff engagingly deals with the problems of contradiction, contending that Norris's fiction is best when disorganized, when Norris's sense of life's complexity escapes the control of the jejune concepts the author provides as organizing principles. *The American 1890s: Life and Times of a Lost Generation* (New York: Viking Press, 1966), p. 251.

4. Frank Norris, *McTeague* (New York: New American Library, 1964), p. 149. Subsequent page references to this Signet Classic will be included in the text.

5. For example, in Stanley Cooperman, "Frank Norris and the Werewolf of

Guilt," *Modern Language Quarterly*, 20 (1959), 252–258, Norris's ideas about sex are attributed to the influence of Calvinistic Christianity.

6. Richard Chase implicitly acknowledges the change in texture when he notes that the characters change from ordinary people to puppets of fate. *The American Novel and Its Tradition* (Garden City, N. Y.: Doubleday, 1957), p. 189.

7. Maxwell Geismar, *Rebels and Ancestors: The American Novel, 1890–1915* (Boston: Houghton Mifflin and Company, 1953), pp. 3–66; and Kenneth S. Lynn, *The Dream of Success* (Boston: Little, Brown and Co., 1955), pp. 158–207, provide a psychoanalytical perspective on the biographical origins of Norris's attitude toward women. Both stress the absent father who refused to see his sons after he divorced their mother and the possessive mother who went so far as to take a room in Cambridge to be near Frank when he entered Harvard. Dillingham, p. 10, also notes the recurrence of the "Destructive Woman" in Norris's fiction, but he attempts to deal with it in moral rather than psychological terms.

Frank Norris's *The Octopus*:
Some Observations on Vanamee,
Shelgrim and St. Paul

Richard Allan Davison*

While preparing to put together a collection[1] of key essays and statements on *The Octopus*, I surveyed virtually all the extant criticism on Frank Norris to better my understanding of this, his most celebrated novel. I discovered how most of the critics have affected each other as well as how they were all affected by *The Octopus*.[2] Unfortunately, much of the vigorous disagreement that a complex and stimulating work of art inspires often throws more light on the critics than on Norris. Least offensive are the critical weaknesses that come from strong personal viewpoints; worse by far are those resulting from murky-minded reasoning and careless reading of the novel. So-called pivotal passages are read with the blurred subjectivism of an Ishmael seduced by the artificial light of the try-works. Frequently, like the proverbial blind men in their encounter with the elephant, the critics have been seized by a single tentacle of *The Octopus* and have strangely managed to elude its other wriggling appendages, not to mention that massive head! that Cyclopean eye! Many of the diverse and contradictory opinions warrant a brief sampling.[3]

I

The earliest known reviewer of *The Octopus*, Wallace Rice, called the novel "a work of realism" whose "philosophy [was] hideous" and whose "purpose [was] self-defeated." He felt that "the episode of Vanamee and Angèle . . . [had] no possible relevance" to the work and saw Shelgrim's speech as "wholly converting [Presley] the most intelligent character" in the book. Over the next fifteen months or so contemporary reviewers further complicated the issues. F. T. Cooper saw Norris as "farther away from real life in *The Octopus* than he was in

*Reprinted from *Literature and Ideas in America,* edited by Robert Falk, (Columbus: Ohio University Press, 1976), pp. 182–203. By permission of the author.

A *Man's Woman,* just as in that novel he was farther away than in *Mc-Teague.*" William Dean Howells felt each of the characters "most intimately and personally real, physically real, but also psychically real." B. O. Flower saw Norris's novel "exhibiting the strength, power, vividnesses, fidelity to truth, photographic accuracy in description, and marvelous insight in depicting human nature, together with that broad and philosophic grasp of the larger problems of life, that noble passion for justice, that characterizes the greatest work of Emile Zola, without that sexualism or repulsive naturalism which the French writer so frequently forces upon his readers. . . . " Another reviewer felt *The Octopus* "too visibly determined by Zola and often too diligently brutal in style . . . [but] tremendous in strength and scope." The early disagreement over Norris's inclusion of Vanamee and Angèle was even more violent. While the *Overland Monthly* praised "the delicate love Idyll of Vanamee and Angèle Varian, touching upon phases of the most modern psychological thought, the shadowy world of the mind," the *Independent* attacked the subplot for dwindling "away into the regions of the most artificial and unconvincing supernaturalism." Just as William Payne of the *Dial* praised Norris for "the vein of mysticism that. . . . is not only distinctly Zolaesque, but also provides a welcome relief from the oppressive atmosphere of the narrative . . .", so H. H. Boynton of the *Atlantic Monthly* attacked Norris's handling of Vanamee and Angèle as "the sort of romantic vulgarity of which only the realist of the French School is capable." The mass of later criticism has followed most of these early reviewers' guidelines, if not always their piety and concern for poetic justice. Until the 1940s *The Octopus* was generally attacked, particularly for alleged philosophical inconsistencies.

Writing in 1915 Frederick Lewis Pattee claimed *The Octopus* was "not literature" and came to "no terminus or conclusion." Eighteen years later Norris's biographer Franklin Walker, while seeing a good deal more merit in the novel than did Pattee, referred to it as "an imperfect synthesis . . . a ragout . . . parts of which are nutritious, others indigestible." Granville Hicks wrote, the next year, that "*The Octopus* can scarcely be called a great book; it is too confused, and in the end too false." By the early 1940s H. Willard Reninger and George Wilbur Meyer had somewhat cautiously argued for different kinds of philosophical consistency in *The Octopus* but Ernest Marchand in the second booklength study of Norris (1942) saw the author bewildered and confused regarding the philosophy of his novel. To this day critics disagree as to the novel's aesthetic and philosophic values. Warren French sees philosophical consistency but flawed structure. Richard Chase has called *The Octopus* "a sub-novel" and Kenneth Lynn has claimed that "measured by any architectonic standard" it is "a literary chaos." Donald Pizer and William B. Dillingham seem most in agreement about the merits of the novel but each has certain reservations.[4] Pizer sees philosophical unity in what he views as a Le Contean reconciliation of "evolutionary science and religious faith"—a kind of "evolutionary theism" stressing divine immanence in the wheat, transcendentalism and utilitarianism.[5] His most serious reservations concern Norris's embodiment and reinforcement of his ideas.

II

Although so many critics have disagreed over *The Octopus'* rank in American literature, no one to my knowledge has denied its vast energy, scope and power. Norris may not be a great novelist but he could be a very good one.[6] *The Octopus* almost embraces the greatness it reaches out for. Norris tells an exciting, profoundly compelling story and he tells it well. Furthermore, Norris was more consciously in control of the philosophy and structure of *The Octopus* than even the most recent favorable critics seem to believe. Almost all critics agree that the weakest aspects of the novel are in the Vanamee-Angèle episode and the conclusion. They are also not sure how to interpret Presley's interview with Shelgrim.[7] As interrelated as these issues are they are worth examining, to an extent at least, one at a time. But to provide a broader context for the discussion, a review of Norris's meticulous concern for the unity of his novel may prove enlightening. What Norris thought he was doing in *The Octopus* may help us to evaluate his actual achievement.

Particularly during the last years of his short life Norris evidenced rather acute awareness of the strengths and shortcomings of his novels.[8] In his critical essays on the novel in general he demanded a structural concentration that was Aristotelian in its unity. "The Mechanics of Fiction"[9] offers a handbook description of some of the unity Norris believed he had achieved in *The Octopus*.

He calls for "a beginning, and end, which implies a middle, continuity . . ." and then elaborates in some detail:

> . . . it is hard to get away from that thing in every novel which let us call the *pivotal event*. All good novels have one. It is *the peg upon which the fabric of the thing hangs*, the nucleus around which the shifting drifts and currents must—suddenly—coagulate, the sudden releasing of the brake to permit for one instant the entire machinery to labour, full steam, ahead. *Up to that point the action must lead, from it, it must decline.*
>
> But—and here one holds at least one mechanical prob-

lem—*the approach,* the leading up to this pivotal event *must be infinitely slower than the decline.* For the reader's interest in the story centers round it. . . .

The unskilled, impatient of the tedium of meticulous elaboration, will rush at it in a furious gallop of short chapters and hurried episodes, so that he may come the sooner to the purple prose declamation and drama that he is sure he can handle with such tremendous effect.

Not so the masters. Watch them during the first third—say—of their novels. Nothing happens—or at least so you fancy. *People come and go, plans are described, localities, neighborhoods; an incident crops up just for a second for which you can see no reason,* a note sounds that is puzzlingly inappropriate. The novel continues. There seems to be no progress: again that perplexing note, but a little less perplexing. By now we are well into the story. There are no more new people, but the old ones come back again and again, and yet again; you remember them now after they are off stage. You are more intimate with the two main characters. Then comes a series of incidents in which these two are prominent. The action still lags, but little by little you are getting more and more acquainted with these principal actors. Then perhaps comes the first acceleration of movement. The approach begins—ever so little—to rise, *and that same note which seemed at first so out of tune sounds again and this time drops into place in the progression, beautifully harmonious, correlating the whole gamut.* By now all the people are on; by now all the groundwork is prepared. You *know the localities* so well that you could find your way about among them in the dark; *hero and heroine are intimate acquaintances.*

Now the action begins to increase in speed. The *complication* suddenly tightens; all along the line there runs a sudden alert. An episode far back there in the first chapter, an episode with its appropriate group of characters, is brought forward and, coming suddenly to the front, collides with the main line of development and sends it off upon an entirely unlooked for tangent. Another episode of the second chapter—let us suppose—all at once makes common cause with a more recent incident, and the two produce a wholly unlooked for counter influence which swerves the main theme in still another direction, and all this time the action is speeding faster and faster, the complication tightening, and straining to the breaking point, and then *at last a 'motif' that has been in preparation ever since the first paragraph of the first chapter of the novel suddenly comes to a head, and in a twinkling the complication is solved with all the violence of an explosion,* and the *catas-*

trophe, the climax, the pivotal event fairly leaps from the pages with a rush of action that leaves you stunned, breathless, and overwhelmed with the sheer power of its presentation. And there is a master work of fiction.

The master work of fiction Norris so vigorously described follows the structural patterns of a Greek tragedy with its exposition, inciting action, rising action, climax, catastrophe, and falling action. The novel he actually wrote also follows this basic pattern. The scope of his theme, however, prompted him to add more characters and more fully develop the falling action. In *The Octopus* Norris achieved a "progression" that is "beautifully harmonious" largely through an intricate analogical structure reinforced by what E. M. Forster has called inner stitching or rhythmic repetition with variation.[10] Just as Melville employed countless rhythmic patterns embodying the numerous themes in *Moby Dick* and Twain used incremental repetition to impose form on otherwise picaresque incidents in *Huckleberry Finn*,[11] so Norris coordinated his epic, elemental struggle between the ranchers and Pacific and Southwestern Railroad. He begins the preparation of various of his motifs "in the first paragraph of the first chapter." Norris realizes in *The Octopus* a full artistic development of man's struggles with himself and his society. He portrays a complex world whose inhabitants are clearly responsible for their actions. *The Octopus* (along with *The Pit*) is the culmination of Norris's growing belief in a morally ordered universe. By refining devices already present in earlier works,[12] he reveals the far-reaching implications of St. Paul's optimistic philosophy. As the novel progresses the motifs become increasingly meaningful through his manipulation of repeated comparison, contrasts, ironic juxtapositions, and a masterful handling of detail.[13]

III

The first chapter is largely unified by Presley's bicycle trip over the terrain that is to become so familiar to the reader. Norris included a "Map Of The Country Described In *The Octopus*" that at once enhances the visual conception of his novel and reinforces many of its major images.[14] In the opening sentence of *The Octopus* Presley passes Caraher's saloon (where the anarchist is to press both Dyke and Presley into violence). Derrick's ranch, Los Muertos, is mentioned as the "prolonged blowing" of a railroad whistle reaches Presley's ears. Within the first ten pages Norris established the post harvest time (the "last half of September") and the sparsity of the recent wheat crop. Presley passes the life-giving watering tank on which a fresh sign, "S. Behrman, Real Estate, Mortgages, Main Street, Bonneville, Opposite the Post Office," is "all but finished." Hooven is introduced along with his fear that Magnus Derrick will remove him as tenant; Presley rides past the greyhounds that will participate in the rabbit hunt and massacre following Dyke's capture and preceding the climactic ditch fight. He passes the giant live-oak which remains in towering majesty impervious to changing human circumstances.[15] He passes the Derricks' broken-down, rusting seeders and the Railroad's box cars that are to take the Derricks' new plows on a costly, circuitous route. Presley rides past the unfinished irrigation ditch, potential bringer of water and life, that is to be the site of bloodshed and death. The moral flaws in Minna Hooven are hinted at. Dyke is introduced with news of his recent firing by the Railroad. Presley meets Annixter, who complains of Derrick's exploitive ranching methods. He also announces his own upcoming barn dance. Presley meets Vanamee and Father Sarria and recalls the shepherd's tragic loss of Angèle. Chapter one ends with the slaughter of Vanamee's neglected sheep by a speeding locomotive.

Throughout chapter two the exposition continues at its slow and steady pace. The inciting action does not occur until chapter three when, at a ranchers' meeting at Derrick's house, Osterman suggests their counter use of bribery to combat the Railroad. With the rising action Norris's novel gains momentum as pivotal incidents pile one upon another: Vanamee's meeting with Father Sarria and rejection of St. Paul's hopeful words; his first attempt to call Angèle from the grave; Annixter's thwarted attempt to kiss Hilma; the celebratory barn dance (where all the characters literally or figuratively join hands and circle round, a device much like the scaffold scenes in *The Scarlet Letter* or the Corey dinner party in *Silas Lapham*);[16] the art show at Lyman Derrick's San Francisco club where the joyful cries of the raffle winner merge with the news of the ranchers' major setback in the higher courts;[17] Annixter's thwarted overtures to Hilma; Dyke's ruin; Annixter's realization of a love beyond the purely physical the same day Presley writes "The Toilers" and Vanamee sees Angèle's daughter for the first time and the young green sprouts of wheat break through the brown earth; Annixter's marriage and Dyke's train robbery; Lyman Derrick's betrayal of the ranchers; Genslinger's blackmail of Derrick; Dyke's capture and the rabbit hunt followed by the climactic irrigation ditch battle. The falling action involves the sorting out of thoughts and the inexorable working out of what human beings have set in motion: the catastrophic scene of Magnus Derrick disgraced and driven from the stage of the opera house to a claustrophobic actress' dressing room that reeks of sachet;[18] Presley's astounding interview with Shelgrim; Minna Hooven's downfall and her mother's starvation; the Gerard dinner party; Vanamee's enlightened

restatement of St. Paul to Presley; Behrman's death; Presley's departure on the wheat-filled ship destined to relieve starving people in India
and his concluding statements of hope. Norris has carefully developed
the implications of Presley's concluding optimistic speech. The omniscient author and the reader can better appreciate the appropriateness
of this ending than can the convalescing protagonist and speaker.

IV

Claiming that the "Conclusion" of *The Octopus* is neither prepared
for nor convincing, Norris's detractors have inevitably used it to cap
their arguments for his muddled philosophy and loose artistic control.
Yet Presley's semi-enlightened echo of Vanamee's enlightened restatement of St. Paul represents the culmination of a motif that Norris established in the fourth chapter of the first book of a sixteen-chapter novel.
And the seeds of this optimistic philosophy begin their growth in the
very first chapter. When Vanamee continues to despair of the loss of
Angèle, Father Sarria tries in vain to comfort him by quoting from St.
Paul's letter to the Corinthians:[19]

> "Thou fool! That which thou sowest is not quickened except
> it die, and that which thou sowest, thou sowest not that body
> that shall be, but bare grain. It may chance of wheat, or
> of some other grain. But God giveth it a body as it hath
> pleased him, and to every seed his own body. . . . It is sown
> a natural body; it is raised a spiritual body. It is because
> you are a natural body that you cannot understand her, nor
> wish for her as a spiritual body, but when you are both
> spiritual, then you shall know each other as you are—know as
> you never knew before. Your grain of wheat is your symbol of
> immortality. You bury it in the earth. It dies, and rises again
> a thousand times more beautiful. Vanamee, your dear girl was
> only a grain of humanity that we have buried here, and the
> end is not yet. But all this is so old, so old. The world learned
> it a thousand years ago, and yet each man that has ever stood
> by the open grave of anyone he loved must learn it all over
> again from the beginning."

The truth of these words has not yet reached the bereaved lover (i, 139).
Before the end of Book I Vanamee himself draws the parallel between his mystical awareness of what seems to be Angèle's growing
presence and " 'the very first little quiver of life that the grain of wheat
must feel after it is sown, when it answers to the call of the sun, down
there in the dark of the earth. . . . ' " Now it is Vanamee who quotes
St. Paul to a noncommittal Presley: " 'That which thou sowest is not

quickened except it die . . . ' " (i, 209). But he rather fuzzily associates this phenomenon with a kind of sixth sense until the night Angèle's daughter appears to him in the Mission garden. Then even Sarria's assurance that the beautiful girl is not Angèle but her daughter does not dampen Vanamee's new spiritual affirmation:

> Life out of death, eternity rising from out of dissolution. There was the lesson. Angèle was not the symbol but the proof of immortality. The seed dying, rotting and corrupting in the earth; rising again in life unconquerable, and in immaculate purity. . . . Why had he not had the knowledge of God? Thou fool, that which thou sowest is not quickened except it die. . . . The wheat called forth from out of darkness . . . from out of the grave, from out of corruption, rose triumphant into light and life. So Angèle, so life, so also the resurrection of the dead. . . . (ii, 106–107)

By the end of the novel Vanamee has generalized his new awareness into a transcendental philosophy. He reads Presley a lesson that is gradually to dissipate the young poet's confusion and bitterness: " 'the good never dies; evil dies, cruelty, oppression, selfishness, greed—these die; but nobility, but love, but sacrifice, but generosity, but truth . . . — these live forever. . . . Never judge of the whole round of life by the mere segment you see. The whole is, in the end, perfect.' "[20] The words have taken root in Presley's mind by the time he is bound for the open sea and India: "The larger view always and through all shams, all wickednesses, discovers the Truth that will, in the end, prevail, and all things, surely, inevitably, resistlessly work together for good" (ii, 361). Throughout Norris's book, the moral implications of St. Paul's message grow into a kind of incremental refrain which vibrates through the very backbone of the novel. What is more, St. Paul's statements provide a central frame of reference for almost all of the characters, particularly the major ones.[21]

Early in the novel when Annixter attempts to convince a vacillating Magnus Derrick that bribery is the best way to combat the Railroad, his argument is a kind of mock version of Presley's concluding restatement of St. Paul. Annixter's remarks smack of Shelgrim's sophistry. It is a viewpoint he is to transcend: " 'But, Governor, standards have changed since your time; everybody plays the game now as we are playing it—the most honorable men. You can't play it any other way, and, pshaw! if the right wins out in the end, that's the main thing' " (i, 177). Nowhere in the novel does Norris condone dishonest means as justified by their ends. Annixter, himself, is to repudiate this position.[22] Magnus Derrick's own confusion reveals an inherent misunderstanding of St. Paul's message: "He was hopelessly caught in the mesh. Wrong seemed indissolubly knitted into the texture of Right. He was blinded, dizzied, overwhelmed, caught in the current of events and hurried along, he knew not where. He resigned himself" (II, 8). This is also redolent of Shelgrim's rationalizations concerning the absence of human responsibility amidst the inevitability of Force. Shelgrim's speech to Presley toward the end of the novel contains only the sense of inevitability in St. Paul and none of the hope (II, 283–86). The railroad president's apotheosis of Force is a kind of irony of self-deception, a weak counterpoint to Vanamee's eventual realization and the central truth Presley speaks in the last paragraph of *The Octopus*. Annixter, Magnus Derrick, Vanamee and Presley all repudiate this tissue of expediency and half-truths. And through them so does Norris.

V

Both the Vanamee-Angèle episode and Shelgrim's function are crucial to an understanding of Norris's use of St. Paul and hence the consistency of the novel's conclusion. Vanamee is a much more reliable philosophical frame of reference for the author than is usually granted.[23] His reactions are a barometer for the moral implications of *The Octopus*. Just as Annixter, for a time, may be an externalization of Norris's Victorian struggle with sexuality,[24] Vanamee seems to epitomize the novel's central spiritual struggle. In a letter written just three months before he completed *The Octopus*, Norris expressed strong feelings as to the importance of the Vanamee-Angèle inclusion: "You'll find some things in it that for me—are new departures. It is the most romantic thing I've yet done. One of the secondary subplots is pure romance—oh, even mysticism, if you like, a sort of allegory—I call it the Allegory of the Wheat."[25] Norris places Vanamee in important locations throughout most of the novel. He keeps the "subplot" before the reader as Vanamee gradually changes along with Annixter[26] and, to a lesser extent, Presley. Although there are certain weaknesses in Norris's execution of Vanamee's story, the transformation is rendered convincingly. On close observation even the most questionable facts surrounding Vanamee's career are scarcely unacceptable.[27] It *is* somewhat odd that Vanamee seems unaware of Angèle's growing daughter until the night he first sees her as a full grown replica of her mother. He left for distant wanderings, however, even before Angèle's grave was filled, perhaps without having seen the newborn baby. For sixteen years he stayed away long periods at a time, returning only intermittently. When he meets Presley at the beginning of the novel he has been away for perhaps six years.[28] Since there is no evidence that he ever met Angèle at her home but always rendezvoused in the Mission garden, it is not strange that he does not seek the daughter at her home.[29] Furthermore, he is a loner, a mystic with whom odd habits and strange lapses are as common as his spiritual insight.

Norris continually underlines Vanamee's physical and spiritual resemblance to the Hebraic prophets.[30] He is at the outset an appropriate vehicle for Norris's philosophy in *The Octopus,* for life in accordance with natural goodness, Christian morality, and St. Paul's statements on immortality. From the beginning he is an editorial spokesman. He registers uncondescendingly positive reactions to the Homeric scene of the ranch workers' feasting and drinking after a hard day's involvement in the planting stage of nature's cycle of growth, its continuum. To Vanamee, but not Presley, the feasting is as natural as the songs and sleep that follow (1, 127).[31] Not so the overindulgence and drunkenness at Annixter's barn dance. The atmosphere and unnatural circumstances cause Vanamee to become "more and more disgusted" (1, 261).[32] Presley merely remains aloof.

Vanamee's importance is evident in many other ways. He is philosophically linked directly or indirectly with almost every major character and many minor ones. It is Vanamee who sparks Presley's thoughts about the great poem of the West (1, 37–39) and to whom Presley takes "The Toilers" for an honest judgment. Norris gives to Vanamee the last prophetic words in Book I,[33] just as his "words" end the novel. It is Vanamee who brings the news of the Railroad's march on the ranchers but remains a neutral pacifistic figure.[34] Even Angèle and Hilma are associated through image motifs and parallelism. Hilma, a continual reinforcement of the goodness that Vanamee attributes to unspoiled nature, is seen in almost constant sunlight.[35] Until the moment Angèle's daughter meets Vanamee she and her mother are continually associated with moonlight. When Vanamee meets the daughter, Norris externalizes the simple profundity of the shepherd's new spiritual insight: "It was no longer an ephemeral illusion of night, evanescent, mystic, but a simple country girl coming to meet her lover. . . . She stood forth in the sunlight a fact, and no longer a fancy."[36] By this point Norris has traced Vanamee's essentially Christian spiritual progression from that of knowledge of evil (Angèle's rape by the Other), to despair (his aimless wanderings and denial of God's goodness), to penance (his ascetic life and the long nights of contemplation in the Mission garden), to rebirth and deepened spiritual insight first realized in the love of Angèle's grown daughter. Vanamee struggles many years before his epiphany. The results of his transformation allow him to throw off self-pity and despair and rejoin the human race with new spiritual breadth. A kind of microcosm of the novel, the Vanamee-Angèle episode in its ultimate "Reality"[37] is an allegorical comment on each of the other plots as well as "the Allegory of the Wheat."

VI

In fact the five most central plots in *The Octopus* are structurally and thematically interwoven. The plots involving Vanamee, Annixter, Hooven, Dyke, and Derrick are all, in varying degrees, microcosms of the novel's major plot, side mirrors for the various attitudes toward the wheat in the struggle between the ranchers and the Railroad.[38] All the characters are thematically linked.[39] Annixter repents of his desire for purely physical gratification and is on his way to spiritual fulfillment in Hilma's love at his death. Vanamee achieves an earthly fulfillment through his love of Angèle and her daughter. Presley is groping toward the truth that he speaks by the novel's end. Magnus Derrick asks God's forgiveness for his dishonesty to others and to himself. The misguided Hooven dies nobly for "the Vaterland," the dwelling place of his wife and children. Dyke alone seems merely pathetic in his attempt to save his family by striking back at the Railroad. But in the context of "the larger view" is the assurance that he, along with Hooven, will rise up out of the earth as did the corrupted wheat.[40] Norris likens the fallen ranchers to the seeds in Paul's letter to the Corinthians; they too await the fulfillment of promised resurrection. The astute reader is not to be taken in by Shelgrim's explanation of the Universe as a combination of mere conditions and forces to which man must acquiesce. Man is responsible for combatting evil and moving toward the good. The Railroad and the wheat are neither responsible nor irresistible as mere forces. It is man's use of these forces that results in evil or good. Men bribe railroad commissioners and exploit the land. Neither tenant farmers nor railroad presidents are immune to responsibility.

Although Shelgrim is physically present in only one scene, it is a vital one. Whenever he is mentioned before this scene there is a suggestion of something worse than S. Behrman, something worse than the Other. He is the Octopus, the embodiment of the Railroad, the title of Norris's novel incarnate. During the first meeting of the ranchers Shelgrim's name falls "squarely in the midst of the conversation" (I, 99). He is described as "a giant figure . . . hated . . . dreaded . . . " with a "colossal intellect operating the width of an entire continent. . . . " After Lyman Derrick has been so speedily elected as the ranchers' railroad commissioner, Annixter is distrustful of such an apparent victory: "It's too easy. . . . No I'm not satisfied. Where's Shelgrim in all this . . . There's a big fish in these waters somewhere" (II, 8). And just before Presley's interview with Shelgrim Norris again places a nonhuman image before the reader: "How far were the consequences of that dreadful day's work at the irrigating ditch to reach. To what length was the tentacle of the monster to extend" (II, 278).[41] Norris has consciously played up the monstrous aspects of Shelgrim before he is seen. During the interview Presley is mesmerized by the man and his forceful pronouncements. Norris is not; nor, hopefully, is the reader. Consciously satiric description reinforces the suggestion that Norris is undercutting Shelgrim's half-truths.[42] For the gigantic president of the P. and S. W. Railroad is given the physiognomy and attributes of the very creature that gives the novel its title:[43]

> He was large, almost to massiveness. An iron-grey beard and moustache that completely hid the mouth covered the lower part of his face. His eyes were a pale blue, and a little watery; here and there upon his face were moth spots. But the enormous breadth of the shoulders was what, at first, most vividly forced itself upon Presley's notice. Never had he seen a broader man; *the neck, however, seemed in a manner to have settled into the shoulders,* and furthermore *they were humped* and *rounded,* as if to bear great responsibilities and great abuse.
>
> At the moment he was wearing a silk skull cap. . . .
> (II, 281)

> Presley, his senses never more alive, observed that, *curiously enough, Shelgrim did not move his body. His arms moved, and his head but the great bulk of the man remained immobile in its place,* and as the interview proceeded and this peculiarity emphasized itself, *Presley began to conceive the odd idea that Shelgrim had, as it were, placed his body in the chair to rest, while his head and brain and hands went on working independently.* A saucer of shelled filberts stood near his elbow, and *from time to time he picked up one of these in a great thumb and forefinger and put it between his teeth.*
> (II, 283)[44]

Norris was undoubtedly aware of precedents for such a portrayal in the numerous political cartoons depicting the actual prototype for Shelgrim (Collis P. Huntington) with the body and tentacles of an octopus. One such cartoon shows his tentacle grasping figures and papers labeled: "Honest Vote, Manufacturer, Farmer, Merchant, Orange Raiser, Subsidized press and the cities of Oakland and San Francisco."[45] Certainly Norris's juxtaposition of Presley's meeting with the fallen Minna Hooven after his meeting with the railroad president gives the lie to Shelgrim's claims that Force and not men are to blame. Even Shelgrim's possibly sentimental gesture to save Tentell's job suggests man's ability to act justly, if he so chooses. That one villain is society's potent Indifference becomes clear as one by one the ambassadors of society—the landlady, the sexton, the flophouse attendant, potential employers, policemen, and people on the street—all turn their backs to the Hoovens' plight. Here indifferent men, not Forces, are to blame.[46] Significantly, it is outside the mansion of Shelgrim's Vice President, Gerard, that Mrs. Hooven starves and her daughters are orphaned.[47]

Norris proposes no easy solution to the agony of living in an imperfect society. But a transcendental view of the world is necessary before his characters can come to terms with themselves. Possibly the social evils can be partially conquered by the Unity of the People aroused from lethargic Indifference. Perhaps this can only be realized through the kind of human sacrifice the ranchers suffer. In Norris's framework, when man acts for the good, even when he dies tragically, he is in harmony with a Christian universe transcending the Railroad and ranches. Regardless of all the vacillating, capricious, or indifferent men, there will always be an Annixter, a Hilma, a Vanamee, an Angèle, a repentant Magnus Derrick. The cause of truth and justice will eventually triumph over evil as certainly as the buried wheat rises to life and Angèle's daughter appears to fulfill Vanamee's love. For, in *The Octopus,* when man lives for goodness or dies tragically aware, he does so in the matrix of a well-ordered universe. But the order is not immediately apparent to all men. In this real world Norris creates, it is possible for a mystic to vibrate with the fecund rhythms of nature—Emerson's or Whitman's vast continuum. It is possible for a man of the dignity and worth of Magnus Derrick to fall tragically and for a lustful, self-centered Annixter to rise through humility. It is also possible for one to be taken in by the high-sounding malarky of a Shelgrim. Norris was saddled with his own frailties. He struggled with personal prejudices that prompted him to see individuals as better or worse than they really were. He, like Presley, was very much at home dining with the Gerards; he was also imaginatively capable of seeing the "frail, delicate . . . fine ladies with their small fingers and slender necks, suddenly transfigured into harpies tearing human flesh" (II, 317). The "clink of wine glasses" could, in his mind, be "drowned in the explosion of revolvers" (II, 317). Norris's personal attitude toward both the ranchers and the railroad owners contained an ambivalence that, transmuted into art, enriched the texture of his epic novel. The complexity of his view of man and the fine artistic embodiment of it are what brings him in *The Octopus* far closer to Hawthorne and Melville than to his contemporary muckrakers.

Notes

1. *The Merrill Studies in The Octopus.* Columbus, Ohio: Charles E. Merrill, 1969.

2. Among the most perceptive critics of *The Octopus* are Franklin Walker, Ernest Marchand, H. Willard Reninger, George W. Meyer, Warren French, Donald Pizer and William B. Dillingham.

3. Commentary on *The Octopus* will be surveyed in the following order: *Chicago American Literary and Art Review* (April 16, 1901), 5–6. *Bookman*, 13 (May 1901), 246. *Harper's Monthly*, 103 (October, 1901), 824. *Arena*, 27 (May, 1902), 542. *Land of Sunshine*, 15 (July, 1901) 58. *Overland Monthly*, 37 (May, 1901) 1050. *Independent*, 53 (May 16, 1901), 1140. *Dial*, 31 (September 1, 1901), 136. *Atlantic Monthly*, 89 (May, 1902), 708. *A History of American Literature Since 1870.* (New York, 1915), 400. *Frank Norris: A Biography* (Garden City: Doubleday, Doran, 1932), 259. *The Great Tradition* (New York: Macmillan, 1933), 172. "Norris Explains *The Octopus*: a Correlation of His Theory and Practice," *American Literature*, 11 (May, 1940), 218–27, "A New Interpretation of *The Octopus*," *College English*, 4 (March, 1943), 351–59. *Frank Norris: A Study* (Stanford University Press, 1942). *Frank Norris* (New York: Twayne, 1962). *The American Novel and Its Tradition* (Garden City, New York: Doubleday, 1957), p. 203. Introduction to *The Octopus* (Boston: Houghton Mifflin, 1958), p. v. *The Novels of Frank Norris* (Bloomington: Indiana University Press, 1966). *Frank Norris: Instinct and Art* (Lincoln: University of Nebraska Press, 1969).

4. *The Novels of Frank Norris*, p. 160; *Frank Norris: Instinct and Art*, pp. 119–21.

5. "The Concept of Nature in *The Octopus*," *American Quarterly*, 14 (Spring 1962), 73–80.

6. Mr. Pizer is one of many who have made this judgment. See *The Novels of Frank Norris*, p. 179.

7. Other weaknesses in *The Octopus* frequently attacked, and with some justice, are the treatment of the "little tad," Sidney Dyke, who in her hissings at passing trains is rather frighteningly reminiscent of Elsie Venner; Mrs. Hooven's starvation scene and S. Behrman's death. In the last two instances, particularly Behrman's death, Norris may be descending to melodrama; but his writing is so effective (as it is in "the death in the desert business" in *McTeague*) that the reader is too caught up in it to be adversely critical. If Behrman's suffocation by the wheat seems too contrived, it is an appropriate death. For the greediness that prompts him to lean close to the hold and finger the wheat, as a miser would his gold, has been thoroughly established.

8. Norris wrote to his friend Isaac Marcosson of the *Louisville Times* insightful statements about two of his novels. Regarding *Moran of the Lady Letty*, he said: "When I wrote Moran I was, one might say, flying kites, trying to see how high I could go without breaking the string. However I have taken myself more seriously since then and in my next novel [*McTeague*] I have tried to do something really worthwhile." Norris called *A Man's Woman* "a kind of theatrical sort with a lot of niggling analysis to try to justify the violent action of the first few chapters. It is very slovenly put together and there are only two people in all its 100,000 words." See items 9 and 28 in Franklin Walker's edition of *The Letters of Frank Norris* (San Francisco: The Book Club of California, 1956).

9. *The Responsibilities of the Novelist*, Volume VII, *The Complete Edition of Frank Norris* (Garden City: Doubleday, Doran, 1929) pp. 113–117. Hereafter page references to *The Complete Edition* will be incorporated into the text. *The Octopus* comprised Volumes I and II of this ten-volume edition. The italics are mine.

Norris later admitted that an overly strict adherence to this formula is not always advisable (I, 117).

10. E. M. Forster, *Aspects of the Novel* (New York: Harcourt, Brace, 1927), Chapter VIII.

11. See Frank Baldanza's "The Structure of *Huck Finn*," *American Literature*, 27 (November, 1955), 347–355.

12. Norris manages to sustain his control more effectively than in his best earlier novels, *McTeague* and *Vandover and the Brute,* where the control is often sporadic and the technical effects generally more heavy-handed.

13. Notice how Norris controls the function of such minor details as Annixter's bronco, which is a linking device. Delaney's "breaking" of it in front of Hilma triggers off Annixter's jealousy. Delaney steals the horse and rides it during his humiliating defeat in the gunfight at Annixter's barn dance. Annixter gives the horse to Dyke as he tries unsuccessfully to outride the posse. It carries Annixter to the irrigating ditch and his death. All who ride it suffer some calamity.

14. Neatly drawn and labeled are, among many other items Norris chose to stress, the watering tank, the live-oak tree, the irrigating ditch and the Long Trestle. It is by the Long Trestle that the sheep are mutilated as Presley dreams. It is underneath the Long Trestle, "an oasis of green shade,' that Hilma goes to gather water cresses and receives Annixter's ugly proposition. At the Long Trestle the hot steam of the railroad meets with the cooling waters of the Earth. The climactic gunfight takes place by the irrigating ditch that flows under the railroad tracks in full view of the live-oak tree.

15. The healthy oak tree is recalled when Mrs. Hooven dies near "a few stunted live-oaks" (II, 319) outside the railroad Vice President's mansion.

16. In Norris, as well as Hawthorne and Howells, the major characters are changed as a result of these gatherings.

17. The winner is, significantly, Mrs. Cedarquist: industrialist's wife, philanthropist and do-gooder.

18. Another indication of Norris's concern for detail in *The Octopus* is in his use of smells. He associates sachet, for example, with downfall or defeat. After the calamity of the barn dance the smell of buckskin (also associated with disaster) is blended with the "stale perfume" of sachet. Magnus Derrick's dishonesty is exposed in a room smelling of "stale grease paint" and sachet. Minna Hooven surrenders her virtue to an enameled madame who exudes an atmosphere that is "impregnated with sachet."

19. Wallace Rice has pointed out that Norris has a Catholic priest quote from the Protestant King James Version of *The Bible*. This is but one of many relatively unimportant inconsistencies in *The Octopus*. Along with the slips in chronology that Pizer has alluded to (*The Novels of Frank Norris*, p. 196) there is, for example, Norris's comment about Annixter only months before his death: "For years he could with little effort reconstruct the scene [of his fight with Delaney]." (I, 252–53)

20. For an indication of the transcendental elements in *The Octopus* compare Vanamee's last words with the conclusion of Emerson's "Each and All:" "Beauty through my senses stole; / I yielded myself to the perfect whole."

21. Norris underlines the important figures by including, along with his map, a list of "Principal Characters in the Novel."

22. This is particularly evident when the once volatile Annixter tries to settle matters peacefully just before the bloodshed at the irrigating ditch (II, 222).

23. Vanamee proves a far mellower spokesman for Norris than the vacillating, unstable Presley. Except on some literary matters Presley's judgment is almost consistently unreliable. See, for instance, I, p. 10 and II, pp. 275–76.

24. See, for instance, Kenneth Lynn's "Introduction" to *The Octopus* for mention of repressed sexuality in Norris's characters.

25. Franklin Walker, *Letters*, pp. 67–68. Norris was writing to Isaac Marcosson on September 13, 1901.

26. Although there is some preparation for Annixter's transformation it is more sudden than Vanamee's.

27. For the more popular opinion see Donald Pizer's *Novels of Frank Norris*, p. 160. It may be strange that Vanamee has never noticed Angèle's daughter; but then only at the end does he seek her in the light of day.

28. See, for example, I, pp. 31, 36–37, 139–140, and 146.

29. There is also some confusion concerning Angèle's home life. Presley remembers her "as a girl of sixteen . . ., who lived with an aged aunt in the Seed ranch back of the Mission." (I, 33) But the "little babe was taken by Angèle's parents. . . ." (I, 36) Neither the aunt nor the parents are again mentioned.

30. Father Sarria, Presley and the narrator all point this out at various times.

31. As Presley grows toward Vanamee's insights he becomes more tolerant of such natural activities. (II, 216)

32. See also I, 240–241.

33. "I think . . ., I think that there was rain in Brussels the night before Waterloo." Rain falls on the ranchers as they leave Annixter's barn.

34. Vanamee is conspicuous by his absence from the rabbit slaughter.

35. Sunlight represents the truth and reality Vanamee and Annixter came to realize in the light of day.

36. Not only does Angèle move toward Hilma's sun (as Hilma gains some of the complexity of darkness) in a symbolic sense; she, as well as Hilma, is described as a sensuously attractive woman of flesh and blood. (I, 79–80, 150–51, 144, 233–34; II, 347). The parallel between Hilma's strong simple love and Angèle's becomes vividly apparent.

37. Norris emphasizes the importance of seeing Vanamee and Angèle's daughter as real flesh and blood human beings rather than ethereal creatures subsumed in the realm of the fantastic. They are spiritually *and* physically united. See II, 346–47.

38. Presley, like Magnus Derrick, Dyke and S. Behrman, has understood the wheat purely in physical terms. Only later does he begin to realize the spiritual significance that is at the core of St. Paul's letter.

39. Dyke's train robbery parallels Derrick's moral compromise. Hooven's shot which precipitates the ditch battle underlines Annixter's early impulsiveness.

40. Dyke is essentially a good man who is misguided and directed toward evil deeds. His "Eden" (security and happiness for Sidney and his mother) has been violated along with Magnus' (personal integrity and his love for his son), Annixter's (Quien Sabe and his love for Hilma), Hooven's ("The Vaterland"—wherever "der

wife and der kinder" are) and Vanamee's (his idyllic relationship with Angèle). According to St. Paul, in the end the good that is a part of all of these men will triumph.

41. The phrase "nucleus of the web" (II, 279), describing Shelgrim's office, gives him a spidery dimension but this is not the dominant image. Shelgrim is also described in passing as an ogre and a tiger, with both animals seemingly transformed into an octopus: " 'It is an ogre's vitality' he [Presley] said to himself. 'Just so is the man-eating tiger strong. The man should have energy who has sucked the life-blood from an entire People.' " (II, 280). Norris's later description of a broken Magnus Derrick is a kind of pathetic analogue to the vital picture of Shelgrim. (II, 331)

42. Shelgrim's speech has been prepared for by similarly deceptive words and actions by many other men, including Osterman, and all the Derricks, excepting Annie. I cannot agree with Mr. French's claim (*Frank Norris*, p. 94) that the Shelgrim interview distorts "the structure of the novel and begins to make us suspect the artistic integrity of a writer who peremptorily introduces a new viewpoint into a nearly completed work."

The core of Shelgrim's claims is as follows:

"You are dealing with forces, young man, when you speak of Wheat and the Railroads, not with men. There is the Wheat, the supply. It must be carried to feed the People. There is the demand. The Wheat is one force, the Railroad, another, and there is the law that governs them—supply and demand. Men have only little to do in the whole business. . . . If you want to fasten the blame of the affair at Los Muertos on any one person, you will make a mistake. Blame conditions, not men" (II, 285)

43. Marston LaFrance first brought Norris's device to my attention. It is the same technique that Norris uses to draw parallels between both Angèles and stalks of wheat. See I, pp. 33–34, 136–37; II 104–05 and 347.

44. The italics are mine.

45. For samples of these cartoons see Oscar Lewis' *The Big Four* (New York: Alfred A. Knopf), pp. 136–137. Huntington died in August, 1900, some four months before Norris completed *The Octopus*.

46. The theme of Indifference is first discussed by Cedarquist. (II, 19–22).

47. Shelgrim's earlier gesture to Tentell may be as insidious as Indifference in its capricious paternalism.

Romance in *The Octopus*

William L. Vance[*]

Attempts have been made to demonstrate that Frank Norris's *The Octopus* has a coherent philosophy.[1] Other, and sometimes conflicting, attempts have been made to relieve Norris of responsibility for its inconsistencies by ascribing them to a naive point-of-view character, Presley.[2] I believe that neither effort is wholly convincing, and that, in any case, neither can establish the artistic integrity of *The Octopus*. The very multiplicity of fictional modes in this book illuminates both what the modes have in common and the limits of their compatibility. Of the five discernible modes involved, four relate without much friction because some of their assumptions coincide and because Norris exercises tact in managing them. But a close analysis of one of these modes, the Romance which has for protagonist the character Vanamee, indicates that both the conventional assumptions of Romance and Norris's practice in this instance cause it to disengage from the other modes. Moreover, Norris's handling of the problem of point of view, in contrast to Melville's and Faulkner's, is inadequate to relate the antithetical modes without violating the integrity of Romance.

I

The four modes providing the context for the Romance of Vanamee are Allegorical Melodrama, Naturalism, Tragedy, and Realism, the last dominating the whole.

On the most elementary level of Allegorical Melodrama, we discover Behrman, the local banker. He is a simple villain, a black-mustached, fat personification of covetousness or greed. He has no human reality or complexity, and he literally cannot be killed by human agencies; although he is fired upon at point-blank range and has a bomb thrown into the room where he is dining, only an equally unhuman force—the Wheat, the Hero itself—is able finally to dispatch him and grant the reader the specific moral and emotional satisfactions of the melodramatic mode.[3]

The Naturalistic Mode in its most conventional sense is only slightly

[*]Reprinted from *Genre*, 3 (June, 1970), 111–136, by permission of *Genre*.

116

more complex than Allegorical Melodrama; it is employed in telling the story of Dyke, the discharged railroad engineer turned hops-farmer. He is a "little" man from the world of Hamlin Garland concerned only with caring for his aged mother and little daughter. He struggles on his own quite apart from the big ranchers with whom he has only an antagonist—the railroad—in common.[4] He is uneducated, inexperienced, and not very intelligent. He is not shown to be capable of moral deliberation, and he responds instinctively to protect his loved ones when a vastly superior and inexorable force moves to crush him. His conscious love alone defines him as human, and in his final extremity he is reduced to an animal fighting "bull-like with his head," while the posse closes in on him "like hounds upon a wolf."[5] Annixter expresses the precise response to this Naturalistic Tragedy: "Poor fool! The pity of it" (I, 194).

Norris assays the Tragic Mode itself in the story of Magnus Derrick, "The Prominent Man."[6] Derrick is distinct from and above all the other ranchers by virtue of his great personal dignity, courtly Southern manners, and immense wealth. His ethical stance is pridefully commensurate. All the other ranchers both respect and fear him, and by making him their leader, merge their fates with his. The situation is such that Derrick must compromise his honor in order to meet the community responsibility imposed on him. His flaw is explicitly depicted: he has a "sub-nature of recklessness," which, like Othello's flaw, is "inconsistent, all at variance with his creeds and tenets" (II, 14). He is, however, a free agent, and frequently deliberates on his course of action and the moral issues involved. For all the force of his specific flaw united with compelling circumstances, Derrick nevertheless chooses his fate. And the dilemma he faces is fully tragic, since whatever choice he makes is sure to incur guilt: "Wrong seemed indissolubly knitted into the texture of Right" (II, 8). Derrick's wife is the sympathetic vehicle of tragic emotion; it is she who experiences "sudden terror" in perceiving the direction of her husband's action and feels "the pity of it, the tragedy of it!" in contemplating the spectacle of Magnus's "financial ruin, moral ruin, ruin of prestige, ruin of character." And chorus-like she feels it is "better to submit, to resign oneself to the inevitable," than to challenge a superhuman Power (I, 171–173).[7]

The most fully developed of the worlds of *The Octopus* is that of Annixter, in the Realistic Mode.[8] The chief character is typical without being ordinary; his actions, what happens to him, and the changes he undergoes are rendered with a high degree of probability. His is a fully rounded, dynamic portrait from life, and his world is a "balanced" one with contrasting elements of humor and distress, and with external scene and action related to interior thought and feeling. The plot is compounded: a personal love story is interwoven with a public, political and economic story of social contention and violence. The way one impinges on and affects the other, with resulting complication of motives, is a defining aspect of Realism, as the themes of love, moral growth, and death are characteristic. Although at one point a rhetorical paean to the Wheat is forced into service as a symbolic coda, climaxes are usually narrated with perfect control and simplicity; the event is relied upon to convey its excitement without stylistic inflation. In the great chapter that closes Book I, for example, in a moment of vividly realized danger Annixter and Hilma involuntarily reveal their mutual love. The moment has a concrete unvoiced lucidity which undoes at once the entangled misunderstandings caused by Annixter's clumsy courtship and Hilma's shyness and disbelief, Annixter is not the Hero protecting the Heroine from the Bad Men; on the contrary, his success in shooting Delaney's gun from his hand leaves him "overwhelmed with astonishment" (I, 257). The humorous, non-satirical mock-heroism is characteristic of the Realistic Mode.[9]

In his struggle with the railroad, Annixter has neither the pretensions of Derrick nor the humble aims of Dyke.[10] He exists in the middle ground of Realism, just as Quien Sabe, his ranch, is in size halfway between the baronial spread of Derrick's El Rancho De Los Muertos and Dyke's hop-fields. His is a world of wicker slippers, walnut washstands, unframed lithographs, and cigar butts, and he lives comfortably in the milieu of the lively and characteristic Western town which is described with concrete local detail primarily in relation to him. To make his life and property secure is Annixter's only concern. Untroubled by ethical dilemmas, he has but one objection to the bribery-scheme, the pragmatic one of the average man that it won't work, it is "crazy, wild-eyed." When finally convinced, he does all he can, freely and consciously, with full awareness of the forces involved. He is not inevitably doomed and seems at any moment to have at least half a chance of success. The truth of this is only emphasized by the manner of his death. He blunders into it when the odds are better than even. A few men on one side confront a few men on the other; all are armed and suspicious, but wish to effect a compromise and postpone the real "showdown"; uneasiness naturally grows as the confrontation is prolonged; positions are shifted and suspicion mounts; a horse shies, knocks a man over, and this, indistinctly witnessed by the men in the ditch, is misinterpreted; a foolish minor character leaps out of the ditch and starts firing, and the fight erupts. A series of simple statements narrating the consequences concludes the chapter. The last sentence is: "Annixter, instantly killed, fell his length to the ground, and lay without movement, just as he had fallen, one arm across his face" (II, 233). The extreme understatement employs what we think of as the "realistic" technique for dealing with such events, from Thackeray to Hemingway. Like the rendering of the action immediately preceding it, it carries the force and shock of the simple truth.[11]

The four modes so far discussed are related to each other in *The Octopus* by the plot. Some of them coincide without difficulty. There is little incongruity between the tragic and realistic worlds, and these are the worlds which most frequently coincide in *The Octopus*. Tragedy arises from daring aspirations and greater ethical claims on the part of an exceptional man, who may be and usually is surrounded by more ordinary mortals. There is no ontological difference between them. Antipathies such as those between Derrick and Annixter arise from differing values held by the men themselves, and what differences in experiences and actions occur are consistent with the differences between equally credible characters.

If it is admitted that "the little man" is in fact more helpless in the face of the great forces of life which affect everyone to some degree, then the world of Dyke may be assimilated partially with the former two. Yet the improbable alacrity with which Dyke turns to drink and crime, and the assumption of his eventual doom from the very moment of his reversal of fortune, make of him a fictional creation of a different kind from Magnus and Annixter, not merely a less fortunate character of the same kind in the same world of realistic causality. His friends seem to recognize this when, instead of trying to help him, they merely pause to foresee "the slow sinking, the inevitable collapse and submerging of one of their companions, the wreck of a career, the ruin of an individual; an honest man, strong, fearless, upright, struck down by a colossal power, perverted by an evil influence, go reeling to his ruin" (II, 73). He is so clearly intended as an illustration of the minimal "struggle for survival," as they are not in the least, that the philosophical dogmas of naturalism begin to control both their reactions and the ensuing events entirely apart from any question of probability. Dyke becomes a pawn illustrating an idea, and his gun fails him simply because in his fictional mode he has absolutely no chance of prevailing.

It is especially instructive to observe how the melodramatic world enters into the three others involved with it by necessity of plot. It can assert itself least successfully in the concrete, complex, rounded world of Annixter. This is graphically illustrated by the completely ancillary role Behrman plays in the confrontation at the ditch. The spokesman for the forces opposing Annixter is not Behrman, but an ordinary man who happens to be sheriff of Tulare County, who, with his posse, is carrying out his legal duty. Annixter dies in realistic conflict with men of his own kind, not melodramatic villains.

In contrast, Behrman is vividly present as the central antagonist in bringing about Dyke's ruin and at his capture. The difference is not coincidental. Almost inevitably in Naturalism the abstract forces of determinism are felt so vividly to dominate the usually sensational ends of human victims that a sense of the abstract, allegorical, and melo-dramatic easily arises where it would be felt to be false in a realistic scene. There is thus an affinity between Naturalism and Melodrama. It was toward their point of meeting that Norris had gravitated in his early fiction, and this was not a reflection merely of his own peculiar temperament. As a tendency of Naturalism itself it occurs even in the superior works of Zola; in, for instance, *L'Assommoir*, where the story of Lalie Bijard and her father is as melodramatic as anything in Norris.

Finally, in the world of Magnus, whose conflict in its tragic aspects is not with Behrman at all, but with himself, the "Villain" Behrman can be fully realized only *after* Magnus has fallen, when the rancher can no longer speak to him curtly and look the other way. He must now respond to Behrman as a Power dominant over him, a vehicle and sign of his degradation, but not a sufficient cause.

II

While the worlds of Melodrama, Naturalism, Tragedy, and Realism may thus supplement each other, the world of Vanamee's kind of Romance is a thing wholly apart. The problem is then one of seeing how this is so, and of considering what possibilities for unity exist.[12]

E. M. Forster has remarked on the degree of inflammation which would occur if characters from the world of one novelist were transferred to the worlds of another.[13] Something similar happens when Vanamee uncomfortably descends to meet realistic men. For a long time Norris does not require him to do so; he sets him off in a pastoral scene—on a hillside with some sheep—or else in the old Spanish garden after all the other worlds have gone to sleep. When, rather unaccountably, Vanamee chooses to attend the barn-dance to which he has not been invited, he "disassociates" himself and does nothing but look on (as Norris twice remarks) "a little contemptuous," growing "more and more disgusted" with this realistc "uproar" which becomes "too boisterous, savoring of intoxication" (I, 258). Vanamee, of course, drinks a liquor never brewed in the punch-bowls of Annixter. The other characters are understandably suspicious of such an other-worldly type. Dyke, "country-bred," makes familiar objections to this bearded nonconformist:

"Why did he never wear a hat...? Why did he not cut his hair? Above all, why did he prowl about so much at night?" (II, 55). Annixter says simply, "Vanamee is crazy in the head....He's a crank" (I, 195–196). The mysterious world of miracles is not for them.

There is no reason, of course, why an eccentric cannot exist in a realistic world, find his own sympathetic and isolated environment, and even be shown by the novelist to have a qualitatively different kind of experience, arising from a deeper and more complicated psychology. But Norris invents a separate world of causality for Vanamee which is more than an extension of an eccentric's perception of things, which exists in the narrative in its own right.

In Faulkner's *The Sound and the Fury*, the perceptions and interpretations of life alter radically from part to part, and Naturalism, Tragedy, and Comic Realism play complementary roles within the whole. But the facts of the action the reader infers are of a consistently realistic kind, and they are absolute. *Absalom, Absalom!* goes further. Outrageously romantic and melodramatic legends are introduced as increments upon the tragic story, which never does achieve existence in objective historical reality. But here the demonic improbabilities are clearly the self-serving inventions of a neurotic old woman, and other later imaginary versions of the truth characterize their conceivers. Faulkner uses all for meaningful atmospheric and thematic purposes, but does not assume responsibility for their literal truth. In contrast, Norris presumes to be the responsible narrator throughout *The Octopus* and is equally enthusiastic whether he is drawing characters and inventing action according to the conventions of Melodrama, Naturalism, Realism, or Romance.

Norris's own commitment to Romance, which now concerns us, is imbedded in the style he employs as well as in his characterization, plot, and point of view. The total world created is one in which the distinct moral outlines of Melodrama are replaced by the indistinct Hawthornesque boundaries between categories of reality: the material, the psychological, the imaginary, and the transcendental. Vanamee does not embody a moral abstraction; he represents the bewildered striving of the psychic personality for some meaning in life, some compensation for the gratuitous violence and suffering in the mundane world. His story exists in its own dimension, the legendary. His first love had been "so fine, so pure, so marvellous that it seemed...a miracle, a manifestation, a thing veritably divine..." (I, 129). When this ended in violent desecration and death, Vanamee had at first behaved melodramatically. "With knife and revolver" he had sought to be the avenger of innocence. But the Evil had escaped: "The Other had withdrawn into an impenetrable mystery" (I, 36). And here, in mystery, we have something higher than Melodrama. The elusive violator also had become legend, existing in the same unreal dimension as the love itself. Thus Vanamee, unable by simple revenge to reduce the experience to the levels of either crude Naturalism or crude Melodrama, goes to the desert and becomes himself "a mystery, living a life half-real, half-legendary" (I, 32). His spiritual quest leads him back occasionally to the scene of its origin, and as the book opens he is on one such visit, recollecting the time when, in the other-worldly and perfectionist terms of the romantic, he had thought that "the mingling of their lives was to be the Perfect Life, the intended, ordained union of the soul of man with the soul of woman, indissoluble, harmonious as music, beautiful beyond all thought, a foretaste of Heaven, a hostage of immortality" (I, 129). But "God had not meant it"; the love had been only "the flimsiest mockery." In a "paroxysm of sorrow," he must suffer his dark night in the Mission garden, "asking 'Why?' of the night and of the stars" (I, 129).

Norris has supplied this story with a setting fully and exclusively romantic, quite isolated from the others: ". . . shut off, discreet, romantic, a garden of dreams, of enchantments, of illusions. Outside there, far off, the great grim world went clashing through its grooves, but in here never an echo of the grinding of its wheels entered to jar upon the subdued modulation of the fountain's uninterrupted murmur" (I, 135). The fountain, the flowering trees with their perfume, the crumbling sun-dial, the graves, the ancient church, the moon: these are the Gothic furnishings of his world, in which are located also Rappaccini's garden and Poe's Dream-Land. The heavy alliteration and assonance of the sentence quoted are used only in describing this world, and they too suggest Poe.

Vanamee's imaginative life is co-ordinately lush: "the mind, concentrated forever upon one subject, had recoiled upon itself, had preyed upon the naturally nervous temperament, till the imagination had become exalted, morbidly active, diseased, beset with hallucinations, forever in search of the manifestation, of the miracle" (I, 141). This passage, like the one on the love affair itself, conveys very well the romantic desire for supernatural perfection in natural existence. One thinks of Hawthorne's Aylmer, and also of Emerson and Whitman, for whom the world of sensation was not expendable. Vanamee's desire precludes finding an Answer in the Church's promise of Heaven. "Tell your God to give her back to me!" he demands of the priest (I, 141). To Father Sarria, he is like a "weak-minded girl" in his protests against the "inevitable, the irrevocable," and in his "groping for the supernatural" (I, 142). But Christ is merely a "lamentable vision of tormented anatomy" to Vanamee, with no Answer for his romantic realization of "human distress." He wants not "Grace" or "a formless sense of Peace," but "an Answer, something real, even if the reality were fancied" (I, 146, 145).

Warned against taking hallucinations for reality, Vanamee admits: "Perhaps I want only the delusion, after all" (I, 143). With this admission, he distinguishes himself from Hawthorne's characters and from the Transcendentalists, and applies for full citizenship in the world of Poe. Throwing himself upon Angéle's grave, violently weeping, he seeks an Answer there, "beyond all bounds of reason," in "the domain of hysteria, dementia . . . . The vast egotism that seems to run through all forms of disordered intelligence gave his fancy another turn" (I, 147). He seeks to call Angéle from the grave by force of his own Ligeia-like will. But the Earth is beyond appeal. Unconsciously, Vanamee is turned toward the Seed Ranch by an unseen power, as though his Answer were there. And, indeed, "his imagination . . . found Something . . . . The night was no longer voiceless, the dark was no longer empty" (I, 152).

Obviously, within the terms of Vanamee's world, none of this is far-fetched or foolish. The imaginary world of Poe has its own reality, an hallucinatory, unlimited, yet sensuous reality, appealing to the claims of the soul. Norris does ultimately betray it, but the innocent reader does not know that he will, and follows the author trustingly into the climactic chapter (II: iii) of the Vanamee-plot, wondering only at the increasing insistence on the reality of the arcane in a book whose predominant assumptions are realistic. What Norris seems to be depicting is the actual achievement of Vanamee's Vision, as either miraculous or hallucinatory.

Strange possibilities have been fully prepared for by scenes in which Vanamee previously exercised his mysterious "sixth sense" by summoning Presley and Father Sarria on separate occasions, from a distance and from sleep. Who knows how far such a power may extend? What Vanamee really wishes is to resurrect his dead Angéle. The fictional experience now progresses further into the world of Romance where this might in some way—literally or imaginatively—happen. As Norris himself rather baldly says: "The material world drew off from him. Reality dwindled to a point and vanished like the vanishing of a star at moonrise . . . . He entered the world of the Vision, of the Legend, of the Miracle where all things were possible" (II, 94–95). Norris assumes a freedom from questions of probability that Hawthorne claimed for Romance, going in fact even beyond those demands.

The "atmosphere" established has a particularity combined with indefiniteness that would do credit to Poe: through arches of an ancient tower "slow-burning stars" are seen; and "bats, with flickering wings" make "dancing shadows on the pallid surface" of the tower. The night is illuminated by "silver veils," "a whorl of shimmering stardust," "a lambent disk of pale saffron," "a mysterious sheen of diaphanous light," and even the garden and grave-yard—romantic enough in themselves—become "dim," "half-emerging from the shadows," "uncertain," "blurred," "vague," and "indistinct." This evocation of mood leads into excesses of rhetoric, excesses because while not irrelevant, they do generalize away from the central subject, which is the mental state of Vanamee. For instance, the briefly observed Ursa Major wheeling "gigantic in the north" lends a pertinent cosmic dimension to the setting and is merely an observation, not a concept, while the remark that the fountain is not only "marking off the lapse of seconds" (relevant in the suspenseful context), but also "the progress of hours, the cycle of years, the inevitable march of centuries" goes rather far, even for an old Mission fountain. Vanamee is not thinking about this, and the reader is merely distracted by it.

Norris was faced with two related compositional problems. He needed to give the very simple Vanamee story adequate bulk; its importance seemed to require a proportionate extension and amplification in the telling. And yet Vanamee's experience was almost wholly interior, and relating it could be nothing more than a gradual intensification of a single obsession. It required a different kind of writing from the rest of the book and could not be amplified by the invention of a variety of incidents. Lacking the ability that Henry James displayed in "The Beast in the Jungle" and even more in "The Jolly Corner," finely to analyze an egotistic introspection while at the same time making it progress through actual minute stages of development toward a crisis, Norris sought the answer to his problem in repetition, accumulation, and artificial organization. But his writing here is not wholly without an effect comparable to that of Poe's poetry, and his method is similar. Certainly an actual look at it qualifies Marchand's assertion (and the apparent assumption of most critics) that care for the "shape and ring of sentences" was "forever outside" Norris's intention.[14]

Vanamee's repeated nightly vigils in the garden take on a ritualistic quality which is rhythmically reflected in the style. Four successive sentences begin with the words "Once again," followed by statements which say the same thing in different abstract words. The effect is of a repeated expenditure of psychic energy, as Vanamee sends his mind "out from him across the enchanted sea of the Supernatural" (II, 96). Frequent rhetorical questions serve more effectively, however, (because they are less static), to convey the peculiar mixture of anxiety, foreboding, hope, and faith with which Vanamee awaits his manifestation." Yet these are also perhaps too flatly explicit and too shapely—or too obviously shaped—faithfully to represent the inchoate, tentative manner in which the bewildered Vanamee could have experienced them: "Would he have her again, his love, long dead? Would she come to him once more out of the grave, out of the night?" (II, 97). The style continually forces the reader to remain critically outside the experience, and this undesirable effect is reinforced when Norris resorts to borrowed and not entirely apposite diction: "He waited [repeated four times] . . . hoping all things . . . believing all things . . . enduring all things" (II, 98).

Earlier chapters having related that Vanamee's psychic search was progressing toward Something, the function of this one is to bring the tendency to its fulfillment. But Norris's imagination failed him in his attempt to sustain the effect of passing time during the act of psychic willing. As one means of prolonging the climax, he chose to use exposition and recapitulation of Vanamee's past attempts, and in so doing lost much of the intensity of the present occasion. Such connectives as "Months had passed since . . ." and "Meanwhile, as spring advanced . . ." vitiate any possibility of providing for the reader the single continuous experience at a high and intensifying emotional pitch which Poe sought in his own tales. In fact, the time-sequence becomes incoherent; and it is something of a jolt to be informed, suddenly and flatly, that "It was the same night," (II, 102) and thus to be reminded that all this while Vanamee has been waiting, and we are back where we were.

Within the exposition itself, which is a composite account of Vanamee's previous mystical attempts, there are some good things. The sense of timing, here, is right and meaningful: the Vision's approach must coincide exactly with the gradual flowering of the fragrant blossoms. "The illusion defined itself" as by "imperceptible degrees" the starlight of spring grew brighter and magnolia buds emerged. In a context of concrete but airily romantic imagery of night and perfume, the repeated use of the indefinite pronoun ("It came . . . it passed forward . . . it left . . . it advanced") projects a subtle suspense. The vague awareness of an approaching being as intangible as the fragrant air develops on a later night into something more definite: a sound, "a vibration merely, faint, elusive." Still later, there occurs "an instant of passing light"; something is seen.

Norris uses an analytical development, in which paragraphs in sequence are almost identical except that each focuses on a separate sense. The sequence itself is correct, however, in that a sound gives the effect of greater actuality than an odor and a sight still more than a sound. The composition is thus progressive as well as accumulative.

The last three sentences of the paragraph on sound are almost exactly parallel in structure to the last three on sight. A series of indefinite images is negated: (1) "the rustle of a leaf, the snap of a parted twig, the drone of an insect," and "the dropping of a magnolia blossom," as against (2) "the glancing of a moth's wing, the nodding of a wind-touched blossom," and "the noiseless flitting of a bat" (II, 100–101). Both paragraphs end with ingeniously balanced syntactical arrangements: (1) "It was a vibration merely, faint, elusive, impossible of definition; a minute notch in the fine, keen edge of stillness." (2) "It was a gleam, merely faint, elusive, impossible of definition, an intangible agitation, in the vast dim blur of the darkness."

These sentences were written by the man who declared, "I detest . . . 'elegant English,'—tommyrot. Who cares for fine style! Tell your yarn and let your style go to the devil. We don't want literature, we want life."[15] Obviously, he had to ignore his own advice when faced with a "yarn" such as Vanamee's, which would not tell itself. But since his attempt at "elegant English" calls attention to itself rather than to the sensibility of Vanamee, his style goes to the devil anyway—if a style is judged by its success in achieving its end. For Vanamee's experience exists only as "literature," that is, as words, and not as "life," certainly not the deep emotional life characteristic of the great romances. But it would be a mistake to charge Norris with having chosen the wrong style. For Vanamee's world, an elevated "romantic" style, all the elements of which Norris employs, is exactly right. The true charges against Norris are that he uses it ineptly even where appropriate, and that he tries elsewhere (even in the Annixter sections) to use it where it is not.

The three stages of the Vision's approach thus described, Norris returns to the present climactic evening. A certain tension is partially created (and partially merely asserted) between the mystical passivity in Vanamee's "patient waiting" and his intense willing. He both wonders whether tonight "it" will finally come closer, and realizes that perhaps its failure on previous occasions was really a failure of his own strength and desire. "Had there not always been an element of dread . . .? Had he not even allowed the Vision to dissolve . . .?" (II, 103). A relatively detached consideration such as this may seem a little false at the very moment when "it" actually *is* approaching nearer than ever before. But, we are immediately made to realize, Vanamee's own degree of effort is not a free choice on his part. It is a function of the natural seasonal rhythm of the earth with which, prone upon the ground, he is uniting himself. And since this is the most beautiful night—"the full period of spring"—it is on this night that he will experience and even himself contemplate his ecstasy: "lying deep in the grasses beneath the pear trees, Vanamee . . . felt, as it were, his imagination was reshaping itself . . . He saw with new eyes, heard with new ears, felt with a new heart" (II, 104).

At this point Vanamee achieves his Vision, and the ultimate difficulty for Norris arises. What kind of vision can it be? One can hypothesize three possibilities. The first would be for it to be an authentic miracle: Angèle Varian resurrected. Every element in Vana- mee's story has tended toward such a Poesque extreme, and a revivifica- tion would seem only right and logical. But since the story cannot finally exist as an isolated unit, but must be one of the major elements in a predominantly realistic novel, a miracle such as this was not really a live option for Norris. A second possibility would save some of the inherent fictional values of Romance, while effecting a plausible re- conciliation with the "real" world. This would be to have Vanamee truly suffer from the mental delusion with which he said he would be satisfied. Some revision would have been required, with the more improbable experiences and expectations recast so as to exist only in the crazed consciousness of Vanamee, not shared by Norris. This would have approximated closely enough the first-person technique of Poe in "The Tell-Tale Heart" and "Ligeia," or the dream-convention ending that Hawthorne invites realists to use at the end of "Young Goodman Brown." But a serious objection might be made to the con- sequent transformation of Vanamee into a simple madman (which is what most of the other characters regard him as being). This would have either reduced him to complete irrelevance or required Norris to suggest that hallucination is a desirable mode of escape from the un- endurable evil of this world. Since Vanamee is made relevant only with extreme rationalization anyway, and since the philosophy he finally is made to preach is (in my opinion) hardly less evasive than the one just suggested, this choice would have been infinitely preferable to the one Norris made. It at least would have preserved the integrity of the fictional mode in which he had so long indulged.

But the choice he did make—suddenly to introduce a real woman, the daughter of Angèle, of whose presence in the vicinity neither Vanamee nor the reader had ever heard before—is disastrous. Why go to the extremes of Gothicism if in the end all that is offered is a pale, thin theory of compensation? Norris sustains the delusion as long as he can, describing the sleep-walking arrival "out of the darkness" in terms which inevitably deceive the reader into taking her for her dead mother, unchanged, young, and pure (and why not?—this is the world of Poe). Then Father Sarria, who has been conveniently spying on Vanamee and can see the girl entirely without benefit of transforming ecstasy ("new eyes"), steps forward to identify her. Norris's maneuver is self-defeating. In order to give his Romance a realistic resolution, he has resorted to improbable plot developments which would be acceptable only in unrealistic modes of fiction. Moreover, he alienates the reader because without even pretending to limit his point of view, he has willfully withheld information in order to titillate him with a bogus miracle. Given Norris's conclusion, the only possibility for retaining some fictional value in the pseudomysterious proceedings, and of granting Vanamee even a degree of pathetic dignity, lay in the reader's being informed of the facts. The dramatic irony would have been less destructive of the Romance than complete dishonesty ultimately proves to be. While Vanamee thought he was achieving revivification, the reader might have known that it was only long-range hypnotism, which is quite arcane enough. As it is, whatever has been experienced is turned into a sham, because it was so much less than it pretended to be.

Vanamee, however, is satisfied. "It was all one with him. It was She. Death was over-come" (II, 106). Vanamee immediately becomes—and continues to the end to be—the chief expositor of the "positive" transcendental philosophy with which Norris seeks to counterbalance the realistic force of the main action. Thus, although the mode of fiction ceases to be Romance, the philosophy continues to be romantic.[16] But because the assumptions of romanticism are not easily transferable to the other modes (where they inevitably appear quixotic), Norris attempts by rhetorical extension and the device of allowing this view the "last word" in the book, to compensate for want of evidence to support it.

The view is simply a commonplace Whitmanesque restatement of the intuited sense that ever-recurring victory in Nature is *the* truth, sufficient cause for rejoicing. Unfortunately, Vanamee will not even grant that it is romantic. His Vision is "no longer a figment of his imagination, a creature of dreams . . . Romance had vanished, but better than romance was here . . . . her very self . . . . Reality was better than Romance . . . . She stood forth in the sunlight, a fact, and no longer a fancy" (II, 346–347). The reader longs for a good look at this creature, thus exposed to the light of common day; but all he is allowed to see is a mannequin that says (quite improbably), "I love you" (II, 347). He is entitled, surely, to allow his common sense to remind him that what Vanamee claims is false. She is not Angèle's "very self"; she is half Other. Moreover, she has been wooed through suspicious means by a man old enough to be her father. To ignore all this is to be satisfied with the cheapest sort of romance; an opium dream is more respectable. But Vanamee, Norris, and a surprising number of critics seem to be satisfied with a fancied reality after all. When Presley does not reply to a little Emersonian sermon, Vanamee abandons all argument, and delivers a disarming summation which is ungracious to the first Angèle and amusing in its abrupt conclusion: "I believed Angèle dead. I wept over her grave; mourned for her as dead in corruption. She has come back to me, more beautiful than ever. Do not ask me any further. To put this story, this idyl, into words, would, for me, be a profanation. This must suffice you. Angèle has returned to me, and I am happy. *Adiós.*" (II, 345). What will preserve this idyll, no one can say, or had better ask.

While much has been written on how Vanamee's philosophy is or is not consistent with the rest of the book, few have observed that it is not even consistent with his own experience. And after having been ignored or deplored for so long, Vanamee is now in danger of being made too much of. George W. Meyer, for instance, sees Vanamee as an embodiment of those living "in a happy state of nature," a foil to the ranchers, and exemplifying the moral that "As long as men maintain this harmonious relationship with the natural order, . . . their actions are good. . . ."[17] This interpretation of Vanamee is difficult to reconcile with the facts that through most of the book Vanamee is the most anguished character around, and that the evil in his own life has no relation to the question of his harmony with nature. Warren French also fails to observe these facts when he writes that Norris's "characters suffer not because—like Stephen Crane's—they are victims of an indifferent universe but because of their selfish efforts to thwart Nature's benevolent intentions."[18] Vanamee makes no such effort, and he suffers deeply. Actually he is *rewarded* for his persistence in refusing to accept the natural fact of death. French rests his whole thesis for Norris's importance on his continuation of the transcendental faith which Vanamee is said to epitomize, and my own explication of his story in part agrees with this. But it is not possible to make even the generalized moral application to particular men which French claims to find. Nature's "benevolent" intentions operate on so grand a scale that they may easily seem to be the workings of an "indifferent universe." The worlds of Emerson's "Compensation" and Crane's *Maggie* are the same world seen from different angles. Individual men cannot make "selfish efforts to thwart" intentions they cannot even conceive. Even if Vanamee's story had been such as to make us respect his views because they grew naturally out of it, they could not serve as a meaningful foil to, and judgment upon, the actions of other men.

Vanamee's story is interesting chiefly as an anachronistic exploitation of old Romance materials and techniques. But its self-conscious style causes it to fail even in this limited literary way. More seriously, Norris chose a method of concluding it which sought to reconcile it with his other modes, and not only failed in achieving that, but reduced it to a mockery. Over all he attempted to cast a cheery veil of dogmatic faith, as though all were well. Hawthorne, a far better romancer, attempted a similar sleight-of-hand at the end of *The House of the Seven Gables*; but at least he had the honesty—or was it the simple intelligence?—to admit that "After such wrong . . . there is no reparation."[19]

III

It should by now be obvious that the use of a point-of-view character could not possibly bring the various modes of *The Octopus* into artistic coherence, since the *kinds* of *events* which occur—e.g., the deaths of Annixter and Behrman, the "revival" of Angèle—are in no way controlled by point of view, and it is precisely these events and the antithetical conventions necessarily pertaining to them which cause the modes to disengage. Still, Norris did introduce a ubiquitous character who functions partially as a center of consciousness, and we must consider what purposes he serves, particularly in relation to the Romance of Vanamee.

Presley is either a wholly superfluous character or else he is the most important character and the book is essentially about him. If the book is primarily about the growing of wheat and the rancher-railroad war, then Presley is useless and has not even Vanamee's pseudo-significance. He never at any point affects the action of the book, and whatever meanings the actions themselves suggest, or whatever ironies their juxtapositions create, exist independently of him. He only makes them more explicit or reiterates what Norris as omniscient didactic author could more economically have said for himself, which he frequently does anyway.

But there is a second possibility, that Norris introduced Presley merely to serve the structural purpose of providing a person at leisure whose wanderings-about could function as narrative transitions between characters important in the action and then, by making him a literary person and letting him mull over some of Norris's own problems, inadvertently placed him at the center of the book and made his problems its theme. It is a little as though Homer had introduced into the *Iliad* a malcontent would-be bard who complained about the stink of the sacrifices and the difficulty of writing an epic about people who quarrelled over concubines. The *Iliad* might then have ceased to be an epic and become the story of a man trying futilely to write one with such intractable materials to work with.

Whether or not this corresponds to the actual writing of *The Octopus* is unimportant; the fact remains that Presley is interesting only because he allows the novel to discuss itself and because he is in a sense the novel as a whole in his own person. As Norris tell us, he is of "mixed origin," with a "composite" nature and a "complex" temperament (I, 6). His own specific literary aims are self-contradictory in the same way the novel is: "On one hand, it was his ambition to portray life as he saw it—directly, frankly, and through no medium of personality or temperament. But, on the other hand, as well, he wished to see everything through a rose-coloured mist—a mist that dulled all harsh outlines, all crude and violent colours. . . . He searched for the True Romance, and in the end, found grain rates and unjust freight tariffs" (I, 10–11). Vanamee, however, seems to be the living embodiment of Romance, its validation. In recounting his wanderings to Presley in the first chapter, he inspires the writer to believe that the romantic epic is still possible. Exalted, Presley stands on a high hill and in his imagination all the great ranches below him and their people resolve themselves into "mere . . . accessories" of his epic: "he seemed to dominate a universe, a whole order of things" (I, 43–44). "At last he was to grasp his song in all its entity" (I, 46). But the "entity" is not complete after all; at this point "reality" enters. A speeding train in the night roars into a wandering herd of sheep which the dreamy Vanamee—significantly—was supposed to be tending. The terrible slaughter wakes Presley from his grandiose illusion, and the chapter ends with his dilemma thus powerfully restated.

After the first chapter, as the various complications develop in the plots proper, Presley assumes a position in the background. But he is always there, riding along on horseback or lounging nearby on a sofa. Norris's point of view is omniscient, but his scenes are frequently rendered in objective form; and if any interior consciousness is described, it is as likely to be Presley's as anyone else's. The high degree of identification between Presley and Norris is also evident in the way their diction exactly coincides. The first rendering of Vanamee's character is given as Presley's subjective impression of it: "To Presley's morbidly keen observation . . ."; "Presley's vivid imagination chose to see . . ." (I, 30). Yet the same descriptive terms ("ascetic," "recluse," "seer") and comparison ("younger prophets of Israel") are used even when Presley is not present. Similarly the unusual terms describing Angèle are first given as representing Presley's impression of her, but later are reiterated constantly as standing for how she seemed to Vanamee, and also in absolute terms to Norris. All this merely increases the ambiguity of Presley's role.

In those episodes where Presley is entirely absent, little happens that he does not find out about (Behrman's death is the single important exception). Vanamee's private visions, for instance, are afterward fully related to him, and he easily intuits the private experience of Annixter. Despite certain of Norris's intimations to the contrary when he is trying to dissociate himself from Presley, Presley's sympathies are equivalent to the author's. He has romantic affinities with Vanamee, yet he no more identifies with his point of view than any other. When Vanamee tells of his mysterious experiences, Presley is interested but incredulous: "Imagination can do so much and the influence of the surroundings was strong," he says; "How impossible it would be that anything *should* happen" (I, 209). On the other hand, Norris asserts that Annixter and Presley, though "diametrically opposed in temperament," are "the best of friends" (I, 25). Although Annixter constantly thwarts Presley's attempts to see life romantically, Presley more fully appreciates his moral growth than he does Vanamee's visionary affirmations. An increasing interest in the "real" is also evident in his attitude toward Dyke. At first he finds the handsome young engineer merely "picturesque" (I, 14) and enjoys sitting up in the cab with him as a novel experience. But later (I, 214) Presley is urging Dyke to tell him about his economic problems. In face of the later spectacle of Dyke's complete ruin, Presley is outraged and his sympathies at last are fully evoked. It is out of his feeling for Dyke that his "great" poem, "The Toilers," is written. His one important literary work is thus inspired by the most pathetic embodiment of the "immovable facts" he had initially thought the death of literature.

Presley is an eyewitness of the fight at the ditch, and this experience culminates in his declaration, *"By God, I, too, I'm a Red!"* (II, 246). He then spends a passionate night at the desk pouring his outrage into his journal. But his constant desire for "expression" now goes beyond writing. After a long talk with Caraher the Communist, he goes to the Opera House and impulsively interrupts a mass meeting to deliver a wildly rhetorical denunciation of the railroad. Presley is conscious of his own failure in this, however: "he had been literary. . . . He had not helped them [the People] nor their cause in the least" (II, 262). So he goes out and throws an equally ineffectual bomb at Behrman. From a disdain for the facts he has so altered as to become a sordid fact himself: the ineffectual social activist.

All this vacillation (of which there is much more) only intensifies Presley's confusion about his role as a writer. The facts of his experience keep protesting against the high-sounding theories of both Shelgrim, the owner of the railroad, and Vanamee. When Vanamee states that "if your view be large enough, . . . it is *not* evil, but good, that in the end remains," Presley "held his peace" (II, 345).

In the end Presley is still "alone, thoughtful." Shelgrim's self-excusing "truth" is placed against the felt horror of the deaths of so many friends. And a vivid last recall of each of them is followed by a reconsideration of Vanamee's "truth." Presley is left (rather desperately) affirming it, an affirmation which could satisfy only as memory of reality faded. The last paragraphs, whether or not they are Norris's own "final word," are clearly presented as existing within the still tortured mind of Presley. But they are merely the last statement of half the truth, with the order of the two halves as stated in the first chapter reversed. The claims of rosy-tinted idealism and those of blunt realism remain; the reversal only indicates which half Norris might wish were true.

The Octopus is not the romantic epic Presley hoped to write; if it were, he would not be in it. It is a book about a man who wished to write such a work, but could not. Nor could Norris. But neither did he write an entirely successful novel on the problem itself. Presley's temperament and intellect are passive; and in comparison with the action from which he distracts and to which he is irrelevant, he is a bore. He does not shape the worlds he visits, even in imagination; he merely receives them as the far more inventive Norris creates them in all their incongruity. He can perceive how Magnus is tragic, but it is not his perception that *makes* Magnus a tragic character. His bomb and Dyke's gun are ineffectual against Behrman in spite of any views of reality and literature that he may have. And the new Angèle comes wandering improbably into life just when he himself is abandoning his belief in Romance. Norris's novel is richly varied not because Presley is, but in spite of him.

In contrast, Melville's *Moby-Dick*, which has much of the same fictional multiplicity as *The Octopus*, achieves far greater unity and impact because even those scenes which are narrated independently of Ishmael do not seem to be beyond him in conception. We believe in the wide and active range of Ishmael's intellect and symbolic imagination. He may speculate with realistic detachment on the activities of actual whales, or express—in a sense, create—the romantic and tragic reality of Ahab. The book's conventions are unlimited because Ishmael's mind is unlimited, and the book is wholly his.

The failure of *The Octopus* as an artistic creation, we may conclude, goes much deeper than a simple failure in rhetoric which may or may not be explained away when we are properly informed about Norris's literary theories,[20] Social Darwinism, or Evolutionary Theism, or when we conceive of Presley as a developmental or ironic center of consciousness. And it is strange that this failure should be rooted in the excessively literary character of the book, the last thing Norris could have wished. But his preoccupation with literary types—with the epic,

the romantic, the tragic, the realistic, the naturalistic, and the melodramatic—evidently so obsessed him that he indulged himself in all of
them, oblivious to incompatibilities, and even introduced at the center
of his book a character similarly obsessed, but far less brave—or assertive.

Notes

1. See George W. Meyer, "A New Interpretation of *The Octopus*," *College
English*, 4 (March, 1943), 351–359; Warren French, *Frank Norris* (New York:
Twayne Publishers, Inc., 1962), Chapter 6: "A Large Enough View"; and Donald
Pizer, *The Novels of Frank Norris* (Bloomington: Indiana University Press, 1966),
pp. 127–154. The Pizer book incorporates the substance of his several previous
articles on *The Octopus*.

2. Frederick J. Hoffman, in *The Modern Novel in America* (Chicago: Henry
Regnery Company, 1951), first referred to Presley as Norris's "point-of-view character," observing that the book's structure was "naive and unwittingly ironic"
(p. 38). Pizer (pp. 134–140) attributes the inconsistencies to Presley rather than
to Norris, but argues that the two are in accord at the end. French finds the novel
"an exercise in point of view" (p. 92), asserting that "What it contains is what
Presley . . . sees during a summer," which is doubly inaccurate, since the book
contains much that Presley does not see, and he spends an entire year at the ranch,
not a summer. The most cogent discussion of the subject is James K. Folsom's
"Social Darwinism or Social Protest? The 'Philosophy' of The *Octopus*," *Modern
Fiction Studies*, 8 (Winter 1962–63), 393–400. Where Pizer has Presley arriving
at an ultimate perception of "Truth" at the end, Folsom insists on the "highly
ironic" nature of Presley's "gloss on the meaning of the book," adding that
"Presley might just possibly not have the slightest idea of what he is talking
about" (pp. 393–394).

3. Cf. Charles Walcutt, *American Literary Naturalism, A Divided Stream*
(Minneapolis: University of Minnesota Press, 1956), pp. 144–145; Richard Chase,
The American Novel and Its Tradition (Garden City, New York: Doubleday, 1957),
p. 194; French, pp. 103–104; and Pizer, pp. 144–145.

4. Many critics have erroneously equated Dyke's story with those of the big
ranchers. For instance, Lars Ahnebrink, in *The Beginnings of Naturalism in American
Fiction* (Upsala and Cambridge, Mass: Harvard University Press, 1950), in discussing the question of free will, speaks of Dyke as being a "typical case" in *The
Octopus* (p. 202), whereas in fact he is completely atypical in this respect. (But
Ahnebrink [p. 203] even uses the immigrant tenant farmer Hooven as a "case in
point" to illustrate the economic situation of all the characters, whereas Hooven
possesses absolutely nothing of his own.) Meyer, p. 354, and Pizer, p. 120, both
correct the earlier critical tendency to speak of the ranchers as though they were
the downtrodden "People." One must, however, leave Dyke out of the revised
conception of the ranchers; his story remains fully naturalistic.

5. Frank Norris, *The Octopus: A Story of California* (Garden City, N. Y.:
Doubleday, Doran & Company, edn. 1930), II, 197–198. All references hereafter
within the text are to this edition, the pagination of which coincides with that of
Volumes I and II of *The Complete Edition of Frank Norris* (Garden City: Doubleday, Doran & Company, 1928).

6. Magnus as a "tragic" character has been discussed by Meyer, p. 334: "The noblest rancher of them all, according to conventional ethical standards"; Walcutt mentions his "tragic flaw" (p.   144); and Ernest Marchand, in *Frank Norris: A Study* (Palo Alto, Calif.: Stanford University Press, 1942; reprinted New York, 1964), writes of the "fatal error" which is the "source of his personal tragedy" (pp. 148–149). Marchand, p. 150, ably replies to Granville Hicks's specific objections to Norris's handling of Magnus's dilemma in *The Great Tradition* (New York: The MacMillan Company, 1933), p. 173.

The multiple-choice quality of *The Octopus* is well indicated by the fact that while Walter F. Taylor, in *The Economic Novel in America* (Chapel Hill: The University of North Carolina Press, 1942), can see Magnus as the "focal and typical figure" of the novel (p. 295), Kenneth S. Lynn's long introduction to the Riverside Edition (Boston: Houghton Mifflin Company, 1958) does not so much as mention him. On the other hand, Maxwell Geismar's lengthy discussion of the book in *Rebels and Ancestors* (Boston: Houghton Mifflin and Company, 1953) completely ignores Vanamee.

7. "She paid the penalty," Norris writes, "for being the wife of a great man" (I, 272). But Derrick's story is not convincingly tragic precisely because one cannot believe in his greatness. He seems guilty of bloated pride–a comic trait—rather than of hubris, because his much-vaunted "honor" is depicted as a wholly negative virtue. It is hard to care about it, as one cares about the integrity of Oedipus or Othello. Oedipus proves his character by the very act that brings him down; Othello's most vile act is an extension of his best idea of himself. But when Derrick compromises his honor, there is nothing left. Norris provided a beautifully appropriate setting for Magnus' humiliation: a tiny dressing room, which "only two nights before . . . had been used by the leading actress of a comicopera troupe." "The air was heavy with the smell of stale greasepaint," writes Norris. "Underneath the sofa was an old pair of corsets" (II, 267). These details lend an aura of comeuppance to the proceedings, but since Norris continues in a vein of heavy commiseration, he evidently did not intend the effect. But a "great man" must have the capacity somehow to survive–to rise above—the wreck of his fortunes and life, even if only in a Macbeth's eloquently articulated nihilism. Self-discovery and an unmasking are not equivalent catastrophes.

8. Critics generally agree on the superior merit of Annixter's portion of the book. Chase, p. 194, and Walcutt, pp. 142-144, effectively distinguish Annixter's story from naturalism. I think, however, that they and Lynn, p. xiii, considerably overstate the manner of his death, using such words as "heroic," "epic," "glorious," and "tragic."

9. In this the chapter resembles Stephen Crane's "The Bride Comes to Yellow Sky." On the mock-heroic strain in Realism, see Harry Levin, *The Gates of Horn* (New York: Oxford University Press, 1963), pp. 39–56.

10. Norris's ill-considered and apparently unrevised introductory sketch of Annixter does not coincide in several respects with the character we come to know. Annixter is said to possess extraordinary degrees of intelligence, executive ability, and legal knowledge. Then he is shown as a man who eats prunes as a cure for a nervous malady, fires a ranch-hand without sufficient cause and with foreseeable serious consequences, and is as naive as everyone else about the state of his contract with the railroad. It is known that Norris began writing *The Octopus* with an actual historical event in mind (see Franklin Walker, *Frank Norris: A Biography*

[New York: Doubleday, Doran & Company, 1932; reprinted 1963], pp. 240–245). But at some early point he wrote a series of character sketches (printed as Appendix F.2 in Ahnebrink), evidently without certainly assigning the personages roles in a fully conceived story or without thinking of them much in relation to each other, since he never alludes to action and makes few cross-references. This resulted, I believe, in a certain priority of character when it came to developing the novel, and perhaps explains both the degree to which characters manage to create independent fictional milieux and the several inconsistencies between character and action.

11. The Annixter story is fully completed, and its persistent Realism fully and finally established, only in later developments: Hilma, his earth-goddess wife, suffers a miscarriage. This is in a sense arbitrary and, in view of Hilma's size and health, even unlikely. Yet the pressures of the book as a whole were directly against such an occurrence; considering the deliberate parallel drawn earlier between Vanamee's vision and Annixter's emotional growth, and the importance Norris was immediately going to place on the wheat as a symbol of resurrection and continuing life, the obvious thing would have been for Hilma to have borne a bouncing baby boy. In avoiding such a patently symbolic maneuver, Norris goes to the opposite extreme of depicting her in a state of barren hopelessness and suffering. These are the very elements in life Vanamee had found intolerable and had supposedly transcended. It belonged to Realism to restore them to the novel as a part of the truth. When Presley tells Hilma to start living again, she replies, "I do not understand, . . . but I know you mean to be very very kind" (II, 339). Only Folsom among previous critics has given adequate weight to this aspect of the *total* story of Annixter's love. Most recent interpretations find it convenient to stop with Annixter's transformation and death, because this forces it into the closest relation and hence "unity" with Vanamee's story and the wheat symbolism.

12. For Pizer, the unity derives from similarities between Vanamee's philosophic development and those of Presley and Annixter. Lynn also finds that "Norris's epic is bound together" by the "three young men" who have "only casual connections" but "share certain extremely significant resemblances" (p. v). But while one may admit certain parallelisms exist, I believe they are inadequate to "bind the epic together."

13. *Aspects of the Novel* (New York: Harvest Books, 1963), p. 161.

14. Page 174. On page 180 Marchand rather reluctantly refers to the "lyrical, empurpled prose" and "rhapsodic intensity" of the Vanamee narrative, but does not analyze or characterize it beyond this. Marchand's Chapter V remains, however, the best general discussion of Norris's style.

15. Quoted in Isaac F. Marcosson, *Adventures in Interviewing* (New York: Dodd, Mead, 1923), p. 235.

16. Transcendental (romantic) aspects of Norris's philosophy in *The Octopus* are well delineated by Walcutt, pp. 136–151, and French, Chapter 6. Pizer's interpretation, pp. 127–154, in the light of Evolutionary Theism, expounded on pp. 3–22, expresses them in the particular terms of Norris's time.

17. Meyer, p. 353.

18. French, "Preface."

19. *The Complete Works of Nathaniel Hawthorne*, ed. George Parsons Lathrop, (Boston: Riverside Press, 1883), III, 371.

20. The most explicit attempt to correlate theory and practice is H. Willard

Reninger, "Norris Explains *The Octopus*: A Correlation of His Theory and Practice," *American Literature*, 12 (May, 1940), 218–227. Reninger's errors in interpreting Norris's critical writings are discussed in C. C. Walcutt, "Frank Norris on Realism and Naturalism," *American Literature*, 13 (March, 1941), 61–63. Reninger (p. 227) says that Norris "avoided pseudo-romance, commonplace realism, and pessimistic naturalism" in *The Octopus*. My thesis is that he achieved all of these, and more.

Frank Norris's *The Octopus*:
The Christian Ethic as Pragmatic
Response

Joseph R. McElrath, Jr.[*]

The question of the author's intention and its relevance to what was actually effected in his art has become so difficult a matter to discuss that most critics wisely avoid it when possible. A single reading of the "Intentions" essay in the *Princeton Encyclopedia of Poetry and Poetics* is enough to alert anyone to the risks and trials of even mentioning the term: to speak of the *intended* structure or the *intended* meaning means leaping into a morass of qualifications and very fine distinctions. It can prove an especially unpleasant experience. When one consults available scholarship on Frank Norris and then approaches his novels to see if the critics have accurately gleaned their significance, however, the question of intention seems unavoidable. The critics contradict each other with great frequency. Their radical disagreements tend to suggest that the novels' structures seem amorphous enough to trigger widely various responses; and the themes appear ambiguous enough to put sincere and intelligent readers at odds. It is at such a juncture that the question of what Norris was *trying to do* naturally comes to mind. Then one wishes he could discover in the novels' structures the true intentional indicators and thus herald in a golden age of agreement among the Norriseans.

In regard to Norris's *The Octopus,* though, there has been little reason to believe that singly or collectively we will ever "definitively" discover what was *the* intention behind the novelistic enterprise. Norris was seized by the wheat trilogy idea early in 1899, and by July he had begun his research and writing. It was finally published in 1901, apparently after an unsuccessful attempt to have it serialized in a magazine or in newspapers. The data of the published book suggest that during composition many intentions were at work. This was not an uncommon phenomenon in Norris's novels, as readers of the earlier *Moran, McTeague* and *A Man's Woman* well know. Only *Blix* is a simple, straightforward

[*]This essay was written specifically for this volume and appears here by permission of the author.

realization of an obvious intention. *The Pit* (because of its structure) and *Vandover* (because of its impressionistic point of view) are also puzzling works, and they have produced a good deal of squabbling over what Norris was trying to do and trying to say. But nothing approaches the degree of argumentativeness that characterizes debate over the meaning of *The Octopus*.

The crux of the problem is the conclusion of the novel. *The Octopus* closes with Vanamee's and Presley's points of view. This has led critics to conclude—with approval as well as with distaste and incredulity—that Norris argues for a bizarre distortion of St. Paul's view concerning death (Vanamee) and/or an exaggeratedly bright belief in Emersonian compensation to which Presley comes after a flirtation with a dark, Stephen Crane-like view of man's insignificance. What troubles commentators is that Norris obviously devoted much of the novel to the pathos of apparently significant individual situations—such as Dyke's, Annixter's, Hilma's, and Magnus Derrick's—only to have his characters stridently declare that, after all, such pathos is not substantially real (Vanamee) and that individuals count for nought (Presley).

The critical predicament is complicated by other apparent contradictions within the novel. For example, villainous S. Behrman, willy nilly, ends up doing "Good" by supplying grain to the starving masses of the Far East. The supreme villain, Shelgrim, who wreaks havoc in the lives of the Ranchers, proves an extraordinarily compassionate man in his treatment of an alcoholic employee. And those self-conceived martyrs, the "Good" Ranchers, are as capable of abusing those below them on the economic ladder as the "Bad" Railroad is with its victims. Moreover, neither the Ranchers nor the Railroaders are at all reluctant to gouge wheat consumers. In terms of economic behavior neither group attends to the concerns of morality unless it pays. Readers seeking simple moral melodrama of the muckraking variety in *The Octopus*, then, are in for a disappointment. There are no untainted heroes in this portrait of American economic realities; rather, the main characters are self-serving participants in the more or less controlled situation of rapacious interaction which was the free enterprise system at the close of the century.

What Norris pictures is a complex dilemma which results in much suffering for a good many characters. The suffering is real; and, as troubled readers from 1901 on have pointed out, Vanamee's and Presley's reactions neither convince nor truly make any sense. Both explain away death and suffering; both refuse to recognize them as significant actualities. Consequently, we must ungraciously ask the questions, was Norris punch-drunk when he finally brought the lengthy *Octopus* to a close, or had he actually adopted a "transcendental" point of view expressed in Vanamee's and Presley's orphic conclusions? Neither question merits an affirmative reply. Norris seems to use neither Vanamee nor Presley as a spokesman. The more likely function of each is to sensationally illustrate the kind of extreme reaction that is necessary if one insists upon providing an immediate, absolute solution to the predicaments that have been pictured during the course of the novel. Norris's own response is not to provide an all-encompassing answer to the problems of the San Joaquin Valley; instead, it seems his intention to establish the fact that there is no *immediate* solution to the problem of inhumaneness in the economic order. The legislatures, the California and Supreme courts, the Ranchers, the Railroaders and, indeed, Nature herself offer no panaceas; as a matter of fact, they are all parts of the problem. There are no legal and moral solutions that will actually work available, and the economic system itself offers no truly dependable checks. Briefly, Norris seems to have been stumped during the composition of *The Octopus,* including the time at which he wrote the conclusion. He knew that the macroeconomic order does work: while its means cannot be sanctioned and its inhumaneness cannot be condoned, it does finally produce the products—financial gain and essential commodities—that are its *raison d'être.* The system does require alterations which will minimize its deleterious effects; but, regarding specific and immediately effective remedies for the socioeconomic disaster in the San Joaquin Valley, Norris does not know how to prescribe. Long before Vanamee and Presley began pontificating, Norris understood that his dominant point of view had to be that of the critical Realist. He could insightfully describe a complex problem. He could delineate the bizarre ends toward which one would have to move if he sought to explain away or immediately "cure" the situation. But he could not sanction Shelgrim's, Vanamee's, or Presley's facile answers to the questions raised by the plot.

The result was that Norris assumed the point of view that informed the major theme of *Vandover and the Brute.* When one reads that earlier novel, he ultimately puzzles over the question, what might Van have done to avoid the calamity that his life became? As has already been suggested, the possibilities are moot.[1] In *Vandover* modern life is depicted as so complex that it nearly defies analysis and certainly eludes any easy strategies for melioration. Having admitted the difficulty inherent in determining the author's intention in several of Norris's novels, one hesitates to proclaim that *Vandover's* theme is a major, intended theme of *The Octopus*; but the data provided by Norris do point in that direction, especially in the first half of the work.

If anything is clearly established in the first half of *The Octopus,* it is that one cannot enjoy a quick, traditional response to the predatory

Trust as the *bête noire* and to the "poor" farmers as the "little men" who are victimized by the beast. Norris's fictional world is not the one Garland depicts in *Main-Travelled Roads*. Life, in the San Joaquin Valley, is not so simple, and Norris refuses to allow Garlandesque melodrama as he reveals the group personality of the Ranchers.[2] Magnus is the self-styled leader, the grand representative of what he likes to imagine as "The People." Actually he is nothing more than the principal of a special interest group. He looks and publicly acts as though he is wearing a toga and sporting laurel; but Norris deftly strips him of that guise through direct comment and the fashioning of self-revelatory action. Eventually we come to look past the obvious dissimilarities between Magnus and his nemesis, S. Behrman. The common denominator is that Magnus, the other Ranchers, and Behrman are engaged by the business of making a profit. They are economic creatures, and they spend most of their time and energy attempting to maximize gains. Behrman's personality is, of course, almost totally repulsive, and little need be said here about the particulars of his behavior. But what are we told about Magnus? First, Magnus does not care for the land as land or as that focal point of nineteenth-century Romanticism, Nature. We may thus check any conditioned responses concerning the pastoral life and Magnus being one of Nature's noble men. Norris does not provide legitimate opportunity for imaginative embellishments of those kinds. Second, Norris bluntly explains that Magnus's quite unpoetical instincts are those of the '49er: his aim is to make a strike not in the gold fields but in the golden fields of wheat. Third, his instincts are also those of a frequently encountered Norrisean personality type, the gambler. Gamblers do not fare well in Norris's fiction and when Magnus attempts to stack the deck for the sake of financially beating the Railroad and earning the accolades of "The People," Norris allows us to fully sympathize with him only after he has lost his son and suffered a complete mental breakdown. (See Curtis Jadwin in the next volume of The Epic of the Wheat for a similar situation.) Magnus speaks nobly and thinks noble thoughts, usually about himself; but Genslinger is quite correct in his factual account of Magnus's chicanery and his motivations.

Then there is the second major Rancher, Annixter, who undergoes a remarkably positive personality transformation in the middle of the novel because of his relationship with Hilma Tree. In the first half, however, Annixter is neither a noble husbandman of the soil, nor a potentially fine husband, nor even an admirable "Western" figure. In a Dickensian way he is designed as an irascible misanthrope, a childish misogynist, and an all-around nuisance. The data provided stop us once again in our possible tendency to romanticize. Like Magnus who, early in the plot, abruptly dismisses his sharecroppers so as to maximize profits, Annixter is quite capable of abusing those within the sphere of his economic control. Delany, for example, is a capable and loyal employee whom Annixter verbally abuses and then fires simply because of jealousy; and the fact that the unquestionably good young lady, Hilma Tree, finds much that is likeable in Delany reinforces the conclusion that Annixter's behavior is indefensible on any grounds. In fact, Annixter irrationally abuses everyone: he is famous for it. Within his domain he is as arbitrary as a feudal lord in his exercise of absolute power, almost to the point of employing his *droit du seigneur* with Hilma. Thus, even before Magnus and he resort to political corruption, Norris has depicted Annixter negatively in terms of his egotism, insensitivity, and bullying disposition. The result is that, when S. Behrman and his agents begin to squeeze Magnus and his comrades, it is difficult to imagine the Ranchers as flawless victims unfamiliar with the abuses of power. When the Railroad unfeelingly acts, it is all too easy for the reader to recall how unfeelingly and selfishly the Ranchers themselves behave toward those under their control in the economic system. And is there any doubt that the Ranchers would exploit the Railroad if they could? The major differences between the Ranchers and the Railroad are the scale on which power is avariciously wielded and the superior abilities of the Railroad in using and abusing power.

Needless to say, the early commentators did not focus on these thematic developments in the first half of *The Octopus,* and the apparent result has been the largely sympathetic reading the Ranchers have received in Norris criticism. Anti-Railroad, yellow newspapers such as the San Francisco *Examiner* described the Rancher-Railroad relationship in the simplistic Good vs Evil terms that Norris had carefully avoided.[3] Reformers described what they wanted to see in *The Octopus*: a Thomas Nast cartoon in prose. Thus were the shortcomings of the Ranchers ignored by the early commentators; thus was the Ranchers' bribery mainly excused as "necessary"; and thus was one other bit of culpability pushed into the background. That final fault high-lighted by Norris was the plain-and-simple poor business sense, or greed-induced myopia, of the Ranchers. Norris's field research regarding the Mussel Slough Affair— the origin of the main plot—apparently opened his eyes to some unpleasant aspects of 1880s economic life. The novel tells us that he judged his growers less than pure and noble; it also tells us that the growers directly contributed in large measure to their own predicament. They were grossly unprepared to competently enter the arena of economic competition, and their incompetence did them in. What early and later commentators have not duly emphasized is that Norris clearly pictures the ranchers as having no actual defense for their position: the courts, up to the Supreme Court, correctly recognize that the Ranchers have no legal claim to a low price on the Railroad's sections of land. The Ranchers were thick-witted to the degree that they actually construed the Railroad's *handbills,* advertising low-priced land, as "legal paper." The price of such foolishness is ruination. That is how the competitive situation (*caveat emptor*) works, as Norris seems to clearly realize. The irony is that Magnus, the time-tested gambler who should have known better, accepted the hand craftily dealt by the Railroad without understanding the nature of the game—its spoken and unspoken rules. To have proceeded in improving the Railroad's land without *the* essential safeguard of the economic system—a mutually binding contract—is as sensible as entering a poker game when one's experience includes nothing more complicated than a hand or two of Old Maid. Like Vandover and McTeague, the ranchers are not sophisticated enough to flourish in a harsh world in which the maladapted naturally and regularly perish at the hands of "the fittest." The Ranchers thus suffer calamity, and the suffering is finally great enough to evoke a sympathetic response; but, at the same time, Norris has tough-mindedly explained how it was that the Ranchers greedily and blindly rushed in where competent capitalists would never tread. They voluntarily ran the gambler's risk; and, predictably, they lost to the truly professional sharpers.

The main plot, then, reveals an unpleasant reality: a rural version of the greed-dominated San Francisco depicted in *Vandover* and *Mc-Teague* (where Charlie Geary and Marcus Schouler function in much the same predatory role as S. Behrman). It is a complicated reality which is designed to evoke a complex response from the reader—a reaction of hard-headed realism as well as one of some sympathy for the duped Ranchers.

When the debacle at the irrigation ditch occurs, Norris further complicates the reader's experience; for both the Railroad agents and the Ranchers are then presented as victims of a disaster which participants on both sides regret deeply. It is in light of the pathos of the post-irrigation ditch events that we move forward in the novel to view Vanamee's and Presley's reflections on life and then consider them in terms of Norris's authorial intention and point of view. For the reasons presented below, it seems that Norris's point of view at the conclusion is ironical and his intention is to illustrate that only a madman and a chronic neurasthenic are capable of denying the tragedy of the present *comédie humaine* and of transforming real disaster into imagined triumph.

Regarding Vanamee, what should be obvious is that he is not responding to the events of the main plot. He is responding to his own very peculiar experiences, which are not truly integrated into the central story line—as readers with an eye to structure have long recognized. Like the Grannis-Baker subplot in *McTeague*, the Vanamee-Angèle story runs parallel and then radically tangential to the main plot. By the close of *The Octopus* Vanamee has mentally left the real world behind. In the "world" Vanamee has created for himself, death has become an illusion—and not in the sense that a Pauline perspective may allow, but in the sense that it is truly a nonentity for Vanamee. Meanwhile, back in the real world, Hilma has lost an actual husband and an actual, stillborn child; they are real losses for which there are no soothing consolations or denials available. She experiences profound sorrow because there is a reason for the sane, natural response of unmitigated grief. Vanamee, the incompetent who could not manage the simple matter of keeping his flock off the P. & S. W. tracks at the beginning of the novel, further loosened his hold on reality's particulars bit by bit as the subplot progressed: at the end he has drifted off into a world of meaningless abstractions. The mystical madman turned away from the problems which remain present for Hilma and the others whose lives have been devastated. His final thoughts, therefore, are irrelevant to the principal concerns of *The Octopus*.

Who leads Presley to his happy solution? His mentor is Vanamee. That is the first thing to remember when evaluating Presley's vision and considering its relation to Norris. The second salient point to recall is, when Presley comes to the conclusion that in the larger view Evil vanishes and Good dominates, he is in a condition of nervous prostration, and his breakdown is of approximately three months duration. Norris clearly describes his pathological condition and characters, such as Cedarquist, directly comment on it. The neurasthenic poet of the opening of the novel has become bewildered, physically debilitated, and without a hold on life when Vanamee provides him with the means to construct a trauma-alleviating fantasy. Presley is ill, very ill, and when he leaps to metaphysical "certainties" as a cure, Norris does not join him.

In fact, Norris let Presley go his own way shortly after the climax of the novel, the irrigation ditch episode. For it was in the events surrounding that episode that Norris had his say as a meliorist; and his very qualified and tentative meliorism is distinctly more pragmatic, modest, and reasonable in its aims and assumptions than Presley's. The difference is roughly that between William James's approach to problem-solving and the early Ralph Waldo Emerson's. As James would, Norris seems to have asked the questions, what is remediable in American life as depicted in *The Octopus*, and what is not? What can be positively altered and what must be accepted as "necessary" for the present? Neither Vanamee nor Presley—who behave as metaphysicians rather than pragmatists —posed such questions. When Norris did, he came to the conclusion that the macrocosmic situation could not be transformed overnight. Economic special interest groups do not typically manifest miraculous changes in their outlooks and programmatic behavior; and the economic system is characterized by its inertia and will naturally run over anyone who stands in its way. That is, the San Joaquin conflict will, as Literary Naturalists phrase it, move toward its inexorable end at the irrigation ditch and the surviving Ranchers will be driven off the Railroad's land.

What, then, is remediable? All that is possible, Norris determines, is change at the individual and personal relationship levels: it is within the relatively tiny microcosm of self and one-to-one relationships within the local commuinty that any hope for change lies. While the system resists modifications, an individual such as Annixter can be transformed, literally overnight. While special interest groups seem destined to remain antagonists, Annixter can almost immediately refashion his relations with his neighbors by choosing to do so and then putting some effort into the task. This is the positive insight, and the rudimentary step toward problem-solving, that Norris offers in *The Octopus*. Principally through Annixter's experience, Norris makes his proposal for reform, and the larger framework for it is the widely-known but rarely-tested ethic expressed in the Sermon on the Mount (Matthew 5:8). One needs to quickly add that Norris is not promising pie-in-the-sky when he introduces the Sermon's concepts; but, as we would expect from a pragmatist, he does demonstrate what James termed their "cash value" in realizable experiential terms. The Sermon ethic does not prove a cure-all. But Norris does show the potential and real value of an experiment in Judaeo-Christian living. It proves the best solution he can come up with; in fact, it seems the only promising alternative to dog-eat-dog living that he could imagine in 1901.

The practical usefulness of the Sermon ethic is illustrated in two ways in the second half of *The Octopus*. First, Annixter's experience is presented as a paradigm. To experience love in the classical terms of *agapè*, Annixter must eliminate the egocentric outlook so characteristic of him in the first half. He at first merely wants to use Hilma Tree as a kept woman. When she refuses and flees his ranch, he finds a void in his life. After a night-long period of reflection he discovers that he has unwittingly fallen in love with her and he must do something about it; then he finds that he must deal with his bloated pride because some painful humiliation is required to reconcile her to him; and then, after righting the situation, he realizes that his chief joy lies in making *her* happy. Once he reorients himself, he discovers that the new orientation of selfless living produces unexpected results in regard to others. He begins treating his neighbors humanely, for the first time in his life. He brings those whose lives have been ruined by the economic struggle into his own home and cares for them. Hilma explains the change when Annixter decides to take in the Dykes: " 'You wouldn't have thought of being kind to Mrs. Dyke and Sidney a little while ago. You wouldn't have thought of them at all. But you did now, and it's just because you love me true, isn't it? Isn't it? And because it's made you a better man.' "[4]

Presley too notices the change: " 'There was a time when you would have let them all go to grass, and never so much as thought of them' " (p. 320). In response, Annixter clarifies the point that Norris intends:

> I was a machine before, and if another man, or woman, or child got in my way, I rode 'em down, and I never *dreamed* of anybody else but myself. But as soon as I woke up to the fact that I really loved [Hilma], why, it was glory hallelujah all in a minute, and, in a way, I kind of loved everybody then, and wanted to be everybody's friend. And I began to see that a fellow can't live *for* himself any more than he can live *by* himself. He's got to think of others. . . . That ain't much of a religion, but it's the best I've got, and Henry Ward Beecher couldn't do any more than that.[5]

Having allowed the idea to clearly emerge, Norris then renders judgment on Presley who realizes that, in contrast to Annixter's new vision, his "own vague schemes, glittering systems of reconstruction, collapsed to ruin, and he himself, with all his refinement, with all his poetry, culture, and education, stood, a bungler at the world's workbench" (pp. 320–21).[6]

In the problematic world of *The Octopus*, the Annixter-response is *the* answer proffered by Norris. But Norris-the-Realist is not so foolish as to suggest that heaven on earth is just around the corner. Again, the focus is on only a microcosmic development and not the macrocosmic status quo. For example, Annixter's personal revelation cannot check the al-ready-in-motion events leading to the bloody confrontation at the ditch. Annixter, in fact, does not himself see the slightest connection between his new personal behavior and his public actions in the economic arena. When the rifles are delivered to the Ranchers, he knows that they most likely will have to use them, and there is no hesitation when the time comes. Like Shelgrim, who demonstrates the same inability to connect personal morality with public behavior in the economic order, Annixter fails to even see the need to synthesize a consistent, all-inclusive philoso-phy. As Curtis Jadwin in *The Pit* turns from Sunday School work to guilt-free predation at the Board of Trade, Annixter turns from his new life to continue his old ways in the struggle with the Railroad.

When Annixter fails to make the connection, Norris does not overtly criticize him. After all, Annixter is a wheat-grower, not an urbane intellectual, social philosopher, or novelist. Moreover, even if he had been schooled to perform such a task, the on-rushing events do not allow him the time necessary to test possible macrocosmic applications of his new orientation. The most important reason, though, for Norris's positive treatment of Annixter is that the author of *The Octopus* himself seems not to have been able to intellectually proceed much farther than his character did.

Norris was, by 1901, no longer the "boy Zola" whose hard Darwinism was voiced in *Moran* and whose other early works were set in a Godless universe of insentient forces. As his personal life became more stable (largely because of his 1900 marriage) and his future as a successful writer began to seem assured, he turned from the sensational negativism, flamboyant hard Darwinism, and lurid ultra-Realism of his apprentice days to a more sober and thoughtful analysis of contemporary issues.[7] The first fruit of this new phase is seen in his turning away from the fashionable, attention-winning clichés of Naturalism to a more common-sensical, tradition-tested investigation of broadly applicable verities. One would suppose that by 1900 he had asked himself, what do the lessons of *Moran, McTeague,* and *A Man's Woman* really have to do with life as most Americans live it? Only in *Blix* had he come close to addressing life in normative terms—in the widely relevant terms suggested by William Dean Howells. In *The Octopus* he finally attempted to picture life in a truly representational fashion with "roses" *and* the "thistles" which Howells claimed must be included in any balanced portrait of experience.[8] Norris also tried to provide a useful, positive response to life's predicaments; but in *The Octopus* he was only beginning to develop this new concern of his.

This is not to say that he "killed off" Annixter because he did not know what to do with his Sermon ethicist once he had created him. But there is some truth in the idea. For, when Annixter dies, one looks in vain to discover any sophisticated authorial development of the Sermon theme or any significant transference of Annixter's function to another character. Norris's theme remained embryonic; and when Sermon-related notions do emerge, Norris is mainly elaborating upon, but not logically developing, his initial insight.

Norris's uneasiness over the theme seems manifested some twenty pages after Annixter's profession of his new "faith." The point had already been crystallized by Annixter, but Norris intruded upon the story to further clarify and perhaps defensively qualify his theme which would undoubtedly strike some readers as either old fashioned preaching or idealistic moonshine:

>   Where once Annixter had thought only of himself, he now
> thought only of Hilma. The time when this thought of another
> should broaden and widen into thought of *Others*, was yet to
> come; but already it had expanded to include [his] unborn
> child—already, as in the case of Mrs. Dyke, it had broadened
> to enfold another child and another mother bound to him by
> no ties other than those of humanity and pity. In time, starting
> from this point, it would reach out more and more till it should
> take in all men and women, and the intolerant selfish man,
> while retaining all of his native strength, should become toler-
> ant and generous, kind and forgiving [p. 341].

This is, obviously, almost pure repetition. The only new emphasis added
is that such personal reform with its benign micromosmic social consequences involves development over years. If we consider the macrocosmic
application of the Sermon ethic, Norris is also making it clear that his
proposal for socio-economic reform has to be viewed in terms of evolutionary time. He knew that *if* his Sermon solution was accepted as truly
the only practical, pragmatic approach to the betterment of life, the
realization of a better society would involve centuries of deliberate effort.

In 1901, this was the best that Norris could do as a thinker: provide
Annixter as an attractively suggestive example of the real and potential
values of the concepts embodied in the Sermon.

The second illustration of the Sermon's practical value is presented
in the more overtly argumentative terms of the "cautionary tale" tradition. While Norris, in effect, defaults on the need for a fully thought-
through program for the macrocosmic application of Annixter's insights,
he does not back down from the assertion regarding the need to employ
the Sermon orientation as the starting point for positive change. The
debacle at the irrigation ditch and its pathetic aftermath at Magnus's
house are used by Norris to hammer home his point as one worthy of
serious consideration: these episodes dramatically raise the question,
does it have to come to *this* before human beings realize the need to care
for one another? For it is only in the face of pain, the death of loved
ones, the destruction of families, and a shameful loss of integrity that
the Railroaders and the wheat growers realize their common link of frail
humanity and the need for mutual cooperation. In the world of *The
Octopus* it requires the sight of corpses and grieving parents and spouses
to make economic antagonists drop their public roles and revert to a
common condition of simple humanity—which they all do naturally and
without hesitation as they tend to the dead and the dying.

>   The surviving members of both Leaguers and deputies—
> the warring factions of the Railroad and The People—mingled

together now with no thought of hostility. Presley helped the doctor to cover Christian's body. S. Behrman and Ruggles held bowls of water while Osterman was attended to. The horror of that dreadful business had driven all other considerations from the mind. The sworn foes of the last hour had no thought of anything but to care for those whom, in their fury, they had shot down [p. 363].

It is not long, however, before S. Behrman returns to his former personality: he learned nothing of permanent value from the experience. Magnus takes in the Dykes and the new-made widow, Hilma, and thus indicates that he too was capable of the positive transformation of personality experienced by Annixter. Unfortunately, he is a broken man and soon he himself has to be cared for by his wife. In short, life in California and the socio-economic macrocosm goes on pretty much the same as it did before the battle. In *The Octopus* no utopia was ushered in; and the grim tale informs the reader that it is unlikely that one will be created in the near future.

Still, in the face of such realities, Norris does not abandon hope. Like E. A. Robinson in "Children of the Night," he manifests an attitude of patient optimism rather than despair. For all of his modernity in regard to *avant-garde* Continental and American literary and intellectual fashions at the turn of the century, Norris in 1901 proved true to his upbringing. The core of his personality was that of the earnest Victorian ever capable of seeing a glimmer of light on the horizon. As his principal biographer, Franklin Walker, has pointed out, Norris's youth was spent under the cultural influence of the genteel-ideal Gertrude Norris, who did not conceal her enthusiasm for the morality-imbued art of Scott, Tennyson and Browning. His paternal model was the self-made businessman who undoubtedly contributed in large measure to Norris's achievement-oriented personality: "success" is a major concept in every one of his seven novels. But it is especially in *The Octopus* that such lasting parental personality determinants revealed themselves most clearly. It was in the major phase of Norris's brief career that he turned from the high-jinks of being an *enfant terrible* of Ultra-realism and Naturalistic sensationalism so as to apply himself to the "grown-up" task of making positive, constructive sense of the human predicament. By 1901, his view of "the responsibilities of the novelist" in regard to his fellow man was as serious and as exalted as Howells's and Matthew Arnold's views of the moral function of the artist in society.

At "the world's workbench" he initiated the basic design of a solution to the complex problems depicted in *The Octopus*. In his Annixter-theme he blended modern conditions with traditional insights into human nature; and, not surprisingly, the theme echoed one of the major concepts of *the* quintessential Victorian statement on the nature of love's transforming power—undoubtedly well known to Gertrude insofar as it was one of the literary fixtures of the nineteenth century. One can easily imagine Gertrude Norris, in moments away from Scott, Tennyson and Browning, reading to Frank and his younger brother Charles from Coventry Patmore's spectacularly popular *Angel in the House.* The poem directly anticipates the story of Annixter in that Felix Vaughn's personal life is made ecstatically complete through nuptial love. But the more important parallel between the poem and *The Octopus* is seen in Patmore's analysis of the long-range social consequence of *agapè* within nuptial relationships. Patmore sees the beginning of all amicable, healthy relationships between people and within societies in the marital relationship at its best:

> . . . After a while,
> This pool of private charity
> Shall make its continent an isle,
> And roll, a world embracing sea;
> This foolish zeal of lip for lip,
> This fond self-sanctioned, willful zest,
> Is that elect relationship
> Which forms and sanctions all the rest
> This little germ of nuptial love
> Which springs so simply from the sod,
> The root is, as my song shall prove,
> Of all our love from Man to God.[9]

This is precisely the point that Norris makes through his example of the way to begin positive reform: if a society characterized by mutual cooperation and concern for the well-being of all men is to develop, it must be initiated in the microcosm of one-to-one relationships, then extend to multiple-party interactions, and finally inform the character of the macrocosmic nexus of the entire society.

Through the vitality and simple beauty of the Annixter-Hilma relationship and its laudable social consequences Norris makes an admittedly old idea seem very new. This old idea emerges frequently in the Old Testament under the rubric of *hesed,* the Book of Ruth presenting what is probably the best known example. In the New Testament context the dynamic concept is approximated by the Greek term *agapè.* In the nineteenth-century Episcopalian milieu—Norris's—all of the Law and the Prophets are distilled to love of God and love of one's neighbor. And what Norris did was run the risk of seeming unfashionable, or sounding "square," in the *fin de siècle* literary and intellectual world. He had employed with success the marketplace-tested, attention-winning fads in the Stevensonian *Moran*, the Zolaesque *McTeague*, the Howellsian *Blix*, and the Wagnerian *A Man's Woman*. In the Annixter-theme he finally played true to his own background and experience by suggesting what he concluded was the only workable means to the checking of the worst in human nature and the fostering of the best. The fact that Norris could not exactly explain how to carry out the large-scale application of the Sermon ethic should not be held against him. The problem the young author encountered in this regard merely indicates that he had an awful lot in common with other thinkers and believers who had struggled with the same question over the centuries.

Notes

1. See my "Frank Norris's *Vandover and the Brute*: Narrative Technique and the Socio-Critical Viewpoint," *Studies in American Fiction*, 4 (1976), 27–43. In *Vandover* and later in *The Pit* Norris depicted and analyzed problematic situations for which there were no available solutions and he made it plain that problems sometimes must remain problems.

2. See "Under The Lion's Paw" (1889). This superb example of "Realistic" short fiction does not *degenerate* to melodrama, as is the case in George Washington Cable's "Belles Demoiselles Plantation" and much of Bret Harte's best known stories. But it is nonetheless melodramatic in its pitting of good Haskins against evil Butler. Norris seems to have unblushingly incorporated the climactic developments of "Paw" in *The Octopus*: like Butler, the Railroad upwardly adjusts the price of its land after it has been improved. The more "Realistic" development in *The Octopus*, however, is that the Ranchers are not simple victims of Nature and middleman capitalists the way Haskins is.

3. 6 April 1901, p. 3.

4. *The Octopus*, ed. Kenneth S. Lynn (Boston: Houghton Mifflin, 1958), p. 298. Subsequent quotations are from this edition.

5. Once again we must turn to Garland's "Under The Lion's Paw" where Steve Council explains to Haskins why he has so magnanimously chosen to help him. Council relates at the close of section II that his kind of "religion" involves one principle: helping fellow men in dire straits. Norris, of course, expands upon the point and Garland does not, the consequence being the more positive thematic thrust of *The Octopus*.

6. That Presley "learns" from Cedarquist, Shelgrim, Vanamee and even Caraher but never makes use of the impressive truth revealed in Annixter's actions and words suggests that Norris was reserving him for the ignominious function he would perform at the conclusion of *The Octopus*.

7. That is, as I have suggested in "Frank Norris: A Biographical Essay" (*American Literary Realism*, 11 [1978], 219–34), Norris had become remarkably more "conventional" a person after his final flirtation with extremes in *A Man's Woman*. He soon began holding forth on the state of literature in the Boston *Evening Transcript*, the Chicago *American*, and *The Critic* as a solid citizen of the literary

world. The maturing power of serious love, reflected in *Blix* and *The Octopus*, together with career stability, seems to have finally taken him past a prolonged adolescence.

8. See Howells's 1893 introduction to the second edition of *Main-Travelled Roads*.

9. Book II, Canto XII. See my "Coventry Patmore's 'The Angel in the House': The Experience of Divine Love," *Cithara*, 10 (1970), 45–53, for an explanation of Patmore's views on nuptial love and an indication of the massive amount of attention that *The Angel* received.

It's When You Are Quiet That You Are At Your Best

Warren French*

The Pit (1903), Norris's last novel and second volume in the never-completed wheat trilogy, has had a curious history. Until recently, it was by far his most popular work. The original trade edition sold more than twice as many copies as those of all his previous novels combined, and *The Pit* was the first of his works to be made into a successful play and motion picture. Most critics, however, beginning with Dreiser who called it "a bastard bit of romance of the best seller variety," have regarded the novel as a distinct disappointment after *The Octopus*. Such a judgment may, however, only reveal the immaturity of the critic's taste, for the novel is more carefully thought out than its predecessor and is, in fact, the only work in which Norris shows promise of achieving intellectual maturity.

One advantage the author had in writing this novel is that in it—for the only time except in the lightweight *Blix*—he dealt with the kind of people among whom he had grown up and whom he knew best. At last he moves to the center of his stage the people like Cedarquist, whom he handled authoritatively but had relegated to a minor position in *The Octopus*. He also had the advantage of having severely disciplined himself while preparing to write this novel.

Mathematics had always been Norris's weak point, so that financial operations had been a mystery to him. Progressive educators would say—probably correctly—that he had never been adequately motivated to tackle the difficult, abstract subject. If he was to write convincingly of the operations of the wheat market, however, he had to understand something about them. Franklin Walker reports that George Moulson spent many evenings inducting Norris into the secrets of speculative finance with clever "teaching devices." The instruction paid off. If Norris had been equally assiduous in learning something about the construction

*Reprinted from *Frank Norris* (New York: Twayne Publishers, Inc., 1962), with the permission of Twayne Publishers, A Division of G. K. Hall & Co., Boston, and the author.

of long fiction, *The Pit* might be one of the most effective American novels. Because of the author's disdain for "style," however, the work is awkwardly patched together in a manner that obscures its "message." Even in this ungainly pile—something like the Jadwin mansion that plays a large role in it—we can, however, trace the outlines of the story Norris had so long been trying to tell of the struggles of the *nouveau riche* to understand themselves.

The novel is usually treated as the dramatic story of Curtis Jadwin's effort to corner the Chicago wheat market, based on the famous attempt in 1897 by Joseph Leiter. Actually, however, the story of the corner provides only background for understanding the critical episode in the education of Laura Dearborn Jadwin.

Laura is another girl like Blix and Lloyd Searight (*A Man's Woman*), for she, too, rebels against the petty restraints of a hidebound society. Born in a small Massachusetts town where the "New England spirit" prevails, this spirit appears to her "a veritable cult, a sort of religion, wherein the Old Maid was the priestess, the Spinster the officiating devotee, the thing worshipped the Great Unbeautiful, and the ritual unremitting, unrelenting Housework" (IX, 40).

When the neighbors begin to interfere actively in Laura's life, she flees to Chicago, where she finds three suitors. When one of them is too bold, she rejects them all; but Curtis Jadwin, a financier, will not be refused. Dazzled by the promise of the opulent life his wealth will make possible, Laura marries him; but the life of "conspicuous consumption" proves insufficient to hold the couple together. Bored, Jadwin—who had renounced speculation—begins to plot a corner of the wheat market. As he becomes more and more engrossed in his scheme, he drifts further and further from his wife. Laura, affronted, feels that he no longer thinks her beautiful and plans to run off with a doting artist, Sheldon Corthell. Jadwin's corner almost succeeds; but, encouraged by the rising prices the corner has produced, farmers plant heavily. Unusually favorable growing conditions result in a bumper crop that Jadwin cannot corner; again the Wheat has triumphed over man's selfish machinations. Ruined, Jadwin returns home on the night that Laura has agreed to run away with her lover; but she—seeing at last where her duty lies—chooses instead to go West with her husband to help him build a new life.

Ernest Marchand echoes the views of many critics, beginning with William Dean Howells, when he says that Laura's marital problems are "overprominent" in the novel. Charles Walcutt in *American Literary Naturalism* even goes so far as to say that "obviously, she is . . . merely a foil to set off the great struggles in the Pit." Yet although the Pit scenes are the most exciting in the book, far more of the story is devoted to

Laura's problems; it would be odd for a novelist to devote most of his book to a side issue. In "Norris and the Responsibility of the Novelist" (*South Atlantic Quarterly*, October, 1955) Charles G. Hoffmann soundly surmises that the love story is the central matter in the novel, but that its importance has been obscured by the expectation of a social message raised by *The Octopus* and by the stylistic effectiveness of the Wheat Pit scenes. He also wisely compares the book to *The Rise of Silas Lapham,* for which Norris has Curtis Jadwin express admiration. Hoffmann does not, however, treat in detail the evolution of Laura's attitude, and only by following her story closely can we see why the book reaches the conclusion it does.

Laura's troubles begin when her adventurous spirit is cramped by the decadent busybodies in her home town in New England. Her neighbors are suspicious of her because she belongs to the Episcopal rather than the Presbyterian church and employs servants, but the "crisis" comes when she travels alone to Boston to hear Modjeska in *Macbeth* and upon her return broaches the idea of acting herself:

> A group of lady-deaconesses, headed by the Presbyterian minister, called upon her, with some intention of reasoning and labouring with her.
>
> They got no farther than the statement of the cause of this visit. The spirit and temper of the South, that she had from her mother, flamed up in Laura at last, and the members of the "committee," before they were well aware, came to themselves in the street outside the front gate . . . all confounded and stunned by the violence of an outbreak of long-repressed emotion and long-restrained anger, that like an actual physical force had swept them out of the house (IX, 40–41).

Within a month, Laura leaves her home town for Chicago.

What Norris succeeds in doing in this novel that he had not before is to show the tremendous expense of spirit necessary to carry out such a rebellion. The stubborn pride that makes the gesture possible lingers on after the revolt has succeeded, in the form of excessive love of self and suspicion of others. Having struggled desperately to achieve individuality, Laura finds it difficult to assume a satisfactory role in society. She could easily have become a fanatic like Olive Chancellor in James's *The Bostonians*.

She shies away from marriage because she fears that, in the "pitiless" man's world of the turn of the century, she will lose through marriage the individuality that she has purchased at the price of exile from her home. Having escaped one oppressor—bigoted New England society—she is not anxious to submit to another. Yet, paradoxically, she is attracted to forceful men; in them she sees kindred spirits. Although Corthell, who designs stained-glass windows, would do her bidding, she cannot bring herself to love him: "The figure that held her imagination and her sympathy was not the artist, soft of hand and of speech, elaborating graces of sound, and colour and form, refined, sensitive, and temperamental; but the fighter, unknown and unknowable to woman as he was; hard, rigorous . . . conspicuous, formidable . . ." (IX, 60).

When one of her suitors kisses her without permission, she feels that her suspicion that men will exploit her is confirmed, and she decides to break with all who are courting her rather than tolerate indignities. Corthell, who takes her at her word, goes off to Europe; but Jadwin refuses to be put off. Spurned, he pursues her more assiduously than before. At last he wins her.

Laura is still not willing, however, to admit that she loves him. She is depressed that "love" is not so exciting and flattering to her vanity as she had hoped; she still thinks of love as based primarily on physical attractiveness. She has already had doubts about Jadwin because, although she prefers the fighter to the artist, she prefers the sensuous self-indulgence of the studio to the Sunday School that Jadwin teaches. In learning to look out for herself, Laura has lost interest in looking out for others.

Although an older married woman tells her that the kind of "love" she is looking for is "what you read about in trashy novels" (IX, 153), the young woman says that she is marrying Jadwin for what he can give her: "Think of it, the beautiful house, and servants, and carriages, and paintings, and, oh honey, how I will dress the part." Warned that she should not marry for "things," she scoffs, "I would marry a ragamuffin if he gave me all these things—gave them to me because he loved me" (IX, 161–62). In return she vaingloriously supposes that she is desirable because her "grand manner" becomes a wealthy hostess, who should be "respected," despite the fact that in actuality her manner "never helped her popularity" (IX, 164, 338).

She still thinks of love as a one-way street. When her sister asks if Laura loves Jadwin, she is told: " 'Indeed not. I love nobody. . . . I wouldn't give any man that much satisfaction. I think that is the way it ought to be. A man ought to love a woman more than she loves him. It ought to be enough for him if she lets him give her everything she wants in the world . . . it's her part, if she likes, to be cold and distant. That's my idea of love' " (IX, 159). She marries and, despite her fantastic egotism, things proceed smoothly for three years. The couple's energies are consumed in getting accustomed to living on the grand scale in the mansion Jadwin builds on fashionable North Avenue. That they are basically still small-town people is illustrated by Laura's aunt's bewildered speech when she sees the house: " '. . . it's all very fine, but, dear me, Laura, I hope you do pay for everything on the nail, don't run up any bills. I don't know what your dear father would say. . . . Thirty-three [electric lights, which she supposes "new-fangled" gas devices] in this one room alone. . . . I'd like to see your husband's face when he gets his gas bill' " (IX, 206).

Affluence, like independence, proves a strain upon a girl reared in a traditional, frugal community:

> For very long [Laura] found it difficult, even with all her resolution, with all her pleasure in her new-gained wealth, to adapt herself to a maner of living upon so vast a scale. She found herself continually planning the marketing for the next day, forgetting that this was now part of the housekeeper's duties. . . . She was afraid of the elevator and never really learned how to use the neat little system of telephones that connected the various parts of the house with the servants' quarters. For months her chiefest concern in her wonderful surroundings took the form of a dread of burglars (IX, 200-1).

There is something pathetic about these people with "too much, too soon" who are overwhelmed by wealth they had not been trained to enjoy. Norris's persistent fears of getting too far away from nature were probably largely inspired by the hot-house atmosphere in which he had been reared. Eventually, however, the Jadwins become acclimated to "conspicuous consumption." When they do, he gets bored with showing off the house and yearns for more excitement ("I just about know [the neighboring] park by heart . . . how would you like to go to Florida?" he asks Laura.) She succeeds in fitting herself into her new surroundings by exercising "a curious penchant toward melodrama," which enables her to act the part of "a great lady" with "all the superb condescension of her 'grand manner' " (IX, 202). She begins to think of herself as "two Laura Jadwins"—"one calm and even and steady," who "adored her husband, who delighted in Mr. Howells's novels, who adjured society and the formal conventions, who went to church every Sunday" and "the Laura of the 'grand manner,' who played the role of the great lady from room to room of her vast house . . . who was conscious and proud of her pale, stately beauty" (IX, 239–40).

Although Jadwin had promised to stop speculating, boredom drives him to begin again:

> "What are we fellows, who have made our money, to do? I've got to be busy. I can't sit down and twiddle my thumbs. And I don't believe in lounging around clubs, or playing with race

horses, or murdering game birds, or running some poor helpless fox to death. Speculating seems to be about the only game,
or the only business that's left open to me—that appears to be
legitimate. . . . It's fine fun" (IX, 221).

His rapid rise to success has not been accompanied by a corresponding intellectual development. Nor could Laura be the expected help to
him because, as Corthell points out when she indicates her fondness for
a painting by Norris's old master Bouguereau, her tastes are shallow.
She likes it, she says, "because it demands less" than others, "pleases you
because it satisfies you so easily" (IX, 235–36).

A later sentimental novelist would have straightened matters out by
hinting the approaching patter of tiny feet. Norris even intimates at one
place (IX, 190) that matters might have been improved if the Jadwins
had started a family; but, as William Dillingham points out, Norris is
still too much in the genteel tradition to discuss sexual problems openly.[1]
Although Norris mentions rape in *The Octopus*, he is as reluctant as
Howells to refer to the normal sexual intercourse of a married couple.

The breach between the couple widens. As Jadwin becomes more
and more obsessed with his effort to corner the wheat market, Laura
takes up various fads and even entertains Corthell in her private rooms.
She makes a desperate effort to win back her husband's devotion on her
own terms, for the idea of considering another's feelings is still as alien
to her as to most of Norris's characters. Supposing that lack of beauty
and glamour is her defect, she lures Jadwin to spend one evening at home
and entertains him not as "a calm wife" but as "a grand lady."

In one of the most effective evocations in any fiction of the garish
taste of the *nouveau riche*, Laura first appears before her husband costumed as the Emperor Justinian's consort Theodora and recites a passionate scene from Racine's *Athalie*. Then as Bizet's Carmen, "a red rose in
her black hair, castanets upon her fingers," she dances a passionate Bolero.
Jadwin simply finds what can only be described as his wife's attempt to
seduce him "sort of overwrought" and protests, "I like you best when
you are your old self, quiet, and calm, and dignified. It's when you are
quiet that you are at your best" (IX, 298). Still the country boy at heart,
he has too much respect for this elegant woman he has won to realize
that she may be more than another public showpiece.

But even the old, calm, quiet self fails to hold Jadwin when his
broker calls; although her husband maunders about the good, old, simple
life back on the farm, neither of the two Laura Jadwins can distract him
from the pit. Still convinced that American women lose their hold over
their husbands because they cease to fascinate them with superficial
beauty, Laura tries to win back Jadwin with an ultimatum that if he

loves her, he must spend her birthday, June 13, with her. But this is the day that Jadwin's attempt to corner the wheat reaches its climax.

Despite her high-handed tactics, Laura has had, even before the critical June day, a vague intimation of approaching disaster and has decided that "if anything happened to Curtis, her place was at his side" (IX, 337). Her resolution is, however, still not firm; and, when Jadwin fails to come home as promised one night, she is tempted to send for Corthell.

On her birthday Laura begins to see the light. Her sister Page, who has been an uncomprehending observer at the wheat pit that morning when Jadwin's corner collapsed, tells Laura that she has failed her husband because she does not care enough about his business: " 'Just think he may be fighting the battle of his life down there in La Salle Street, and you don't know anything about it—no, nor want to know. "What do you care about wheat," that's what you said. Well, I don't care either, just for the wheat itself, but it's [her fiance's] business, his work; and right or wrong . . . good or bad, I'd put my two hands into the fire to help him' " (IX, 383). At first Laura is simply angry, thinking "even if he had been very busy, this was her birthday. . . . She had known the humiliation of a woman neglected. But it was to end now; her pride would never again be lowered, her love never again be ignored" (IX, 385–86). Afterwards, however, she begins to have misgivings:

> Was it—after all—Love, that she cherished and strove for—love or self-love? . . . Was this, after all, the right way to win her husband to her—this display of her beauty, this parade of dress, this exploitation of self? . . . Had she been selfish from the very first? . . . Dimly Laura Jadwin began to see and to understand a whole new conception of her little world. . . . She had been accustomed to tell herself that there were two Lauras. Now suddenly, behold, she seemed to recognize a third—a third that rose above and forgot the other two, that in some beautiful, mysterious way was identity ignoring self (IX, 387–88).

Although the language is overblown, Norris is attempting to describe Laura as a person who has risen above selfish considerations and learned to love another well enough to put the other's interests before her own. The transformation of Laura's personality, however, is not unbelievably abrupt. Despite her dawning realization of what selfless love is, she still wishes to hold her husband to her demand that he spend this night with her. He fails to appear, and Corthell arrives instead. In a last fit of self-pity, Laura pleads that the artist make her love him and forget all that has happened. They agree to run away together the next night.

No sooner has Corthell gone, however, than Jadwin appears "his eyes sunken deep in his head, his face dead white, his hand shaking." As they sit close together, "groping in the darkness," she hears the newsboys crying, "Extra . . . all about the Failure of Curtis Jadwin!" (IX, 394–95). Instead of running off with Corthell, Laura sells her property and goes west to start a new life with her husband, who tells her that "we both have been living according to a wrong notion of things" (IX, 400).

Jadwin's false notion is more apparent and has often been discussed. His attempted corner succeeds as long as his manipulations do not boost the price above what wheat is actually worth; but his troubles begin when he reckons without the forces of nature and, driven by the same kind of self-love that makes Laura wretched, begins to scoff at expert reports of a bumper crop and to feel that he can drive wheat to the abnormally high price of two dollars a bushel.

He rationalizes his folly by telling his wife. "I corner the wheat! Great heavens, it is the wheat that has cornered me. The corner made itself. I happened to stand between two sets of circumstances, and they made me do what I've done" (IX, 270). Obviously, though, he is using this deterministic argument (as Norris himself was likely to use talk of "forces") to avoid accepting the responsibility for his personal vanity and "wrong notions." Although it is sheer volume of wheat flowing into the market that breaks Jadwin's corner, he would never have gotten into trouble if he had stayed home in bed.

Although *The Pit* contains one passage, which—like the end of *The Octopus*—talks about the wheat "obeying" laws of supply and demand (IX, 358), Norris, by the time he wrote his last novel, was ceasing to rely upon the notion that man was a passive agent helpless in the hands of the vast impersonal forces of nature. He offers, through the broker Gretry, the explanation—much more convincing than Jadwin's—that the speculator "put wheat so high, that all the farmers planted it, and are getting ready to dump it on us" (IX, 353). How Jadwin has literally been driven mad by his infatuation with speculation is evident from his physical attack on the faithful but cautious Gretry for "selling out."

The title of *The Pit* is not often recognized as having a double meaning. Besides referring to the room where wheat trades are consummated and around which much of the action of the novel whirls, it refers also to the abyss that Norris has spoken of as early as *Vandover*—the pit toward which people are hurled as the indulgence of their self-love causes them to attempt to thwart what the novelist calls "the resistless forces of nature." Both Jadwins head for this pit; the husband topples over; but, as more convincing evidence of Norris's theory that good comes out of evil than he had been able to provide in *The Octopus*, the wife hears the news of the husband's disaster just in time to prevent her from following his course to a disastrous end. Ernest Marchand is unfair when he calls the end of the novel "anti-climatic, too trivial"; it is the climax that Norris has been building up to from the beginning—the wheat corner entered halfway through the action—and is trivial only if domestic relations are less consequential than business deals.

Norris accomplishes his purpose in *The Pit* without recourse to the mystical trappings and remarkable coincidences of *The Octopus*. There is an occasional mention of a "sixth sense," but generally Norris uses the term in this novel only as a metaphor to describe Jadwin's knack for correctly evaluating situations until his lust for power blinds him.

Because the characters and events are convincingly human—drawn from observation rather than myth—*The Pit* is the only one of Norris's novels that can be read enjoyably today except as a period piece. Although it preserves a splendid picture of the *nouveau riche* of the period (excellently illustrating what Veblen meant by "conspicuous consumption"), the preservation of a vanished mode of life is not the principal justification for reading it today.

Norris in most of his novels approaches his ideas about universal principles of good behavior through specific problems that have either diminished in significance (*The Octopus, A Man's Woman*), or that he was not equipped to understand (*Vandover, McTeague*). In *The Pit*, however, he deals with people he knows well (there are remarkable superficial resemblances between his parents and the Jadwins) and with problems that are still urgent. Ernest Marchand points out that the Jadwin story is essentially an anti-gambling tract. Although the regulations of the Securities and Exchange Commission have largely eliminated utterly irresponsible speculation, the gambling instinct and the over-confidence bred of temporary success are related problems that are not only still with us in everything from personal to international relations, but that probably always will be with us.

The increasing flow of fictional and factual writing about marital dissatisfaction and the discord resulting from self-love and self-indulgence also shows that these problems are constantly looming larger or are more frequently recognized than before. While writing his last novel, Norris seems to have realized at last that appealing as the desire to return to a kind of unconscious, uncivilized life might be, it was wishful thinking. Only at the end of his short life does this man who is often classified as a naturalist seem to have absorbed the basic premise of scientific thought—that any program for reform must begin with a dispassionate acceptance, not an emotional rejection, of things as they are found. Jadwin's unsound intuitions about the wheat suggest that Norris may even have begun to distrust "feelings."

We wonder if Norris may have been conscious of the extent to which Laura Jadwin's problems paralleled his own. Like her, he had been torn at the beginning of his career between a concept of art as something detached from life (which led to his absorption in the Middle Ages) and the magnetic attraction of the street (which accounts for his fascination with the McTeagues). Like her, he decided in favor of the street; but still he was repelled at the same time he was fascinated.

His attempts to court the favor of the "street" led only to a pulp adventure like *Moran,* and Norris may have recorded, through the story of Overbeck's seduction by the "literary women" in his short story "Dying Fires," an experience like Laura's temptation to give up Jadwin and run away with Corthell. Certainly the small success of Norris's efforts to write for the "street" and to share his views about the proper relationship between man and woman must have distressed him as much as Laura's failure to reclaim Jadwin from the Wheat Pit.

Whatever unidentified spark ignited his desire to write the Epic of the Wheat led him back, however, to his concept of the novelist's responsibility. Possibly his shocked reaction to the dreadful sights he had seen while a war correspondent in Cuba awakened him to the need to try to get back on the "right track," the "natural course." Possibly his marrying and becoming a father awoke a sense of mature responsibility.

Whatever happened, *The Pit* seems more genuinely the result of intensive self-analysis than any of Norris's earlier novels. Although this last novel is less immediately gripping than *McTeague* or *The Octopus,* it is a more notable achievement because Norris, while writing it, appears for the first time to have been really conscious of the precise implications of his story. It is also to *The Pit's* credit that it has been the most often misunderstood of Norris's novels, since the more searchingly a book probes the motivations underlying human behavior, the less likely it is to yield its secrets to superficial readers. Like Laura Jadwin, Norris— despite his penchant for melodrama—was at his best in his quiet moments when he promised to become an author who would explore rather than merely denounce the problems of urbanized society.

Note

1. William B. Dillingham, "Frank Norris and the Genteel Tradition," *Tennessee Studies in Literature,* 5 (1960), 15–24. Jadwin still cannot discuss anything about his relations with his wife with others. His attitude is that of the embarrassed juvenile in "The Opinions of Leander" (*Frank Norris of "The Wave": Stories and Sketches from the San Francisco Weekly, 1893 to 1897* [San Francisco: The Westgate Press, 1931], pp. 220–250). As his inability to stop speculating also shows, although he is a "self-made man," he is still emotionally adolescent.

[Eroticism in *The Pit*]

Joseph Katz*

It astonishes critics to discover that *The Pit*, Frank Norris's last novel, was a bestseller almost immediately: it sold 100,000 copies during its first year of publication in America alone. Their astonishment comes from the reasoned conviction—shared without exception—that the novel splits apart. The consensus is that Norris muddles the novel by intruding Laura, Curtis Jadwin's younger wife, into the story of Jadwin's monomaniacal attempt to corner wheat:

> She is both important and unimportant. Though she seems real enough at times, her character is nevertheless intellectually rather than emotionally apprehended. One feels that Norris thinks of new things to do with her as he proceeds with the story: he makes dialectical discoveries of ways to write pages of reasoning about how she should feel and act at particular times. These reasoned pages do not make her come to life. Her whole role, to be sure, is vitiated by the supreme importance of Jadwin's fight over the wheat. Obviously, she is there merely as a foil to set off the great struggle in the Pit, to show the other side of Jadwin's public failure. Thus the story breaks completely in two when Norris devotes considerable time to her connection with Sheldon Corthell, the understanding artist to whom she goes for comfort when Jadwin is deserting her more and more for the Pit.[1]

In fact, Laura Dearborn Jadwin goes to Corthell for much more than "comfort"—and receives it.

Norris began *The Pit* as the story of Laura, not of Jadwin. "*She occupies the center of the stage all the time*," he wrote to an acquaintance at the end of the novel's planning stage, "and I shall try to interest the reader more in her character and career than in any other human element in the book. The two main themes, consequently, are the story of Jad-

*Reprinted from Joseph Katz, "Eroticism in American Literary Realism," *Studies in American Fiction*, 5 (Spring 1977), 35–50, by permission of *Studies in American Fiction*.

win's corner in May wheat and the story of his wife's 'affair' with Corthell."[2] This is not an occasion appropriate to explicating any one work
in detail, even a novel that has been generally misunderstood by modern
critics. But *The Pit* offers so good an example of the ways in which a
realist not only could treat erotic materials successfully, but also could
use them as integral in an extensive work of fiction, that it does deserve
consideration as a specimen for analysis.

To be fair, there are good reasons for misreading *The Pit*. One is
that it was the second volume in Norris's Trilogy of The Epic of the
Wheat, preceded by *The Octopus* and to be succeeded by the never-
written *The Wolf*. This setting seems to imply a focus on the wheat.
Norris, however, was doing something quite different: he was focussing
on people whose lives were affected by attempts to manipulate the wheat
for industrial purposes. "These novels," he said in a brief preface to *The
Pit*, "while forming a series, will in no way be connected with each other
save only in their relation to (1) the production, (2) the distribution,
(3) the consumption of American wheat." Read *The Pit* as emphasizing
Curtis Jadwin's failed attempt to corner the wheat market—the distribution of wheat—and the novel is indeed a failure for just the reason
critics have offered. In that reading, Laura Dearborn Jadwin's story is
superfluous.

But *The Pit* is a much more complex and carefully wrought novel
than it seems to be for modern critics. Of course it is partly the story of
Jadwin's failed corner. Mainly, however, it is an exploration of development in a woman with great beauty who has limited capacities in most
other areas of life. Laura is ill-educated, egocentric, and without real
understanding of her own sexuality or its effects on others. Drawn into
marriage with Jadwin almost by whim, therefore, she is unable to make—
or even to understand the need to make—the loving compromises that
define marriage. *The Pit* is the story of an illumination, an awakening,
and like all of Norris's novels its direction is to support middle class
values. Extremes of any kind are intolerable to that value system. So,
like novelists in the mainstream from Jane Austen on, Norris takes his
characters to the extremes in order to bring them back to the middle
way. The title of his novel is important. It refers literally to the floor of the
wheat exchange, on which men manipulate the grain for their own advantage. Metaphorically, it is a reference to an arena in which beasts tear one
another apart for sport. And allegorically it evokes the place to which
sinners are relegated.

Most of this will appear to be critical hocus-pocus to the reader who
does not recognize the explicit sexual aspects of the novel. Laura is
introduced in the first chapter as a beautiful, strong-willed young woman

who waits impatiently with her sister Page and their Aunt Wess' for their hosts to arrive so that she can see her first opera. When she hears the opera begin and they still have not appeared, she boldly introduces herself to Jadwin (whom she had not met, but who she knew was one of the party) and asks him to help. While Laura intentionally makes him feel awkward in punishment for his initial reserve at being accosted by a strange woman in a public place, the rest arrive. Among them is Sheldon Corthell, the comfortably-fixed artist who had been wooing her. He had sent her flowers for the evening; not seeing one on her cape, he asks if she did not like them. She replies that she selected the most beautiful, parts her cape, and shows him the rose pinned to her gown. By the time the group hustles to their box, the first aria of the second act is just finished. "She'll sing it over again, though, just for you, if I have to lead the applause myself," Corthell says. "I particularly wanted you to hear that."

All commentators have acknowledged that first chapter of *The Pit* as a *tour de force*. Always behind the social intercourse and the music of the opera are rumblings about the failure of a wheat corner, presaging what will happen to Jadwin later. But more—much more—is happening. Again, Norris is qualifying his readers. Everyone recognizes that Corthell is courting Laura. Neither The Iron Madonna nor The Young Girl would be repelled by a good love story; romance, in fact, was what they wanted —so long as it did not involve the bedroom. They could find such good, clean romance in *The Pit*. More sophisticated readers, however, would recognize the bounty of literary, musical, pictorial, and mythological symbols with which Norris develops the erotic context in which everything else is to be interpreted. The affair did indeed involve the bedroom. So textured is the novel with this erotic motif that is its base, that it is impossible here to work through its full development and effect. All that is possible are some slight indications.

The opera that Laura hears is Gounod's *Faust*, by Norris's time a cliché. There is no doubt about the identification: in one of the few surviving pages of the novel's manuscript—the first page—he had originally written the title, then canceled it and substituted the words "one of the most popular pieces of its repertoire" (referring to the opera company). The cancellation presumably resulted in part from the technique of qualification; mostly, however, the knowledgable reader of Norris's day could have been counted upon to recognize the opera from his burlesque of it and from clues such as two different libretti being intermixed on stage. For such a reader, interesting things happen in the first chapter.

Corthell's gift of flowers to Laura, for example, reveals both his intentions and her inability to understand them clearly. He particularly wanted her to hear the first aria in the second act because it is "Faites-lui mes aveux," Seibel's plea that his flowers speak his love for Margarita. Corthell evidently wanted Laura to make the connection, but she does not because she had been tutored only to read French, not to converse in it. Her entire education, in fact, had been deficient. But Corthell's miscalculation is just that. He accurately recognizes Laura's smoldering sexuality. Although she has little idea of what really is going on in the opera, its music and embraces stir her. She herself does not identify her capacity for sexual passion, but Corthell does.

When the marriage between Laura and Jadwin begins to disintegrate, Corthell is there patiently educating her. He teaches her the nature of better painting, literature, and music than she knew before; simultaneously, he cultivates her passions with music like Lizst's *Mephisto Waltz* and conversations about subjects that allude to erotic love, even evoking such figures of feminine sexuality as Phedre and Isolde. In chapter 8, Laura's marriage completely breaks down. Jadwin is so caught up in the pit that he neglects her almost entirely. Despite repeated direct requests that he spend particular evenings with her, he absents himself on business. "Let those who neglected her look to it," she finally declares, considering adultery. That is in her mind one evening when Jadwin is away and Corthell calls. Past visits had been spent in the formal rooms of the house; now she impulsively invites him into her sitting-room, the room off her bedroom that is considered her next most personal and intimate room. There, after a few moments in harmless conversation, she begins to tell Corthell her loneliness, unhappiness, and need for love. His response is to offer her himself. Laura immediately changes the subject, but neither eases him out of the room nor rejects his offer. She is taking time to consider it. With his invariable tact and patience, and his instinctive understanding of her emotions, Corthell participates in the change of subject and waits. Laura invites him to smoke and points him towards matches.

> But Corthell, as he lit his cigarette, produced his own match box. It was a curious bit of antique silver, which he had bought in a Viennese pawnshop, heart-shaped and topped with a small ducal coronet of worn gold. On one side he had caused his name to be engraved in small script. Now, as Laura admired it, he held it towards her.
>
> "An old pouncet-box, I believe," he informed her, or possibly it held an ointment for her finger nails." He spilled the matches into his hand. "You see the red stain still on the inside; and—smell," he added, as she took it from him. "Even the odour

of the sulphur matches cannot smother the quaint old perfume, distilled perhaps three centuries ago."

An hour later Corthell left her. She did not follow him further than the threshold of the room, but let him find his way to the front door alone.[3]

They had had sexual intercourse.

Neither the Iron Madonna nor The Young Girl would understand what happened during the intervening hour between the time Laura accepted the box and the time Corthell left, but any reader of the day capable of accepting the situation unshocked would know it. Norris had carefully developed the episode not only through readily-available cultural symbols, but also through symbols internal to the novel which link its elements together. The shape of the matchbox and the blended odors of sulphur and perfume function obviously enough. What does require noting, in this summary, is a passage in the first chapter that ties the ducal coronet and Corthell's signature. Aunt Wess', more puzzled than Laura by the opera, does not at all understand what is going on between Faust and Margarita at the end of the third act, just before Valentine enters to be slain. She asks about "the gentleman with the beard"—Faust. " 'Why, that's the duke, don't you see, Aunt Wess'?' " Laura explains, wrongly. A few days after Laura's episode with Corthell, Jadwin begins to feel that all is not well. He comes to her, looking odd enough for her to enquire about his health. " 'Sick?' he queried. 'No indeed. But—I'll tell you. Since a few days I've had,' he put his fingers to his forehead between his eyes, 'I've had a queer sensation right there. . . .' " The allusion is to the cuckhold's horns. But by the end of the novel both Laura and Jadwin had risen from their respective pits, obviously battered by their experiences but just as obviously determined to make their marriage work. Laura dismissed Corthell, Jadwin lost his fortune, and they are waiting for the movers to take them to a more modest house that would become a home. While they wait, Laura asks if Jadwin would like to hear a letter that had arrived from her sister Page and which Laura herself had not had time to completely read. There are things in the letter that recall painful parts of the past, but Jadwin asks her to continue. The most painful reference comes in a postscript—a reference to Corthell. Laura quickly puts the letter away. Jadwin covers her awkwardness by feigning vagueness about Corthell. "I told you—told you all about it," she responds. Jadwin replies that his only memory is that he himself had been to blame for everything: "I told you once—long ago—that I understood." Certainly, *The Pit* is concerned with Jadwin's failure to corner the wheat. But its real concerns are far larger than only that.[4]

Notes

1. Charles Child Walcutt, *American Literary Naturalism, A Divided Stream* (Minneapolis; University of Minnesota Press, 1956), pp. 153–154. But any modern critic of the novel could have been cited as well. Walcutt is representative of the consensus.

2. Norris to I. F. Marcosson, [November, 1901]; in Donald Pizer, "Ten Letters by Frank Norris," Book Club of California *Quarterly News-letter*, 27 (Summer 1962), 59–60.

3. *The Pit* (New York: Doubleday, Page, 1902), p. 267.

4. Ed. Note: Portions of the essay dealing with Realism and other Realistic authors have been omitted here.

The Naturalism of
Vandover and the Brute

Charles Child Walcutt°

Frank Norris's *Vandover and the Brute* was written for Professor Gates's composition class at Harvard in 1894–95. It was Norris's first long work and an attempt to imitate the method of the French naturalists with a particularly naturalistic subject—the destruction of an individual by a degenerative disease. *Vandover* has not the scope of *The Octopus* or the primordial violence of *McTeague*, but it contains some of Norris's most effective writing; it has, indeed, been considered his most memorable work. It stands at the opposite end of the scale of naturalistic motifs from novels dealing with the broad external workings of social and economic forces. Here the forces are internal and physiological; the book purports to be a "clinical" study of a disease.

The novelist's reason for dealing with a mental disease would seem to be his enthusiasm for science. He would, perhaps, be inspired by the experimental zeal which Zola described, the desire to show in detail how certain psychoneurotic manifestations could be clinically diagnosed and systematically presented—subjected to the clear light of knowledge so that man would know for at least one malady whether he had germs or "lesions" to cope with. This would, then, be a factual scientific report, rich with information vital to human welfare. Its interest would depend upon the new subject matter and the reader's roused zeal for human betterment. This hypothetical description, with its implication that the facts of the case will be scientifically related and established, leaves no place for an unpredictable element like the free human will. A disease is strictly physical; it is a problem in material causes and effects. Spiritual values, morality, or personal struggle would not seem to be relevant to an understanding of it.

Vandover is the son of a prosperous San Francisco businessman. He

°Reprinted from *Forms of Modern Fiction*, edited by William Van O'Conner (Minneapolis: University of Minnesota Press, 1948), pp. 254–68, by permission of the author. This essay also appears in the author's *American Literary Naturalism, A Divided Stream* (Minneapolis: University of Minnesota Press, 1956). The first half of the essay, which deals with the origins of Naturalism, is omitted here.

is a painter, but he neglects his art. "Vandover was self-indulgent—he loved these sensuous pleasures, he loved to eat good things, he loved to be warm, he loved to sleep. He hated to be bored and worried—he liked to have a good time." His disintegration begins when a girl he has seduced commits suicide in terror at the prospect of having an illegitimate child. Next his father, weakened by the shock of Vandover's deed, dies. When the reason for the girl's suicide becomes known, Vandover is socially ostracized and loses the love of Turner Ravis, a fine girl who had been a powerful influence for good in his life. After his father's death, his income is greatly curtailed. At this point Vandover resolves to reform, and throws himself into his painting with furious energy. But too late. The disease, lycanthropy, first appears in a terrifying scene when he finds that he can no longer paint, that his hand will not reproduce the image in his mind; and thereafter his descent is rapid and inexorable. The dead girl's father sues him for a large sum. One of his friends, on the pretext of "handling" the case out of court, cheats him of money and property. What is left from the sale of his father's house Vandover squanders in reckless gambling and debauchery, his unnatural life punctuated by attacks of lycanthropy, during which he creeps about naked on all fours, snarling and yapping like a wolf. Finally he is living from hand to mouth, dirty, unkempt, estranged from friends, sometimes near starvation—a hopeless wreck. The story ends with a pitiful scene in which Vandover is cleaning a filthy kitchen for the friend who had defrauded him.

An appearance of factual reality is created by the method Norris employs. The style and tone of *Vandover* suit the commonplace unromantic people and setting of the story admirably. Details of Vandover's life and activity are accumulated with meticulous and dispassionate thoroughness. This was a new note in American letters. The quantity and "meanness" of the detail, with the objective tone, give the effect of authentic "documentation" in the best naturalistic tradition. We are shown, step by step, how "In his idleness he grew to have small and petty ways. . . . It became a fad with him to do without matches, using as a substitute 'lights,' tapers of twisted paper to be ignited at the famous stove. He found amusement for two days in twisting and rolling these 'lights,' cutting frills in the larger ends with a pair of scissors, and stacking them afterward in a Chinese flower jar he had bought for the purpose and stood on top of the bookcases. The lights were admirably made and looked very pretty. When he had done he counted them. He had made two hundred exactly. What a coincidence!"

Structurally, the novel is not "well-made" or dramatic, in the sense of being organized around a conflict between free moral agents. Instead

Norris has conformed his structure to the steady and "inevitable" disintegration of Vandover under a succession of blows from forces over which he has no control. In one passage Norris announces a deterministic philosophy very explicitly. It is when Vandover, after his first attack of the disease, prays for help:

> There was no answer, nothing but the deaf silence, the blind darkness . . . there was nothing for him. Even that vast mysterious power to which he had cried *could* not help him now, could not help him, could not stay the inexorable law of nature, could not reverse that vast terrible engine with its myriad spinning wheels that was riding him down relentless, grinding him into the dust.

There is no climactic choice in the story; it moves evenly on a chain of circumstances.

These elements of style, tone, documentation, structure, and explicit determinism constitute the naturalism of *Vandover and the Brute*. But they do not really account for the novel. In spite of its explicit determinism, the conflict in this novel is a thoroughly moral one. It is a conflict between Vandover's free and responsible spirit and a series of circumstantial influences (the disease is merely one of several) which win out over him largely because of his *culpable* moral weakness. Examination reveals (1) that Vandover is morally responsible for his downfall, (2) that the forces which thrust him down are circumstantial rather than inevitable, and (3) that the novel has the form and effect of a tragedy. It appears, also, that the tragic effect would have been stronger if Norris had not allowed so much moral condemnation to intrude; if, that is, he had held to a more rigorous determinism!

The tone of moral judgment appears in passages like the following, where Vandover broods on his decline:

> And with the eyes of this better self he saw again . . . the eternal struggle between good and evil that had been going on within him since his very earliest years. He was sure that at the first the good had been the strongest. Little by little the brute had grown, and he . . . luxurious, self-indulgent . . . had shut his ears to the voices that shouted warnings of the danger, and had allowed the brute to thrive and to grow, its abominable famine gorged from the store of that in him which he felt to be the purest, the cleanest . . . [pp. 214–15].

Again:

> It was gone—his art was gone, the one thing that could

save him. That, too, like all the other good things of his life, he had destroyed [p. 229].

And:

It was the punishment that he had brought upon himself, some fearful nervous disease, the result of his long indulgence in vice, his vile submission to the brute that was to destroy his reason . . . till he should have reached the last stages of idiocy [p. 243].

Although these passages are presented as Vandover's thought, they come as auctorial comment also, for it is clear that Norris's attitude is represented in these and many other passages like them. One is reminded of Milton's

But, when lust
By unchaste looks, loose gestures, and foul talk,
But most by lewd and lavish acts of sin,
Lets in defilement to the inward parts,
The soul grows clotted by contagion,
Imbodies, and imbrutes, till she quite lose
The divine property of her first being.

Far from illustrating the operation of determinism, Vandover's degradation is presented as the result of some internal failure which *allows* the brutish side to grow and thrust out the good. Vandover's moral responsibility depends on his being a person of intelligence and social position; regardless of the author's intention, the naturalistic approach is disrupted because the human being is more important, more intimately known, and therefore more credible than the forces which supposedly dominate him.

There is no established set of forces, either hereditary or environmental, which can bring about his degeneration in such a way that it appears to be inevitable. Vandover is not shown to inherit qualities from his parents that would make him subject to lycanthropy. He does not move in a society that is notable for the pressure it exerts upon its members. He is free from the sort of influences that obtain in industrial areas, or among the poorer classes anywhere. In all these respects he is free from the forces which can be shown, even in the contrived simplicity of the novel, to have shaped a character or bent it toward an unalterable end. Thus the bars which prevent the invasion of his beast must be withdrawn by Chance, that is, by pressures which are not presented as an inescapable part of the milieu; and half of the book is devoted to the impact of various kinds of chance upon him. There is nothing typical, nothing that might contribute to the science of sociology in the course by which he is destroyed. At any time Vandover might take a turn for the better. The events which thrust him down are more coincidental than the acts of fate that destroy some of Hardy's characters. But nevertheless they are presented with such a wealth of convincing detail that the average reader accepts them as probable.

It appears, then, that the Beast—the disease—is an internal and adventitious factor like the suicide of the girl or the swindle by the friend. The disease is not studied for its own sake. Vandover does not become a mere organism subjected to clinical examination. The shred of manhood, of free will, that he retains is always at the focal point of attention. The question is not what new form will the disease take, or what does one learn from the data about its growth and operation, but what is the last tiny bit of conscious individuality thinking and feeling and suffering as it approaches the moment of final extinction. The reader's attention is not fixed by the progress of the disease but by wonder and pity at the fact that the human spark continues so long to survive and so to suffer.

The conflict, then, is between a free but fallible individual and a fatal but indefinable enemy. We never see the operation of "That vast terrible engine with its myriad spinning wheels." What we see is a real young man with a well-developed personality and a whole set of convincing mannerisms, who succumbs because of the impact of circumstances upon him—and not the least of these circumstances is the disease lycanthropy, for it is not "scientifically" traced to a source or accounted for. Chance, of course, does not exist in the theory of naturalism. When it appears we know that another frame of reference has been introduced, whether intentionally or not.

There are two extreme points of view which produce inferior art. One extreme is the belief in pure mechanistic determinism. When this attitude is "pure," it is expressed in scientific reports dealing perhaps with pathological or physiological disturbances of the human organism. The "person" being described or examined does not, for the purposes of the report, exist. He is merely a certain amount of tissue, part of which is isolated as a breeding ground for germs or tumors. In pure science, this attitude may be essential for the study of diseases *per se*, although even scientists are not so sure as they were fifty years ago that a disease is anything *per se*, apart, that is, from the nature of the organism in which it lives. The same impersonal attitude is pure in statistical studies of social trends, and it is perhaps approximated in sociological reports. It is doubtful whether it can be anywhere near pure in a work of fiction. Employed by a very cynical writer who despised the human race and delighted to portray the helpless wrigglings of men impaled on the pins of Fate, it would in effect be an assertion of the writer's superiority and spiritual independence. If it were free of such ironic overtones, it would produce a dismal and boring novel with little or no feeling for the dignity of man.

At the other extreme, there is plenty of fiction which fatuously assumes that nature is benign and man is perfectly in tune with it and with himself. From this view come novels which present an easy universe where justice is always done, evil punished (but merely for the delight and beatitude of the Good), and ambitions fulfilled. It is the world of easy pleasure, happy people, and barren complacency. It is a moral world, constructed entirely for the protection of little men. Its perfect "artistic" expression is Hollywood's doctrine of the unique temptation, according to which one has to resist evil only once in order to be forever blessed. Because this sort of thinking cannot or will not acknowledge the power and unpredictability of nature, it can have no true sense of the dignity of man.

Between these extremes moves the tragic view, which under-estimates neither man nor the forces against which he contends. The greatest men face the greatest oppositions and suffer most greatly; therein lies the grandeur of the Greek and Shakespearian tragedy—and all great tragic artists show man rising to greatness as he pits himself against forces over which he can never triumph. To acknowledge the might of these forces while not losing faith in the men who challenge them is to possess the tragic view of life.

Vandover and the Brute is in this tragic area. The hero, an ordinary attractive young man, is caught and crushed—not in the "vast terrible engine" that Norris describes, but by social and personal forces which twentieth-century man knows all too well. In so far as he *blames* Vandover for *moral* weakness, Norris moves toward the pole of fatuity, for by doing so he assumes that a moral man would avoid conflict with the moral order. In so far as he talks about the vast terrible engine, Norris moves toward the pole of inhuman mechanism. But in reality the effect of his novel is between these extremes, if only because the reader is pulled in both directions. Vandover is accepted for what he is—not judged—and the reader, I believe, identifies himself with the struggling spirit of the protagonist *as well as* with the social and personal evil which destroys him. The tragic conflict is within the individual and also between him and the society which is composed of the fallible wills of all individuals.

A bold and massive array of external forces demands a corresponding grandeur in the characters who struggle against them. This is Shakespeare's pattern, but it is not so descriptive of the modern dilemma. Instead of man against the cosmos, we now have society against man, which is to say, mankind against mankind. The tragic struggle in *An American Tragedy* and *Studs Lonigan* is similarly conceived. Clyde Griffiths and Studs are modern man, ruined in the milieu which modern man has made, and the reader participates in the tragic *agon,* aware of the dangerous forces within himself; yet in a manner somewhat different from that of the spectator of a Shakespearian tragedy, for the terrible forces against which Shakespeare's heroes contend are viewed with awe and wonder and fear; not only are they unconquerable, they are indeed beyond man's power of comprehension. The catharsis of pity and terror is to be reached *only* through art. The modern tragedy locates the opposing forces in society and the nature of man, where they are not quite so terrible. It is true that the "nature of man" could appear as mysterious and ungovernable as an unknowable Fate, but the fact is that social institutions do appear, in these novels of Dreiser and Farrell, to be subject, however tenuously, to the will and knowledge of man. Hence the conflict they present cannot be as grand as Shakespeare's. The idea of progress, the necessity for social action, creep into these modern tragedies and offer an alternative or added release for the emotions which Shakespeare purges through pity and terror alone. The modern tragedy thus unconsciously presents two orders of symbolic action: One shows man struggling with Fate and his own nature. The other "attacks" the social order as the embodiment of injustice and heedlessness.

Vandover and the Brute is a modern tragedy in a minor and imperfect key. If the book had been more exhaustively "naturalistic," it would have shown more fully the nature of the social (that is, human) forces that destroy the hero—and there would have been correspondingly less need to impose a Sunday school moral censure upon him. Thus the weakness of *Vandover* shows very clearly the potential strength of naturalism as a foundation for tragedy—so long as it is not carried to a point of diminishing returns in lifeless mechanism. In short, so long as it is essentially transcendental naturalism will give full recognition to the power and immensity of the physical world but will also assume a meaning in it that is akin to and ideally accessible to the mind of man; so that man achieves tragic dignity as he strives to penetrate and master his own nature and the physical universe which repeats the tension of actual and potential, real and ideal, fate and will, evil and good, and matter and spirit, that is in the nature of man. Seen in this light, naturalism is no revolutionary departure from the world view of Shakespearian tragedy. It is rather a mode of presenting in realistic "modern" terms the forces, microcosmic and macrocosmic, against which man has always tragically contended. Naturalism is the modern approach to Fate. It is more hopeful in that it suggests rational means of coping with Fate;

if it is "pessimistic" it is so only because it has to accord less dignity to man. When it is confused it is so because the polar attractions of mechanism and social action draw it away, in one direction or the other, from the tragic center.

Frank Norris's *Vandover and the Brute*: Narrative Technique and the Socio-Critical Viewpoint

Joseph R. McElrath, Jr.[*]

The value of critical codifications such as Romanticism and Naturalism is that they provide a shorthand with which to quickly enter into discussion of complicated cultural phases and their modes of expression. At best, they can be very helpful in initiating critical analysis. But obvious problems attend their use. One is that because of their necessarily reductive character, they imply a norm that may never have existed in actuality. Another is that those codifications inevitably produce rigidity in critical outlook; the codifications assume the characteristics of "certainties" and eventually enjoy the status of dogma with the passing of time. A case in point is to be seen in Frank Norris studies, where the apparent legitimacy of particular, time-honored codifications has stultified critical inquiry. Norris was a Realist-Naturalist; Norris was a literary and philosophic Romantic; Norris was a melodramatic, conventional-minded moralist. These are the three major views—though one hastens to add that the categories are not exclusive of each other, as may be seen in the available body of criticism on *Vandover and the Brute*.

The majority opinion is that *Vandover* is a Naturalistic work melodramatically expressed by a mind that never freed itself from the nineteenth-century genteel morality or the style of popular romance literature. The verdict is not unanimous, of course. But this interpretation has proven a comfortable one for many, who can label the plot and setting Naturalistic, the style Romantic, and the theme moralistic in the traditional Judaeo-Christian sense. Pretty much the same has been done to all of Norris's novels, and the end result is the same: classification on the critics' terms, not Norris's.

It works, almost. And the "almost" in the case of novels like *Moran, McTeague, The Pit,* and especially *The Octopus,* concerns the matters of point of view and narrative technique. Norris's perspective frequently

[*]Reprinted from *Studies in American Fiction*, 4 (Spring 1976), 27–43, by permission of *Studies in American Fiction* and the author.

proves elusive, and unsettling to those who want clear codification; and interpreters who *will* clearly categorize tend to gloss over the real problem of dealing with Norris's apparently unclear attitude toward his characters in novel after novel. Only occasionally is there someone like Donald Pizer who openly admits uncertainty, as when he wonders whether *Moran* is an excessive example of adventure-romance writing or a parody of the subgenre.[1] Is Presley in *The Octopus* Norris's philosophical surrogate or the butt of a satire on Le Contean evolutionary idealism; and what of "Naturalist" Norris's comedic attitude toward the hero in the first half of *McTeague?* What *is* Norris's point of view, if there is *one*, in *McTeague?* What is the tone, or what are the tones, involved in the characterization of Presley?

In *Vandover* similar questions arise regarding point of view and, consequently, Norris's theme. For instance, *Vandover* begins with a third person narrator assuming as closely as possible the vantage point of Vandover himself: the narrator initiates the story from a point of view within the consciousness of the hero.

> It was always a matter of wonder to Vandover that he was able to recall so little of his past life. With the exception of the most recent events he could remember nothing connectedly. What he at first imagined to be the story of his life, on closer inspection turned out to be but a few disconnected incidents that his memory had preserved with the greatest capriciousness, absolutely independent of their importance.[2]

After this announcement there follows a series of his remembered experiences, and it is through this medium of remembrance that a sensitively conceived hero is introduced. But later, by the close of the first chapter, Norris's point of view shifts mainly to that of a more detached, conventional third person narrator and, as the consensus of critical opinion has it, to a much less sympathetic tone. The narrator, however, never becomes as detached as the textbook definitions of Naturalistic writing specify. Norris does remain sympathetic. As the narrative point of view moves to without Van's consciousness, this physical shift is at appropriate moments compensated for by the use of a narrative tone which corresponds to Van's subjective condition. Specifically, Norris will employ melodramatic language to closely approximate Van's mental and emotional states to present information about the hero's interior life.

To draw this conclusion concerning the function of Norrisean melodramatic language means crediting Norris with a sophisticated artistic skill for which no one has yet thought him worthy. When critics speak of Norris's melodramatic style, they usually do so in a derogatory way; or, they view his melodramatic language as the vehicle with which he directly expresses his outrage as a genteel-Victorian moralist and with which he lashes Van for his "sins" against conventional morality. That is, critics view Norris in *Vandover* as well as in *McTeague,* as an unquestioning upholder of popular morality who mouths his position badly, in the most embarrassingly melodramatic way. Thus when Norris is describing the formative influences on young Van's personality, particularly Van's traumatic introduction to human sexuality, these critics respond by immediately assuming that Norris is choosing his terminology to describe *his own* reaction, as when he says "it was during Vandover's first year at the High School that his eyes were opened and he acquired the knowledge of good and evil," that is, the knowledge of sexual functions (p. 287).

The way in which Norris's language is interpreted here, and in like instances, will determine any conclusion drawn about the novel's structure and theme. One may take it to be Norris-the-tractarian-moralist's direct response to sexuality. This leads to the conclusion that Norris views the genteel celibacy of individuals like Dolly Haight and Turner Ravis as *de facto* "good" and all sexual phenomena without the bounds of marriage as "evil." Or, one may attempt another point of view: that the statement is one of Norris's many efforts to melodramatically mold his language for the purpose of impressionistically rendering Van's perception and interpretation of sexuality, a response taught to him by the upholders of genteel morality. If the latter interpretation is accepted, Van's story is no longer a conventional melodramatic temperance-tract with an obtrusive narrator. Rather, *Vandover* is Norris's attempt to sensationally illustrate and vividly elucidate the origins of the psychological flaws that cause Van's ultimate destruction from a point of view that bears little resemblance to those of orthodox Victorian moralists.

The experiment involves the hypothesis that Norris, though he may not have clearly enough demonstrated his intentions to satisfy most modern tastes, had a definite end in mind when resorting to hyperbole: he was consciously using melodramatic language derived from the lexicon of contemporary popular morality to depict the conventional mental and emotional responses of a traumatized victim of that morality. In the more melodramatic moments Norris impressionistically conforms his language to Van's consciousness, not his own response to the events that transpire in the novel. Norris's own implied response, unlike Van's, is one critical of the society that is permeated with this morality, as was probably indicated in the subtitle that was not included in the first printing of *Vandover: A Study of Life and Manners in an American City at the End of the Nineteenth Century.*[3] Norris stood in the socio-critical tradition of Balzac, Flaubert, and Zola, not that of T. S. Arthur. And *Vandover* is a psychological study of the way in which a young man's personality is fatally warped by the mores of society, in particular society's view of human sexuality.

The paragraphs following the "good and evil" passage indicate why it is that the young Vandover sees sexual activity, and even the sexual instinct itself, in terms of "evil." While reading the Bible Van encounters a great many things that "filled him with vague and strange ideas" (p. 287). Then one Sunday at church he hears the minister intoning a litany; the phrase, " 'all women in the perils of childbirth' " (p. 287), stands out in his mind and stimulates his curiosity. That this curiosity is a natural response is indicated in a comment by Norris: "By and by he became very curious, stirred with a blind unreasoned instinct" (p. 287).[4] Van feels the "presence of something hidden" (p. 287), a something that his awakening sexual instincts incline toward. When he asks his father, "the Old Gentleman," about it, he will tell him nothing. The hidden remains hidden, and Van comes to "be ashamed to ask him" further questions (p. 287). That the feeling of shame should be associated with his instinctual promptings is, of course, significant to all of his consequent responses to sexuality. The talk of sex by boys at his school thus becomes "abominable" (p. 287) to Van's mind. And when he finally learns the factual truth about procreation, Norris's choice of language in describing Van's reaction reveals how thoroughly his attitude has been molded by his father's and genteel society's view of sexuality. "At length one day he heard the terse and brutal truth. In an instant he believed it, some lower, animal intuition in him reiterating and confirming the fact. But even then he hated to think that people were so low, so vile" (p. 287). With such an attitude Van reads an *Encyclopedia Britannica* article with the innocuous title "Obstetrics." His reaction is to be expected from a boy who has already been conditioned to react in the "moral" fashion of the Old Gentleman:

> It was the end of all his childish ideals, the destruction of all his first illusions. The whole of his rude little standard of morality was lowered immediately. Even his mother, whom he had always believed to be some kind of an angel could never be the same to him after this, never so sweet, so good and so pure as he had hitherto imagined her (p. 288).

Van's reaction is certainly an exaggerated one, and Norris's use of melodramatic language effectively conveys its very traumatic nature.

If one assumes Van's perspective at this early age and views his consequent actions and states of mind throughout the rest of the novel, one can see how the Old Gentleman and the society for which he is a spokesman have given Van a formulaic reduction of life that produces the personal and social schizophrenia which damns his chances of ever achieving fulfillment. To follow his sexual instincts will mean evil-doing and guilt. To live the asexual life of Dolly Haight and Turner Ravis will mean that he is good but instinctually frustrated. What Van does not realize during his childhood and never fully grasps up to the point at which the novel ends is that those first stirrings of sexual instinct were simply natural stirrings to which he has been taught to respond in a particular "moral" way. Although he does satisfy those instinctual promptings, and with great regularity during his twenties, he never abandons the point of view that this sexual craving is "evil." He never loses sight of the image of sexual inclination as a "brute" thing contrary to his "better self." Never does he even consider that the "brute" might be a natural, healthy, and positive tendency within himself (as Norris makes clear that it is in chapter 9). Unfortunately for him, he consistently retains the genteel idea that the evil in man resides in his passions, despite the multiple examples of Charlie Geary's intellectually-contrived evil-doings, and bears the guilt that results from following his passions.

On several occasions Norris makes it obvious that the root of Van's problems does not lie in his instincts. When Van hears of "the perils of childbirth," Norris describes his reaction in non-moral terms, the terms of a natural response: "He puzzled over this for a long time, smelling out a mystery beneath the words, feeling the presence of something hidden, with the instinct of a young brute" (p. 287). It is only after the Old Gentleman makes Van feel ashamed, and thus sets him to *thinking* about the subject, that signs of viciousness appear. Only after the intellectual faculties are engaged does vice become associated with the "hidden mystery" of sex; it is then that "the instinct of a young brute" becomes "brutal" in the sense that societal morality assigns to that term.

In his description of Van's response to the "Obstetrics" article one can most clearly see Norris indicating that the evil "brute" of sexuality is conceived by Van only after he has been taught to think of it as something vicious within himself:

> It was very cruel, the whole thing was a grief to him, a blow, a great shock; he hated to *think* of it. Then little by little *the first taint crept in*, the innate vice stirred in him, the brute *began* to make itself felt, and a multitude of perverse and vicious *ideas* commenced to buzz about him like a swarm of nasty flies (p. 288; italics added).

In the next paragraph Norris again describes Van's view of the viciousness of sex as being intellectually derived rather than based upon an actual inherent quality of vileness in the sexual instinct.

> A certain word, the blunt Anglo-Saxon name for a lost woman,
> that he heard on one occasion among the boys at school,
> opened to him a vista of incredible wickedness, but now after
> the first moment of revolt the thing began to seem less hor-
> rible. There was even a certain attraction about it. Vandover
> soon became filled with an overwhelming curiosity, the eager
> evil curiosity of the schoolboy, the perverse craving for the
> knowledge of vice. He listened with all his ears to everything
> that was said and went through the great city with eyes open
> only to its foulness. He even looked up in the dictionary the
> meanings of the new words, finding in the cold, scientific
> definitions some strange sort of satisfaction (p. 288).

If one were to speak of Van as actually being evil, it would be an
intellectual state that would be described. A "word," "curiosity," "the
knowledge of vice," "a dictionary," and "cold, scientific definitions,"
these terms have intellectual, not instinctual, references. Van has been
taught to translate his instinctual drive into a "perverse craving for the
knowledge of vice" that becomes Faustian in its intensity; unfortunately
for him, he has also been taught that the good man suppresses such
cravings. The result is an unhealthy tension within his mind: he wants to
know a vice, but he "knows better."

The degree to which Van has been conditioned to think of sexual
activity as something sordid is illustrated by his first encounter with a
"fast girl" years later when he is a student at Harvard. The girl takes his
arm and Norris says that Van is at first somewhat delighted at this
attention, but it is not long before his "better self" realizes the low,
"brutal" nature of his actions. Having been educated to the conventional
idea that women should be admired from afar, as vessels of purity and
all that is noble in the world, he revolts at the "hopeless vulgarity of the
girl at his side, her tawdry clothes, her sordid, petty talk, her slang, her
miserable profanity. . . . He felt that he could not keep his self-respect
while such a girl hung upon his arm" (p. 299). To understand the
veritable hysteria that then overwhelms Van, one need only recall his
earlier traumatic reaction to the "terse and abominable truth"; for, as the
"chippie" chatters about her frequent strolls down Washington street,
Van's psychic reaction becomes so intense that it is physically expressed:

> Vandover's gorge rose with disgust. He stopped abruptly
> and pulled away from the girl. Not only did she disgust him,
> but he felt sorry for her; he felt ashamed and pitiful for a
> woman who had fallen so low. Still he tried to be polite to
> her; he did not know how to be rude with any kind of woman.
> "You'll have to excuse me," he said, taking off his hat.

"I don't believe I can take a walk with you tonight. I—you see—I've got a good deal of work to do; I think I'll have to leave you." Then he bowed to her with his hat in his hand, hurrying away before she could answer him a word (pp. 299–300).

This is the "better self" of Van in action. Like Dolly Haight he avoids such contact and thus lives up to the ideal conception of manhood fostered by genteel society. It is the better Van who explains to Geary the same night, " 'She was pretty common, but anyhow I don't want to help bring down a poor girl like that any lower than she is already' " (p. 300). It is the other Van who a short while later violates these high scruples:

On a certain evening, moved by an unreasoned instinct, he sought out the girl who had just filled him with such deep pity and such violent disgust, and that night did not come back to the room in Matthews [Hall]. The thing was done almost before he knew it. He could not tell why he had acted as he did, and he certainly would not have believed himself capable of it (p. 300).

It should be noted here that there is no immediate reaction of guilt. Moved by an instinct's tendency toward its desired object, Van satisfied the instinct in a natural, "unreasoned" fashion. It is only upon reflection that guilt begins to loom large in his mind and that he is overwhelmed "by a sense of shame and dishonour that were almost feminine in their bitterness and intensity" (pp. 300–01). He has violated the code given to him by the Old Gentleman; he has allowed the vile "brute" to dominate the "better self."

Such is the story of Van's life during the first half of the novel, and such is that part of the novel's structure. Up to chapter 9 Van is vacillating between one extreme of behavior and the other. Within chapters 1 and 2 he alternates between "brutal" behavior (sensual indulgence) and the behavior of his "better self" (saying his prayers, playing cards with Turner Ravis, practicing his drawing, and feeling guilt and self-contempt for being a "brute").[5] In chapters 3 through 8 he is uniformly dividing his attentions, and hence his self, between the world of Flossie the prostitute and that of Turner the virtuous Victorian maiden. Because Flossie's and Turner's worlds are so antithetical to each other, and because Van unquestioningly accepts this radical disparity as truly representative of reality at large, he resigns himself to a dualistic vision of life ("good" versus "evil") which corresponds with his vision of his self ("brute" versus "better self"). To Van, everything is to be viewed in the rigid terms of "either/or," and his life-vision leads him to act as though all women can be simplistically reduced to two clearly defined categories. To his mind, women are either sexual objects, sluts who satisfy his "brute" self, or they are non-sexual, unprofaned vessels such as Turner whose virtues gratify his "better self." Van suffers mental anguish because of this neat distinction: satisfaction of one side of his personality always produces frustrations of the other. But his previous agonies become inconsiderable in comparison to those that follow in the wake of the Ida Wade affair. Van makes the mistake of approaching her with his dual vision of woman, and she provides the test that reveals the fallacies of his life-vision.

Ida is an anomaly in the definition of life that Van, with the help of his father, Turner, and society, has arranged for himself. She fits into neither of the two general categories Van uses to understand particular women. Rather than saint or slut, Ida is closest to what may be termed a norm of female behavior. As Norris notes, "there was nothing vicious about her, and she was as far removed from Flossie's class as from that of Turner Ravis" (p. 338). She occupies a large middle ground between extremes of female behavior to which Van, with his bifurcated vision, is blind. She represents a large aspect of human behavior for which he has no convenient category, and Van must make a choice as to which of the two ways possible to him he will respond. He chooses to be the "brute," and thus makes the choice of defining her as a slut. Accordingly he takes her to the world in which one acts as a brute or slut, Flossie's realm: Van seduces her in a back room of the Imperial Bar.

Unlike Flossie, Ida cannot bear being used and discarded. She commits suicide, and Van becomes subject to the dire set of circumstances that that act produces: the events leading up to his father's death; the multiple problems for Van that his death creates; his banishment from polite society; and its many consequences. Working in conjunction with the syphilitic infection he receives from Flossie and his alcoholism, the results of the Ida Wade affair eventually drive him mad. As the novel closes the Harvard man is reduced to a dumb brute state.

In terms of causality, there is a direct line of influence to be seen running to chapter 18 from chapter 1. The novel ends with a tableau in which a child eating bread and butter and a degenerate Van stare into each other's eyes; and Norris thus recalls Van's youth. In that period of his life a prime cause of his psychic and physical degeneration can now be easily identified: the "moral" view of the relation between instinct and reason in man that Van was taught, and the view of life at large that results from it. It is a simplistic vision, the vision of a child who has not yet recognized as such the paradoxes, incongruities, and absurdities that characterize reality. Van never sees these aspects of life for what they are and thus does not see that they invalidate his naive dual vision. He persistently clings to his abstractions, despite the painful consequences that result when they come into conflict with experiential realities. The only questioning of sorts that he does engage in takes the most adolescent forms. At Harvard he becomes a heavy drinker, not because he enjoys alcohol, but because it is a form of revolt against his father. His sexual promiscuity is, at least in part, caused by the same sense of rebellion. Such behavior is natural for an adolescent, but as Van moves to physical maturity he does not undergo a corresponding psychological growth. Self-indulgent, always depending on his father, Charlie Geary, and others to arrange his life for him, he continually avoids asking the hard questions about his life and takes the line of least resistance whenever possible.

As the structure of the first half of the novel indicates, the result is chaotic. As attention moves back and forth between Van's two worlds of activity, and as one reads the pitched melodramatic language indicating the hysteria that often overtakes him, the very precarious balance that he is frantically trying to maintain becomes clear. The balance is not primarily one between the demands of instinct and those of reason; that attempt at coordination is a consequence, a symptom, not the cause, of Van's instability. The cause is the balance he feels he must maintain between his concept of reality and reality itself. It is Van's very difficult task to somehow make life fit the abstract model of reality that has been given him. He has no real problem in intellectualizing this balance: he simply assents to the image of himself as both a "better self" and a "brute"; and he dichotomizes the world into "good" and "evil" parts. The real difficulties begin when he leaves the sheltered life of childhood and must confront a world that does not readily conform to anyone's preconceptions about it, as Van soon demonstrates. According to Van's conception of reality, Ida should not have despaired and killed herself, but should have acted as Flossie by disappearing untroublesomely until her services were again called for. Van is truly surprised when complications develop and he does not know how to respond to her unexpected deviation from what he takes to be the norm of the "evil" female's behavior.

A main theme of *Vandover* is that life is so complex in nature that it nearly defies any formulizations, especially not the glib codification that Van has superimposed upon it. The reader may see how complex it is if he begins to wonder what Van could have done to avoid the calamity that his life became. Given the complicated fictional world that Norris creates for his hero, the question cannot be easily answered. If Van is ever to find fulfillment he *must* ask the question. But, although very unhappy, he never energetically pursues an answer to his problems. Even during the *Mazatlan* episode of chapter 9, when a shipwreck dramatically provides him with enough evidence to firmly conclude that his life-vision does not suffice, as it did not with Ida Wade, he once again does not analyze the evidence fully enough. And what he does discover he refuses to apply to his life.

What Van has the opportunity to see in chapter 9 is a vivid demonstration of the life's-complexity theme that Norris has been developing since chapter 1. As Van proceeds through life with his faulty conception of reality, the reader has been shown repeatedly just how faulty it is. While Van deals in nothing but certainties, Norris consistently depicts the uncertain state of human existence. Van's is a world that is rife with contradictory elements that make pat formulization of life impossible. There are many simple incongruities, such as "evil" Flossie not being a drinker or card player while "good" Turner enjoys a beer when friends drop in to play poker. And there are more complex ones, such as Turner's and her female acquaintances' inability to exercise their much celebrated good influence on the large number of respectable young men of their own social class who regularly frequent the San Francisco brothels. It is a world in which the morally repulsive but eminently successful Charlie Geary is the man who escorts the eminently virtuous Turner when last seen in the novel. In fact, it is a world in which a respectable, sensitive Van can sexually exploit a simple, good, likeable young girl and then put her utterly out of mind until he learns that he is responsible for her pregnancy.

In the structure of chapters 1 through 8, there is the largest indication of Van's faulty absolutism. Van unquestioningly labels Flossie and her world "evil" and Turner and hers "good." Yet, as one observes him moving back and forth between the two worlds that he has absolutely categorized, one may note that these two categorical "certainties" are subject to so many qualifications that they are almost meaningless. It is clear that much "good" is mixed with "evil" in both worlds. Ironically, it is Flossie, of all the women in the novel, who is closest in appearance to the type of woman for whom Norris revealed keen admiration in his other novels. While Van can automatically label her "evil," the student of Norris's total fictional world and his critical moral vision might hesitate when he finds that she shares the physical characteristics of Norris's "man's woman" type. One might recall Moran, or Lloyd, or even earth goddess Hilma Tree when Flossie first appears:

> Flossie stood in the doorway smiling good-humouredly at
> them, without a trace of embarrassment or of confusion in her
> manner. She was an immense girl, quite six feet tall, broad and

well-made, in proportion. She was very handsome, full-throated, heavy-eyed, and slow in her movement. Her eyes and mouth, like everything about her, were large, but each time she spoke or smiled, she disclosed her teeth, which were as white, as well-set, and as regular as the rows of kernels on an ear of green corn. In her ears were small yellow diamonds, the only jewellery [sic] she wore. There was no perceptible cosmetic on her face, which had a clean and healthy look as though she had just given it a vigorous washing (p. 323).

Flossie's unpretentious and natural appearance, which reflects a like personality, recalls one of Norris's most idealized women, Blix, who is "tall as most men, and solidly, almost heavily built. Her shoulders were broad, her chest was deep, her neck was round and firm. She radiated health; . . . there was that cleanliness about her, that freshness, that suggested a recent plunge in the surf."[6] The incongruity is that, while appearing as attractively healthy and clean as Blix, Flossie does not "radiate health." The same evening of her first appearance in *Vandover*, she orally infects Dolly Haight, whose lip is cut, with syphilis; and she later infects Van in a less extraordinary manner. Thus, unlike Lloyd and Blix, she has a degenerative rather than a restorative effect on *Vandover's* hero. So, from one point of view, Van is correct: she is "evil" in terms of *a* physical effect. Yet, from other points of view, she is seen not to be "evil." Aside from the fact that she is a syphilitic prostitute, there is nothing about her that might be deemed pernicious. In many ways, she is like Ida Wade: frank, honest, and natural. Compared to the ruthless Charlie Geary and the self-centered Turner Ravis, Flossie is quite attractive as a person.

That Van's assignment of the absolute category of "evil" to Flossie is untenable is further illustrated when one considers the character who represents the "good" in life. Van sees Turner as the embodiment of that which is fine in the world, and he would immediately agree with those critics who have interpreted Turner to be the "man's woman" of *Vandover*. However, a close examination of Turner reveals that Van is once again uncritically accepting an abstract categorization given to him by society which cannot be experientially validated. Turner *is* "good" in the sense that the Old Gentleman and other spokesmen for societal morality use that term. She does embody the conventional virtues of her ethos. The problem with her personality, however, is that it embodies them too fully. She so clearly shows forth the abstractions that appeal to man's "better self" that she is little more than a medium through which the platitudes and biases of Van's ethos are expressed. Nowhere in

Vandover is there any real *concrete* particulars about her appearance as a human being, as with Flossie and Ida. Van felt "she was a frank, sweet-tempered girl and very pretty, and it was delightful to have her care for him" (p. 309). And Van sees her as one "too sincere, too frank, too conscientious to practise any deception on him" (p. 310). From his point of view, she possesses the qualities of a Blix; yet nowhere in the novel does she actually act thus. When she is in social relationships, she proves to be intellectually and emotionally shallow, and, worst of all, cute. That the admirable qualities she is supposed to possess are communicated by Van's generalizations prompts the conclusion that Van is seeing what his *a priori* assumptions about "good" women dictate that he see. In effect, Van's hallucinations begin long before the final sections of the novel.

Turner is simply not much of a human being. That she is not at all likeable as a character is easily explained: she is not a person but a social demi-goddess, a symbol of abstract virtue mounted upon a pedestal for worship and emulation. And Van is one of her greatest devotees, even though, like all icons, Turner gives nothing in return for dutiful service except the satisfaction of having served well as a member of her cult. And her demands are great, as Van discovers when he violates her codes. When Van approaches Ida with the dualistic vision given him by Turner's world, and unwittingly demonstrates the untenability of that vision, he is driven from the temple. The ethos that guides itself by abstractions will not suffer any man to illustrate the inapplicability of those abstractions to real life. Thus, unlike Blix and Lloyd who actively work to help their men become what they can be in life, Turner does not step down from her pedestal. From on high, she will only carp at Van for being inadequate and summarily dismiss him with the appropriate injunction: " 'live up to the best that's in you; if not for your own sake, then for the sake of that other girl that's coming into your life sometime; that other girl who is good and sweet and pure, whom you will really, really love and who will really, really love you' " (p. 459). Van, of course, takes this as good advice and, feeling greater guilt than usual, goes forth into the world, alone, determined to reform and live up to his "better self," even though he can never enter the social realm of the "good" again.

Even after the crushing blow of being thus assigned by Turner to a social, and hence for Van, a spiritual limbo from which he has no hope of returning, he still does not realize that something may be awry. That Flossie is an amalgam of what he terms "good" and "evil" is not evident to him. That Ida was a normal girl, good in some ways and bad in others, never becomes apparent. That frank and sincere Turner, who once said to Dolly, " 'no matter what happened I feel as though I could not break my promise [of marriage] to Van, even if I should want to' " (p. 354), could prove mean enough to desert him when he most needs help, does not shake his conviction that she is "good." The reader understands Turner when she prefaces a self-justification with, " 'I know it looks as if I were deserting you when you were alone in the world and had most need of someone to influence you for the good . . .' " (p. 458). The reader can see that she *is* consciously doing something that may gravely harm Van for the sake of keeping herself socially afloat. But Van the pariah does not. His certainties inform him that Turner is above such meanness and he will not allow facts to belie those certainties.

The structure of the second half of the novel, chapters 10 through 18, indicates the destructive effect of Van's devotion to his dual life-vision. *Vandover* now becomes a tale of unrelieved physical and psychic degeneration. As his attendance at the opera *Faust* in chapter 14 suggests, Turner's limbo becomes a literal hell for Van, Faustian Van who, in his adolescence, began craving the *knowledge* of a "vice." The point of transition between the structure of the first half of the novel and the second is chapter 9, wherein Van is afforded an extraordinary opportunity to see what life at large is really like and adjust his vision accordingly. It is at this point, the "crisis" of *Vandover's* narrative structure, that Van fails to modify his vision and consequently makes his full degeneration "necessary."

During the *Mazatlan* experience nearly all of Van's certainties are violently contradicted before his eyes. The concept of a Christian God and his relation to man, which constitutes a major justification of Van's and his society's dual vision, is dramatically questioned by the accidental death of a fervently religious young lady on the deck of the *Mazatlan*. After hearing the young lady confidently declare, " 'Jesus is going to save me. I *know* I'm going to be saved' " (p. 396), Van dumbfoundedly watches her become a fatal statistic:

> She started up to follow him [Van] and the boom of the fore-mast, which the accident had in some way loosened, swung across the deck at the same moment. . . . It struck the young woman squarely across the back. . . . Vandover ran forward and lifted her up . . . ; she was already dead. He rose to his feet exclaiming to himself, "But she was so sure—she knew she was certain to be saved . . ." (p. 398).

In this event Van receives a most explicit indication that the certainties he *knows* and lives by are equally open to question. Later, in his life-boat he finds another of his preconceptions contradicted by experience. Cold, wet, and hungry, Van finds that "there was nothing picturesque about it all, nothing heroic. It was unlike any pictures he had seen of life-boat rescues, unlike anything he had ever imagined. It was all sordid, miserable, and the sight of the half-clad woman, dirty, sodden, unkempt, stirred him rather to disgust than to pity" (p. 404). Van is thus forced for the first time in his life to look at reality as it is, not as it is repre-sented in a painting, or imagined, or interpreted by the social moralists of the nineteenth century. More fortunate than the young lady, Van is afforded an opportunity to observe and consider the relationship between his certainties and real life.

The most important lesson that Van is forced to observe is one that contradicts his certainties about the nature of instinct. His interpretation of instinct as categorically "evil" is demonstrated to be false at the moment the *Mazatlan* runs aground a reef. For, in this instance, an irrational response proves to be a good one:

> Vandover's very first impulse was a wild desire of saving him-self; he had not the least thought for any one else. Every soul on board might drown, so only he should be saved. It was the primitive animal instinct, the blind adherence to the first great law, an impulse that in this first moment of excitement could not be resisted. He ran forward and snatched a life-preserver from the pile that was stored beneath the bridge (p. 392).

Like Van's sexual instinct, the instinct for survival prompts him to act in a fashion unmediated by thought. Although he has always been intellec-tually repulsed by the image of man being an animal governed by instincts, Van does act here—as he did when he visited the "fast girl"—in a way that is instinctually natural to him, if not "ethical." In following his instinct for preservation Van performs what turns out to be the "right" action. And this gives rise to the *possibility* that the night spent with the Cambridge chippie *may* have been a "right" response too, or at least not a definitively "wrong" one. This possibility is further suggested by the manner in which the leaders of the *Mazatlan's* "society" react to Van's having acted according to the self-preservation instinct. They respond in the way that society responds to a young man who has followed his sexual instinct.

A steward approaches Van and orders him to take off his life-preserver. He instructs Van that it was wrong to act that way and thus create fear and confusion in their "society." As happens when he follows his sexual instinct, Van feels shame now for having "yielded to the first selfish instinct of preservation" (p. 394). It is not long, however, before the *Mazatlan* rolls over. The leaders of the "society" were wrong, the instinctual response was the correct one in this instance, and Van now has reason to consider that society may have been incorrect in other instances when his instinctual behavior was in question.

That instinctual behavior may be "good" for man is again illustrated when the "society" of Van's life-boat murders a man to preserve itself.[7] At first, most of the people in the boat want to make the "moral" response to the man struggling in the choppy water; it is the response society has sternly taught and demanded them to make—demanded so absolutely that the *Mazatlan's* engineer, who kills the man, finds himself being prosecuted for a capital crime when he returns to San Francisco. But as the man pulls on the oars to reach the life-boat, and begins to tip it precariously, the "society" quickly changes its "good" response to " 'Let him drown!' " (p. 402). The response is instinctive: "It was the animal in them all that had come to the surface in an instant, the primal instinct of the brute striving for its life and for the life of its young" (p. 402). By society's and Van's moral standards, the response is "evil," but in the context of the life-boat situation, it is clearly natural and "good." Because they follow their natural instincts rather than abstract supernatural certainties, the passengers are later saved by a pilot-boat.

In a few hours Van has been shown quite a bit. Norris has designed the episode to illustrate that religious certainty and the neatly structured world-vision that is derived from it are not so certain or infallibly structured. He has shown that the spokesmen for a society are not always correct in their judgments. In two instances he has shown how instincts may prove beneficial in their promptings. In short, he has given Van all the evidence he needs to judge his life-vision faulty, or at least to begin seriously questioning its applicability to all aspects of life. Van is, then, in a position to truly reform his life in a way that will make personal fulfillment possible. But, instead, he rejects the evidence as worthy of consideration and returns to the self-destructive task of "reforming" himself in the old, conventional fashion of becoming his "better self."

When in chapter 10 Van encounters Toby the waiter in front of the Imperial Bar, his decision to return to the old ways is made poignantly clear. Toby terms the engineer's killing of the man who threatened to sink the life-boat "regular murder" (p. 411), and informs Van that the engineer will stand trial. Van knows that it was not "regular" murder, that the action cannot be judged by society's simplistic dual vision of "good" and "evil." He knows, however dimly, that the instinctual response of the people in the life-boat, as it was physically expressed through the engineer, was demanded by the situation. The evidence of the *Mazatlan* experience has suggested that there are no absolute categories by which all human behavior can be judged but only categories given meaning and validity by the unique characteristics of *each* situation in which a man finds himself: murder at a cotillion is quite different from murder during a shipwreck. But Van suppresses any conclusions he may have reached. To Toby's statement, Van responds in a way that indicates he plans to change nothing in his life: "Vandover shut his teeth against answering" (p. 411). Like Turner Ravis, he refuses to do the unconventional thing, and so, he returns to the world he left, just as he was when he embarked for Coronado Beach. He ignores the complexities of life, resumes viewing the world with a simplistic dual vision, and reembraces the old life that will destroy him. Thus the falling action of the novel's second half, and the pathos of what might have been.

Thus also the conclusion that *Vandover and the Brute* is not a tub-thumping tale designed to preach the moral that Van's sufferings are fit punishments for his not having lived up to his "finer fabric." *Vandover* is a Naturalistic tale of degeneration in which Norris uses the basic degeneration-tale structure to psychologically explore the root causes of Van's self-destructive life-vision. As such it is a critical attack upon nineteenth-century popular morality and the archaic life-vision of a world of fixed certainties which informed it. Like the correspondent of Stephen Crane's "The Open Boat," Vandover should have recognized the new world ushered in by the nineteenth century. Frank Norris did and as a result he exhibited in *Vandover* one of the most salient features of one strain of American literary Naturalism: a critical, questioning attitude toward the nature of man's place in the world.

Notes

1. *The Novels of Frank Norris* (Bloomington: Indiana Univ. Press, 1966), p. 96.

2. *Vandover* in *A Novelist in the Making: A Collection of Student Themes and the Novels Blix and Vandover and the Brute*; Frank Norris, ed. James D. Hart (Cambridge: Harvard Univ. Press, 1970), p. 281. Subsequent page references to this text of *Vandover* are made in parentheses in this essay. Hart's text, rather than the 1914 first edition, is referred to because it is readily available to all and the first edition is not. The passages quoted in this essay do not differ substantively from the first edition readings.

3. Hart, p. 3.

4. In the lexicon of Norris criticism there are many "trigger" words. Because past critics have taken it for granted that Norris is a conventional moralist, they make a stock response to certain terms whenever they appear. In this instance, "blind unreasoned instinct" may automatically be judged to denote a sordidly "lower" faculty in Van. Likewise, the term "brute" is taken to have a negative connotation whenever it appears. My revisionary point is that such Victorian trigger words do not necessarily denote or connote Norris's negative response to the nonrational in man. As we shall see, Norris's use of the word "brute" often signifies something

quite different from the meaning that the purely conventional-minded Van would assign to that term. For the other side of this critical point, see Pizer, *The Novels of Frank Norris,* and William B. Dillingham, "Frank Norris and the Genteel Tradition," *Tennessee Studies in Literature,* 5 (1960), 15–24.

5. For another opinion of the first two chapters' significance, see Warren French, *Frank Norris* (New York: Twayne Publishers, Inc., 1962), pp. 53–59. French would just as soon eliminate these chapters because "they really add nothing essential to the narrative. The novel is a more satisfying artistic entity without them."

6. *Blix* in *A Novel in the Making,* pp. 107–08 (reading corresponds to that of the first edition of 1899).

7. Ironically, Turner Ravis's society acts towards Van in the same way. Although it would claim that it acts upon "higher," intellectual principles rather than instinctual impulses, the response is the same. When someone threatens to swamp the boat, he must be dispensed with. Like the Jew who is drowned by the life-boat's "society," Van is the social outcast who must be made to disappear beneath the surface before he can do further harm.

Frank Norris and the
Genteel Tradition

William B. Dillingham*

Frank Norris is often regarded as a pioneer, a ground-breaker at the turn of the century who boldly violated the taboos of the Victorians and prepared the way for our contemporary novelists. According to V. F. Calverton, Norris "marked off the beginning of a new mood in our literature" and "gave early voice to the defeatist mood which has pervaded American literature since his day."[1] Granville Hicks states that Norris "sounds the motif of the new literature."[2] Ludwig Lewisohn writes that Norris, along with Robert Herrick and Upton Sinclair, "definitely and finally broke the genteel tradition and . . . ushered in the period of national expression."[3] Norris himself apparently felt that he was in full revolt against the forces that controlled the fiction of his day. His advice to the novelist is to tell the truth, "independent of fashion and the gallery gods."[4] And he was convinced that he was writing something far removed from the "Realism" which too often smacked of sentiment. There was room for the "Romance" of authors like Zola, but "Sentiment will be handed down the scullery stairs."[5] It was not only the task of this new literature to abandon sentimentalism but also to plumb "the mystery of sex, and the problems of life. . . ."[6]

In the face of such words from Norris, there is a strong temptation to think of him as cleanly breaking with one tradition while pioneering a much different one. Nevertheless, Norris's novels reflect many of the characteristics of the polite fiction that was so popular in his day. That his view of life and his choice of subject matter were sometimes quite different, as in *Vandover and the Brute* and *McTeague*, should not obscure his strong ties with the genteel tradition.

I

Like so many other literary terms, "the genteel tradition" has been used widely and with various meanings.[7] Generally, however, it refers

*Reprinted from *Tennessee Studies in Literature*, 5 (1960), 15–24, by permission of *Tennessee Studies in Literature* and the author.

to that literature in America from about 1870 to the turn of the century which was molded by the "polite" manners and the rigorous taboos of refined society. Despite obvious great differences in the quality of the novels of James, Howells, and such minor authors as Thomas Bailey Aldrich and James Lane Allen, all of these writers of the "age of gentility" were careful not to violate certain rules of polite society. These standards prohibited the use of vulgar language, sordid details, and almost any mention of sexual relationships. Grant C. Knight has summed up the chief characteristics of this period. It was an age "noted for its pruderies, its gloved and scented manners, its sentiment and earnestness of purpose. . . . Mid-Victorian ethics were dominant in the conventions which regulated social behavior and in the rules which made up the canon of good literature. . . . A central point of view [was] a belief in the virtues of self-control and in the innate goodness of a race which, contrary to Calvin's teaching, had the wish and the capacity to achieve its own salvation. . . .[8]

This period, says Ludwig Lewisohn, was "so disgustingly 'pure' because it was so violently sex-conscious. It was so afraid of vulgarity because it was so immitigably vulgar."[9] Whatever the reason, there was an extreme restraint in the treatment of sexual matters. A passionate sexual desire was sinful before marriage; after marriage there simply was no such thing as intense sexual passion. Woman's primary duty was to inspire man to moral conduct. "This moral influence of women," writes Lewisohn, "was a sincere part of the period's creed."[10]

The writers of the genteel tradition, then, chose their subject matter from what Howells termed the "smiling aspects of life." They felt a strong moral duty, as James Lane Allen put it, to do "nothing mean and to do nothing meanly."[11] In the choice of subject and its treatment, the advice of Henry D. Cooke, under whom Howells worked while employed by the *Ohio State Journal,* may be taken as the motto of the genteel author: "Never, *never* write anything you would be ashamed to read to a woman."[12] Their characters are free to play out their dramas in a nondeterministic universe. The portrayal of man's sex life is avoided when possible, and when it cannot be avoided, it is treated with painful restraint. In addition, there is a great deal of emphasis upon woman's role as the moral guide of man and upon what Knight terms the "belief in the virtues of self-control." The novels of the lesser authors are characterized by sentimentality.

Norris's deviation from acceptable subject matter of fiction, his treatment of unpleasant details, and his Darwinianism, especially in *McTeague,* completely blinded his own generation and many critics afterwards to his kinship with the genteel tradition. Admittedly, Norris did not always choose to write of the "cleanly respectabilities" Howells so admired. Furthermore, his characters are sometimes caught up in the deterministic forces of chance, heredity, and environment. These represent important differences from the genteel tradition, and the novels in which they occur do reflect a new trend in American literature. But in others of his novels, and even in these decidedly "naturalistic" works, there are strong indications that Norris did not, as Lewisohn and others suggest, "definitely and finally" break the genteel tradition. More often than not, Norris's novels reveal him as strongly influenced by the same manners, morals, and restraints that molded the work of Howells, Allen, Aldrich and the other writers of genteel literature. This influence is especially evident in Norris's treatment of sex, in his characterization of woman as man's moral support, in his emphasis upon self-control, and in his frequent indulgence in sentimentality.

II

Maxwell Geismar has accurately observed that although part of Norris's early fame "rested on the fact that he had restored the sexual drives to their proper place in human affairs . . . he persisted in viewing them as the creation of the Devil."[13] In only two of his seven novels does Norris discuss sexual matters in a way unacceptable to the genteel readers of his day. And even in these works, Vandover and the Brute and McTeague, he often seems more the Victorian moralist than the impartial reporter. He constantly associates the sex drive with disease or with the brute in man, to be repressed lest it lead to his destruction.

In "plumbing the mystery of sex," Vandover and the Brute is Norris's frankest novel, but even here there is no mystery about it: it is simply vice. Norris includes among his characters a prostitute, allows Vandover to seduce a girl who later commits suicide after she discovers she is pregnant, and has Vandover's friend Haight contract venereal disease when the prostitute kisses him against his will. These matters naturally are not described in detail, nor with the verisimilitude of a Faulkner or a Caldwell, but they were in themselves subjects entirely displeasing to the genteel admirers of John Gray and The Rise of Silas Lapham. If these readers could have tolerated Norris's very brief depiction of the prostitute, Haight's disease, and the seduction, however, they might have been greatly pleased with his constant moralizing on the evils that result from the sins of the flesh. Vandover's sex instinct was a form of "the brute in him," an "unclean passion," and this "vice" along with his other weaknesses should have been repressed. But they were not repressed, and Vandover's resulting deterioration was, Norris writes, "the punishment he had brought upon himself . . . the result of his long indulgence of vice, his vile submission to the brute that was to destroy his reason" (p. 213).[14] In *Vandover and the Brute,* Norris steps boldly forth to deal objectively with a young man who breaks the rules of polite society and is ruined. But by the time the novel is over, we are uncertain, as Maxwell Geismar has pointed out, whether the book was a condemnation of the sexual taboos of the period or a confirmation of them.

In *McTeague,* sexual desire is treated as an unfortunate animal instinct in two incompatible people. Trina and the dentist McTeague are drawn together by the sex drive, but with the exception of two or three kisses, there is no real intimacy in the novel. Here, as in *Vandover and the Brute,* sex is brutish and unnatural. As McTeague stands over Trina, who is unconscious in his dental chair, it is "the evil instincts in him," the "animal in the man," that rises to the surface. Immediately another instinct grapples with this evil force: "Within him, a certain second self, another better McTeague rose with the brute" (p. 26).[15] But the brute wins, and the dentist ends by kissing the unconscious girl. Instead of being uplifted by the kiss, McTeague here, as in the later scenes, experiences a "revulsion of feeling." Norris's own feelings about McTeague's giving in to the brute of sex are made quite clear: "Below the fine fabric of all that was good in him ran the foul stream of hereditary evil, like a sewer" (p. 27). If in *Vandover and the Brute* and *McTeague* Norris breaks the taboos of his society by discussing sex, he indicates also that he was soundly anchored in the Victorian concept of the sex drive as a corrupting force.

Norris retains this attitude toward sex in his other five novels and becomes even more restrained in dealing with this daring subject. Some of his characters are almost as highly refined and as pure as the daughter of Silas Lapham, who blushed violently when her father pointed out to Tom Corey where her room would be in the house under construction. Hilma Tree, of *The Octopus,* is smitten with surprise and remorse when her future husband, Buck Annixter, tries to kiss her. She feels that she has in some way given him the notion that she could be "approached." And when he later suggests, before he proposes marriage, that they live together, she goes to pieces and leaves town. When Laura Jadwin, in *The Pit,* is kissed goodnight "squarely on her cheek" by her young admirer, Landry Court, she is outraged beyond expression, and she writes him a short note breaking their acquaintance completely. Laura's sister Page is even more the prude. She severely scorns Laura for identifying herself to Curtis Jadwin in the first of the story even though they are all in the same party attending the opera. When Laura brings Sheldon Corthell to her private sitting room in order to help her hang a picture and to chat with her, Page is sure, and Laura suspects, there will be a terrible scandal if it is known.

In *Moran of the Lady Letty* and *Blix*, the love affairs are based upon comradeship and respect for the pure and noble qualities which the lovers see in each other. The superwoman Moran commands the profound love and respect of Ross Wilbur because of her manliness, and their mutual love is established when he defeats her in hand-to-hand combat. Moran is frequently contrasted in Wilbur's mind with the delicate girls he has always known, and it is precisely because she is not feminine that Moran so attracts him. He admires her "rough blue overalls thrust into the shoes; the coarse flannel shirt open at the throat; the belt with its sheath knife; her arms big and white and tattooed in sailor fashion; her thick muscular neck; her red face with its pale blue eyes and fragrant hair, that lay over her shoulder and breast, coiling and looping in her lap" (p. 263).[16] Before she is corrupted by the lust for wealth, Moran seems to represent all the strength, purity, and nobility of a superior race, untouched by the curses of civilization. Her lack of ordinary feminine sex appeal and her freedom from disturbing sexual emotions are important aspects of her superiority. Ross "could easily see," writes Norris, "how to such a girl the love of a man would appear only in the light of a humiliation—a degradation."

Blix is Norris's chief contribution to the genteel tradition. Its plot is based upon the Platonic relationship of Travis Bessemer and Condy Rivers, who decide early to avoid all physical contact and simply be "pals." Condy comes to love Travis, or Blix, because of her "clean purity." In *Blix*, more than in any of the other novels, Norris reflects his inheritance of genteel ideas on sex. The sex instincts are not only repressed in his characters but are called by Blix "foolishness."

III

Norris's close tie with the genteel tradition is perhaps reflected most strongly in his continual emphasis upon the moral influence of woman on man and upon the necessity of man's unrelenting self-control. Especially in the popular success stories of Norris's day, there was almost always a wife or mother behind the self-made protagonist, standing beside him in travail and inspiring him to the righteous path. In *The Rise of Silas Lapham*, for example, Lapham attributes his success to his wife Persis, and it is Persis who influences Lapham in making restitution to his wronged partner. Quite often in these novels, the purity of woman produces a rejuvenating effect in the hero, causing him to give up bad habits and to lead a truly Christian existence. In six of

Norris's seven novels, his woman characters are conspicuous for their role as inspirers of men.

Condy Rivers, of *Blix,* is a young writer of talent, but he lacks real inspiration and direction until he becomes the companion of Travis Bessemer. In addition, he has become the slave of gambling. Travis performs the dual function of helping him write a splendid short novel and of curing him of his urge to play cards. She serves as an intelligent critic of his work, pointing out to him his genius and frankly telling him when he is too "showy." When she learns of his difficulty in controlling the desire to gamble, she makes him teach her to play poker and urges him to play only with her. She wins from him continually but surprises him in the end by returning all of his money. The profound influence of Travis is summed up in this passage:

> And the love of her had made a man of him. . . . In those two months he had grown five years; he was more masculine, more virile. The very set of his mouth was different; between the eyebrows the cleft had deepened; his voice itself vibrated to a heavier note. No, no; so long as he should live, he, man grown as he was, could never forget this girl of nineteen who had come into his life so quietly, so unexpectedly, who had influenced it so irresistibly and so unmistakably for its betterment . . . (pp. 161–162).[17]

Ross Wilbur, under the influence of Moran, undergoes a like change in *Moran of the Lady Letty.* Before he meets the Nordic superwoman, he is a shallow youth, attending a constant round of dances, parties, and "afternoon teas, pink, lavender, and otherwise" (p. 177). His life is without meaning, and his manliness lies dormant until awakened by Moran. Then he, like Condy Rivers, becomes suddenly mature. In *A Man's Woman,* it takes the insight and maneuverings of Lloyd Bennett to make her husband really start living again. A born explorer, he has retired after his failure to reach the North Pole. Realizing the importance of his work in keeping him vital, Lloyd helps finance a new expedition and convinces him that he should go even though his absence will mean loneliness for her. Her glance communicates a message which could easily have occurred in almost any of the genteel novels about the self-made man and his helpmate: "She said no word, but all her love for him, all her hopes of him, all the fine, strong resolve that, come what would, his career should not be broken, his ambition should not faint through any weakness of hers, all her eager sympathy for his great work, all her strong, womanly encouragement for him to accomplish his destiny spoke to him in that long, earnest look of her dull-blue eyes" (p. 235).[18]

The innocent and beautiful Hilma Tree, of *The Octopus,* has such a powerful influence on Buck Annixter that his change is scarcely believable. Almost overnight, Annixter changes from a selfish and sometimes cruel eccentric, a hater of women and most men, to a selfless, loving husband. His every action bears out the change he speaks of to Presley:

> She's made a man of me. I was a machine before, and if another man or woman, or child got in my way, I rode 'em down, and I never *dreamed* of anybody else but myself. But as soon as I woke up to the fact that I really loved her, why, it was glory hallelujah all in a minute, and, in a way, I kind of loved everybody then, and wanted to be everybody's friend, And I began to see that a fellow can't live *for* himself any more than he can live *by* himself. He's got to think of others. . . . Just as soon as I can, I'm going to get in and *help* people, and I'm going to keep that idea the rest of my natural life. That ain't much of a religion, but it's the best I've got, and Henry Ward Beecher couldn't do any more than that. And it's all come about because of Hilma . . . (II, 180).[19]

Shades of Augusta Jane Evans' *St. Elmo!* And Buck Annixter is not the only man raised to new heights by this noble woman. Even Presley finds himself aspiring to a better life because of her. He has "a longing to give the best that was in him to the memory of her, to be strong and noble because of her, to reshape his purposeless, half-wasted life with nobility and purity and gentleness . . ." (II, 338). The shepherd Vanamee is also given a new hope and inspiration when he finds the daughter of his dead lover.

Curtis Jadwin of *The Pit* sounds more like the self-made men of Horatio Alger than a naturalistic hero like Dreiser's Frank Cowperwood when he tells Laura Dearborn that everyone in his Sunday School class "would be inspired, and stimulated, and born again as soon as ever you set foot in the building. Men need good women. . . . Men who are doing the work of the world. . . . The men have got all the get-up-and-get they want, but they need the women to point them straight, and to show them how to lead that other kind of life that isn't all grind" (p. 118).[20] Young Landry Court, who finds that "the companionship of one intelligent, sympathetic woman is as much of a stimulus as a lot of men," is "pointed straight" and inspired by Page Dearborn. Concerning their relationship, he tells her: "It's been inspiring to me. I want you should know that. Yes, sir, a real inspiration. It's been inspiring, elevating, to say the least" (p. 211). *The Pit* takes on an excessively moral tone when the saintly influence of Laura over Jadwin is put to a test by his passion for speculating in wheat. Although Norris apparently intended *The Pit*, the second novel in his proposed trilogy, to portray wheat as one of the primal and uncontrollable forces in man's existence, this theme becomes obscured by Jadwin's personal problem. The conflict centers on the battle for Jadwin's soul, with Laura's goodness pulling him one way and his intense desire to gamble on wheat pulling him the other way. Because he refuses to accept Laura's advice, he is brought to ruin. At the end, however, he realizes his error and optimistically begins anew with Laura at his side. The moral Norris preaches in *The Pit* is, as Alfred Kazin has pointed out, identical with that in hundreds of temperance novels of that age. "The hold of the pit over Curtis Jadwin," Kazin states, "was exactly like the hold of drink over the good but erring father...."[21]

A similar situation occurs in *Vandover and the Brute* where the young hero brings on his destruction by not heeding the advice of a noble woman. Vandover feels the goodness of Turner Ravis as he accompanies her to parties and to church, but he allows his passion for corrupting pleasures to overcome her good influence. Still, she tries to lead him to a moral life. "But Van," she pleads, "won't you be better now? Won't you break from it all and be your own self again? I have faith in you. I believe it's in you to become a great man and a good man. It isn't too late to begin all over again. Just be your better self; live up to the best that's in you" (pp. 178–179). Norris seems indisputably committed to the notion that we had better listen when a good woman gives advice, and he furnishes us with the terrible picture of Vandover's deterioration to show what happens when we refuse to listen. For Vandover's destruction, like that of Jadwin in *The Pit* and Magnus Derrick in *The Octopus*, is brought on by his failure to learn from a woman's teachings. In each case, a corrupting passion overcomes the character's self-control. Norris makes it clear in a number of places that these fallen men are themselves responsible for their downfall. He writes, for example, that Vandover had "shut his ears to the voice that shouted warnings of the danger, and had allowed the brute to thrive and to grow...."[22] Like *The Pit*, then, *Vandover and the Brute* points up woman's role as moral teacher and man's need of self-control, two common themes of the genteel novel.

IV

A Puritan view of sex, an emphasis upon the importance of woman in man's moral life, and a belief in the virtues of self-control are recurrent themes which Norris's work shares with much of the genteel literature of his time. In his treatment of these and other subjects, Norris is frequently sentimental, even in his more serious fiction. The degeneration of

Vandover, for example, is accompanied by a great deal of sentimentality. When Vandover asks and obtains forgiveness of the "Old Gentleman," his father, for seducing Ida Wade, it is simply more than the poor boy can stand. " 'Oh, governor!' he cried. It was as if it had been a mother or a dear sister. The prodigal son put his arms about his father's neck for the first time since he had been a little boy, and clung to him and wept as though his heart were breaking" (p. 96). There is much of the same sentiment in the entire relationship of Vandover and his father. This quality is particularly evident, too, in *The Pit* in the relationship of Jadwin and Laura, especially after he has lost his fortune. No doubt the scene where the broken Jadwin returns from the pit to his wife for moral support brought many tears to the eyes of the gentle reader: "Jadwin, her husband, stood before her, his eyes sunken deep in his head, his face dead white, his hand shaking. He stood for a long instant in the middle of the room looking at her. Then at last his lips moved: 'Old girl. . . . Honey.' Laura rose, and all but groped her way toward him, her heart beating, the tears streaming down her face. 'My husband, my husband!' " (p. 394). Among the numerous examples of sentimentality in *The Octopus* the portrayal of Dyke and his little daughter perhaps stands out strongest. Dyke, a model father, works hard to support his mother and daughter. When the railroad causes Dyke to lose his farm, Norris plays upon the reader's sentiment by focusing on the way this cruel deed affects not only a good man but also his little girl: "Not only would the Railroad devour every morsel of his profits, but also it would take from him his home; at a blow he would be left penniless and without a home. What would then become of his mother—and what would become of the little tad?" (II, 64).

V

The widespread reputation of Norris as a pioneer of naturalism in America, as an early "angry young man" who broke with the taboos imposed upon literature by a Mid-Victorian society, has come about primarily through two developments. First, Norris wrote at a time when almost any violation of the genteel restrictions was looked upon as extreme. Thus when Norris wrote in *McTeague* of a deterministic universe and pictured prostitutes and syphilitics in other works, his early readers saw only these improprieties. Since they were so accustomed to the genteel elements in fiction, these readers hardly noticed them in Norris. Norris's reputation as a ground-breaker was then furthered during and immediately after the First World War, when the new poets, novelists, and critics were seeking allies for their own more radical break with genteel literature. They eagerly took up the new in Norris and enthroned him, together with a few other writers of the nineties, as an early fighter against the genteel tradition.[23] Although a few modern critics have examined the totality of Norris's fiction carefully and sometimes pointed out its frequent similarity to the polite literature of his own age and the generation before, there remains a tendency to overlook all but the revolutionary in Norris's works. Admittedly Norris was one of the fathers of a new trend in American letters, but in several ways he was at the same time as much a product of polite society as were Aldrich, Allen, and Howells.

Notes

1. V. F. Calverton, *The Liberation of American Literature* (New York: Charles Scribner's Sons, 1932), p. 350.

2. Granville Hicks, *The Great Tradition* (New York: The Macmillan Company, 1935), p. 168.

3. Ludwig Lewisohn, *Expression in America* (New York: Harper & Brothers, 1932), p. 312.

4. "The True Reward of the Novelist," in *The Responsibilities of the Novelist,* VII of *The Complete Edition of Frank Norris* (Garden City, N. Y.: Doubleday, Doran & Company, 1928), 18.

5. "A Plea for Romantic Fiction," *Complete Edition,* VII, 163.

6. "A Plea for Romantic Fiction," p. 167.

7. Although the term has been overworked, it is still useful if used, as Edwin H. Cady suggests in *The Gentleman in America* (Syracuse: Syracuse University Press, 1949), with "a humility and a caution" which recognizes its "fragmentary and illusory nature" (p. 24).

8. Grant C. Knight, *James Lane Allen and the Genteel Tradition* (Chapel Hill: The University of North Carolina Press, 1935), p. 82.

9. Lewisohn, p. 238.

10. Lewisohn, p. 240.

11. Quoted in Knight, p. 264.

12. Quoted in Walter Fuller Taylor, *The Economic Novel in America* (Chapel Hill: The University of North Carolina Press, 1942), p. 218.

13. Maxwell Geismar, *Rebels and Ancestors* (Boston: Houghton Mifflin, 1953), p. 6.

14. *Vandover and the Brute* in *Complete Edition,* V. All page references to *Vandover* are to this edition.

15. *McTeague* in *Complete Edition,* VIII. All page references to *McTeague* are to this edition.

16. *Moran of the Lady Letty* in *Complete Edition,* III. All page references to *Moran* are to this edition.

17. *Blix* in *Complete Edition,* III.

18. *A Man's Woman* in *Complete Edition,* VI.

19. *The Octopus* in *Complete Edition*, II. *The Octopus* occupies volumes I and II; all page references to the novel are to this edition.

20. *The Pit* in *Complete Edition*, IX. All page references to *The Pit* are to this edition.

21. Alfred Kazin, *On Native Grounds* (New York: Reynal & Hitchcock, 1942), p. 101.

22. For an excellent discussion of the moral tone of *Vandover and the Brute,* see Charles C. Walcutt, *American Literary Naturalism, A Divided Stream* (Minneapolis: University of Minnesota Press, 1956), pp. 119–121. Walcutt points out that the passages, like the one above, which blame Vandover for his decline, are written from Vandover's point of view. Nevertheless, it is clear that "they come as auctorial comment also."

23. For comment on the revival of Norris's work, which took place during and after World War I, see Ernest Marchand, *Frank Norris, A Study* (Palo Alto: Stanford University Press, 1942), p. 229.

Frank Norris's Western Metropolitans

Glen A. Love*

I have great faith in the possibilities of San Francisco and the Pacific Coast as offering a field for fiction. Not the fiction of Bret Harte, however, for the country has long since outgrown the "red shirt" period. The novel of California must be now a novel of city life. . . .[1]

A representative action in Frank Norris's San Francisco novels is the withdrawal of the central character or characters from the city itself out to the Presidio and to the ruins of old Fort Mason near the Golden Gate. There, in a setting of solitary beach, fresh trade winds, thundering surf, swirling foam, and great, bare hills rolling down to the sea—in short, the sort of booming and kinetic natural landscape which embodies the author's sense of the vital force surging through all life—come Norris's troubled San Franciscans to straighten out their values. Here McTeague begins his interior journey back to the Sierra Mountains of his youth as he sits for hours, "watching the roll and plunge of the breakers with the silent, unreasoned enjoyment of a child."[2] Here Norris brings all three of his popular romances, *Moran of the Lady Letty*, *Blix*, and *A Man's Woman*, to a close, and in *Blix* the scene is visited repeatedly throughout the novel. Here Norris envisioned his own recovery from his debilitating experiences in the Cuban War in 1898. As he wrote to a friend,

> I want to get these things out of my mind and the fever out of my blood, and so if my luck holds I am going back to the old place for three weeks and for the biggest part of the time I hope to wallow and grovel in the longest grass I can find in the Presidio reservation on the cliffs overlooking the ocean and absorb ozone and smell smells that *don't* come from rotting and scorched vegetation, dead horses and bad water.[3]

*Reprinted from *Western American Literature,* 11 (May, 1976), 3–22, by permission of *Western American Literature* and the author.

The rejection by the fictional hero of his blighted contemporary surroundings and his rejuvenative withdrawal to a green shade is, of course, a classic ritual in American literature. But Norris's version of American pastoral requires closer examination precisely because it is not the simple praise of natural setting and vilification of the city and industrial society which we have come to expect when the machine and the American garden stand in confrontation. Norris's characteristic treatment of the modern city, as exemplified for him by San Francisco, combines conventional romantic attitudes toward nature with his beliefs in a mechanistic life-force and an evolutionary heritage which included the propensities for both atavism and progress.[4] If Norris can evoke the qualities of grim indifference in the San Francisco of McTeague, if it becomes a city of dreadful night in Vandover and the Brute, if it is the setting of inconsequential society frivolity in Moran of the Lady Letty, Norris's western metropolis is also throughout his works the emblem of an inevitable future, urban and complex, in which the survivors are those who have met the city's strenuous and unique requirements. Thus, Norris resists classification as a conventional defender of the natural world against the threatening city.[5] It may be acknowledged that, to some degree, Norris demonstrates apprehension over the growth of technological civilization. His works often dramatize flight from the city into an exhilarating wild nature, and he could wax lyric in his critical essays over the lessons to be learned by modern, urban man in "the canyons of the higher mountains, . . . the plunge of streams and swirling rivers yet without names, . . . the wilderness, the plain, the wide-rimmed deserts."[6] Still on the deepest and most fundamental level Norris's novels fasten upon the necessity for return to—rather than escape from—the city. For he sees the commercial and urban present as an inescapable stage in evolutionary progress and in the "Great March" of Anglo-Saxon pioneering, he emphasizes the underlying similarities between urban and natural worlds and the possibilities for beneficial interaction between the two, and he posits a hopeful future for those who master their stern lessons.[7] The pattern which emerges, then, from the total design of his novels is of a gradual shift from characters who are either somehow unfitted for modern urban life, or who turn their backs upon it in favor of escapist adventuring in wild nature, to those who can function successfully on both levels but who are primarily committed to an urban existence and who discover in industrialized contemporary life the opportunities for high enterprise.

Norris's three early novels, Moran of the Lady Letty, McTeague, and Vandover and the Brute, sketch the hopes and limitations of his western urbanites, and prepare for their more successfully realized descendants in the later works.[8] *Moran's* romantic plot follows the adventures of Ross Wilbur, an aristocratic San Francisco playboy drawn from Richard Harding Davis, who is Shanghaied onto a shark-fishing boat bound for Baja California. There aboard a derelict ship he finds a girl, Moran Sternerson, an Amazonian Nordic with whom, after a series of adventures, he sails back to San Francisco. The muscular Moran, bested by Wilbur in a knock-down fight, has become his clinging vine, and they plan a life together adventuring on the high seas. After anchoring their ship just inside the Golden Gate, Wilbur goes ashore on business and Moran is knifed by one of the Chinese crew. The wind springs up and the ship pulls free and heads out for open ocean with Moran's body lying on the deck. As the book ends, Wilbur, watching from the shore, refuses to attempt to intercept the ship and allows it to race out into the stormy ocean until it is lost on the horizon.

Summary cannot do justice to the rich absurdity of all of this, but the novel is nevertheless important in setting forth Norris's broad contrasts between primitivistic and urban values. The ending of the novel demonstrates the misgivings of both narrator and hero about the decision to follow the primitive, buccaneering life which Moran represents. As the ship lies off the lifeboat station near the Presidio, Moran grows increasingly uneasy at the distant prospect of the city:

> Wilbur could see she felt imprisoned, confined. When he had pointed out the Palace Hotel to her—a vast gray cube in the distance, over-topping the surrounding roofs—she had sworn under her breath.
> "And people can live there, good heavens! Why not rabbit-burrows and be done with it? Mate, how soon can we be out to sea again? I hate this place."
> (III, 316)

When Wilbur goes ashore to make arrangements to outfit the ship for the planned filibustering trip to Cuba, he instead paces the beach and Presidio worrying about how he is to explain Moran and his own behavior to his San Francisco socialite friends. His inordinate concern for the opinions of those whose world he has just forsworn and from whom he will soon part company forever reflects Norris's difficulty in pressing the novel's atavistic escapism any further. As Wilbur walks the beach, Norris employs the physical setting to drive home the choices open to this western renegade urbanite, with his half-tamed Valkyrie. "There, on the very threshold of the Western world, at the very outpost of civilization," Norris's new man stands poised: "In front of him ran the narrow channel of the Golden Gate; to his right was the bay and the city; at his left, the open Pacific." (p. 318) But the choice is never faced. Instead,

Norris allows the inevitably treacherous coolie Hoang, left aboard the ship with Moran, to dispatch her with his knife, thus conveniently solving Ross Wilbur's problem. As Wilbur hears of Moran's fate from the keeper of the lifeboat station, he rejects the idea of attempting to reclaim the ocean-bound ship or the girl's body. In a rush of Norris's clamorous rhetoric, Moran goes

> out, out, out to the great gray Pacific that knew her and loved her, and that shouted and called for her, and thundered in the joy of her as she came to meet him like a bride to meet a bridegroom.
> "Good-bye, Moran!" shouted Wilbur as she passed. Good-bye, good-bye, Moran! You were not for me—not for me! The ocean is calling for you, dear; don't you hear him? Don't you hear him? . . . good-bye, good-bye, good-bye! (p. 325)

In this heavy-handed disposition of a troublesome problem, a "creature unfit for civilization," Norris intimates the limits to his own, as well as his hero's, commitments to nature-girls and unfettered adventuring. (p. 310) The city on the horizon inevitably intrudes itself and brings an end to adolescent fantasies. Ross Wilbur's final farewell to Moran is a sigh of relief at his own disengagement from the freebooting life. Wilbur will once more take his place in the urban world, but it is a reasonable conjecture from the evidence of Norris's later works that he will no longer lead cotillions. The novel does not pursue Wilbur beyond the moment of Moran's disappearance, and thus closes having presented only the most extreme of contrasts. At this point, neither Norris nor his hero recognizes that modern life may offer alternatives which lie somewhere between tea-dancing in San Francisco and swashbuckling ocean adventure. A few months after the publication of *Moran*, Norris wrote to Isaac Marcosson, in terms which apply to Ross Wilbur as well as to his creator, "When I wrote 'Moran' I was, as one might say, flying kites, trying to see how high I could go without breaking the string. However, I have taken myself and my work much more seriously since then."[9] If *Moran* establishes the restricted possibilities for beneficent primitivism in open-air settings, Norris's later-published novels would bring his heroes back into urban and industrial life and examine the opportunities for meaningful existence there.

McTeague and *Vandover and the Brute* probe more directly the nature and requirements of modern urban life in the far West. Themes raised in *Moran*—a man's need for worthwhile work, for the companionship of a strong woman, and for bracing contact with nature—reappear in different forms in these novels. In *Moran* we are left with a hero who has added to his fine city-bred manners the strength and resourcefulness gained from an immersion into euphoric nature and his contact with an inspirational and firm-willed woman. Vandover shares Wilbur's social advantages, but not the ennobling adventure into nature, and unlike Wilbur he rejects the love of a good woman. And while Vandover has, at the beginning, a worthwhile career as a painter to pursue, he eventually allows the city's hidden sensual life to divert him from it. In Vandover's father, however, and in his friend, Geary, Norris provides two characters who anticipate, in a fragmentary way, the emergence of heroic cosmopolitans in his later works. In *McTeague*, the hero shares, even surpasses, Ross Wilbur's physical prowess, but his intellectual and social shortcomings leave him with only a tenuous hold upon his place in a bewildering urban environment. With the loss of his occupation and his wife Trina's regression, his own descent is assured, and he eventually flees back to the primitive world from which he came, with the city in deadly pursuit.

Subtitles reveal Norris's urban consciousness in both books. *McTeague* is called "A Story of San Francisco" and *Vandover* was originally subtitled "A Study of Life and Manners in an American City at the End of the Nineteenth Century." Despite its clinically naturalistic subtitle, *Vandover* is as much a story of San Francisco as is *McTeague*.[10] San Francisco is named on the novel's opening page, and that city's demimonde, its notorious habits of easy and luxurious living provide the fatal attractions for the weak-willed and self-indulgent Vandover. *McTeague* is indispensably set in San Francisco for a different reason; the city's close proximity to its magnificent natural surroundings provides the appropriate backdrop for McTeague's urban sojourn, first as observer, then as bewildered participant, and finally as fugitive. The primitive and elemental natural world which he typifies stands at the edges of the novel's action, glimpsed in the view of the open Pacific across the ugly mud flats from the B Street Station where McTeague courts Trina, intruding more fully in the scenes on the windy downs near the Golden Gate where McTeague spends his days, and reclaiming McTeague and the novel entirely in the concluding chapters set in the high Sierras and Death Valley.[11] Both books reveal the vibrant and emerging western city in search of its appropriate new man. Vandover is hopelessly weak for its stringent demands as McTeague is hopelesly stupid, a judgment which Norris is at pains to emphasize, applying the term to McTeague six times in the opening chapter alone. It is all done without malice, but should nevertheless caution us against regarding McTeague as Everyman. He is an anachronism, huge, powerful, with a kind of childlike innocence about him, but a throwback nonetheless, and thus unsuited to take part in the evolutionary march.

Indeed, none of the characters in *McTeague* is qualified to grasp the potentialities of urban life, and the first half of the work is a satire upon the Polk Street irregulars and their immigrant counterparts, Trina's family, the Sieppes. With a wink to his audience, Norris as sophisticated cosmopolitan gives us a kind of Newgate pastoral of San Francisco's bumpkin class, detailing their libido for the ugly, the sentimental, and the pretentious. In that tone of repressed amusement with which the high-brow regards the aspiring lower-middlebrow, Norris describes the interiors of their houses, their "admirable" wallpaper, Trina's wedding bouquet, "preserved by some fearful, unknown process," (191) the pictures on their walls, cheap prints of fat English babies and incredibly alert fox terriers, and colored lithographs over the mantel of golden-haired girls in nightgowns kneeling and saying their prayers, their eyes invariably large and blue, rolled heavenward. (IV, 191, 136–7) Trina sums it all up with the inevitable judgment: "Of course . . . I'm no critic, I only know what I like." (p. 170)

With similar detached amusement, Norris presents these unlikely urbanites at their leisure. A vaudeville show featuring pie-in-the-face comedy, acrobats, a "Society Contralto" in evening dress, and a performer with burnt cork on his face who renders "Nearer, My God, To Thee" on the beer bottles leaves them transported. The performance ends with little "Owgoost" Sieppe wetting the pants of his Little Lord Fauntleroy suit, while his mother smacks and shakes him to his howls of "infinite sadness."[12] A picnic depicts the elder Sieppe in his characteristic comic role of inefficiency expert, marshalling the group to its destination with a series of sharp commands, "To one side!" . . . "Vor-wart;" . . . "Silence!" . . . "Stand back!" . . . "Attention!" (pp. 57–64) Another picnic with the McTeagues and their Polk Street acquaintances ends in a murderous fight, leaving a wild disorder of trampled turf, torn clothing, empty beer bottles, broken eggshells, and discarded sardine cans. The long ethnic joke which the Sieppes enact in the first part of the novel is set against their grim downward glide later. We last hear of them unsuccessfully attempting to borrow money from Trina, the father having failed in business in Los Angeles and vaguely considering emigrating with his family to New Zealand.

Trina's cousin, Marcus Schouler, is another inept urbanite who blusters through the early chapters, confusedly mouthing the catchphrases of popular reform, choleric in his defense of ideas which he is incapable of understanding. While he professes toward McTeague (his rival for Trina's hand) the Damon-and-Pythias sentiments of popular fiction, he nevertheless rages against the unwitting dentist and throws a knife at him on one occasion. Finally, he reports McTeague for practicing dentistry without a license, the action which precipitates McTeague's decline. For Marcus, the bungler, the man who can do nothing well, the raging fool of words, Norris reserves an appropriate fate. Like McTeague and the Sieppes, Marcus leaves the city, but for reasons which Norris treats with some derision. Scornful of the "red shirt" school of Western fiction and the yellowback novel shoot-em-ups, Norris depicts Marcus as a victim of their fantasies.[13] He leaves to take up a cowboy's life on the ranches of south-central California. His "entrancing vision" of himself, complete with "silver spurs and untamed broncos" (p. 151) is deflated by Norris in the book's final chapter as, with McTeague, Marcus chases a recalcitrant mule across the blistering sands of Death Valley, shouting and cursing, finally emptying his revolver into the beast, thereby destroying the last canteen of water and the men's hope for survival. This entire scene—a pair of western anachronisms, the cowboy and the miner, fumbling away their wilderness chances in awkward-squad confusion—must rank with Stephen Crane's "The Bride Comes to Yellow Sky" in its puncturing of favorite frontier myths.

At the root of the failure of the Sieppes, Marcus, and the other of the novel's characters to be assimilated successfully into urban life, Norris suggests, is their confusion and insecurity over their own proper place in society: "They could never be sure of themselves," says Norris. "At an unguarded moment they might be taken for toughs, so they generally erred in the other direction and were absurdly formal. No people have a keener eye for the amenities than those whose social position is not assured." (p. 80) In this sense, they bear another resemblance to Crane, this time in the characters of *Maggie*, who, in an uglier urban environment at the opposite end of the country, combined the behavior of "toughs" with the sentiments of Victorian gentility.

To some extent, the failure of Norris's characters to respond success-fully to the demands of urban life may be laid to Norris's notorious racism. Mr. Sieppe and Marcus are excitable and confused Germanic types. Trina's penuriousness is traced to her hoarding peasant forebears. Maria Macapa is a demented Latin, a degenerate type which Norris frequently drew. Zerkow is a quintessential grasping Jew, a virtual medieval allegory of avarice. For good measure, he carries, and uses, a wicked-looking knife, that weapon of the depraved. (When Marcus throws his knife at McTeague, Norris describes the performance as "in the true, uncanny greaser style.") (p. 125) Old Grannis and Miss Baker are requisite Anglo-Saxons, but too enfeebled and reticent to serve as proper models for Norris. Furthermore, their painful shyness and fastidiousness are, at one extreme, as inappropriate to the modern city as are the bungling antics of the Polk Street unwashed at the other. Of course, McTeague, too, is acceptably Anglo-Saxon, but his stupidity renders him unfit for a complex society. Still there is something admirable in his opposition to it; indeed, Norris finds McTeague absurd not when he is behaving least like the perfect urbanite, but when he is falteringly trying to play the role.

McTeague as lowbrow, McTeague in his natural animal state, "salient"-jawed and thick-muscled, is a compelling figure: caught up in the genteel respectabilities of courting, marriage, and getting on in the world, he is usually ridiculous. One recalls his wildly comic attempt to purchase theater tickets from a supercilious cashier, his rapturous post-mortem on the vaudeville performance, the pose he strikes for his wedding-picture, "his chin in the air, his eyes to one side, his left foot forward in the attitude of a statue of a Secretary of State." (p. 191)

McTeague's bewildered response to all of his urban tormentors, "You can't make small of me," foreshadows Norris's marvelously-realized enlargement of the man as, after his murder of Trina, he lights out for the mountains of his youth and takes up, with an inarticulate but profound sense of appropriateness, the monstrous dentistry of placer-mining: "In the Burly drill he saw a queer counterpart of his old-time dental engine: and what were the drills and chucks but enormous hoe-excavators, hard-bits and burrs? It was the same work he had so often performed in his Parlors, only magnified . . ." Here, the great mountains take him back again and "he yielded to their influence—their intensity, their enormous power, crude and blind, reflecting themselves in his own nature, huge, strong, brutal in its simplicity." (p. 328–9)

But if McTeague's reversion to the natural world is beneficial, it is only briefly so, for he intuitively senses that the city is his pursuer and that it is more powerful than his protective mountains. Thus he is forced further and further and further back, finally into a landscape beyond redemptive capacity, the baleful and maleficent wastes of Death Valley, where nature itself is dead. For, it must be understood, there is a larger dichotomy in Norris than that of nature and city. Overarching this conventional distinction is Norris's greater contrast between the quick and the dead, between the vast engine of life, the throbbing heartbeat of both city and country, as opposed to the interior and exterior deserts of silence, stillness, and death. The central image of this life-force, seen in *McTeague* and repeated ceaselessly throughout Norris's fiction, is that of the bourdon or the diapason, a swelling sound which emanates from both urban and wild settings and which represents the animating energy behind all life.[14] In *McTeague* it is the note "which disengages itself from all vast bodies, from oceans, from cities, from forests, from sleeping armies, and which is like the breathing of an infinitely great monster, alive, palpitating." (p. 329) Here the description is occasioned by the colossal mountains of Placer County, but elsewhere in Norris we find the bourdon generated by a city, a crowd of people, a sea, and so on.[15] Norris's frequent inter-changing of metaphors drawn from both industrial and organic sources to describe this deep murmur of the life-force demonstrates how the diapason blends the customarily and apparently opposed worlds of city and nature into one vibrant whole, a vast note whose opposite is the still void of death, the heartbeat stopped, the engine run down. Thus Trina is described as dying "with a rapid series of hiccups that sounded like a piece of clockwork running down."[16] (p. 320) And McTeague flees the voices of life into the true wilderness of Death Valley, where

> The silence, vast, illimitable, enfolded him like an immeasurable tide. From all that gigantic landscape, that colossal reach of baking sand, there arose not a single sound. Not a twig rattled, not an insect hummed, not a bird or beast invaded that huge solitude with call or cry. Everything as far as the eye could reach, to north, to south, to east, and west, lay inert, absolutely quiet and moveless under the remorseless scourge of the noon sun. (p. 356)[17]

If McTeague were indeed "left all alone in this world's wilderness" as his one and favorite song puts it, his death might partake of the dignity of an existential isolation, but the city reaches out to wrench a final irony from this scene. For although Marcus pursues McTeague from a motive of personal vengeance, he is also, in his association with the posse, an agent of civilization, and his dying action in handcuffing himself to McTeague is a dramatic reassertion of the city's ultimate authority. McTeague is a representative modern man in his movement from the mountains of his youth to the city of his majority, although his failure there marks him as unequipped for evolutionary progress. In his regressive return to the mountains he repeats the mythic American pattern of rejection of the threatening metropolis. And in his failure to effect that escape, and to reclaim the healing and protective natural world which ought to be his western birthright, he adds another dimension to the tragic pastorals of our literature.

Norris, then, continues the search for an appropriate urban hero in his later novels. The romantic novel *Blix* (1899) reverses the record of Vandover's decline in the story of another artist, Condy Rivers, a young writer who grasps his western city's potentialities for creative, if not heroic achievement while, with the aid of frequent pastoral retreats and his California girl, he resists its destructive attractions. The novel retains interest for the modern reader as an evocation of a lost moment of youthful optimism, as a memorialization of Norris's own courtship of his wife, the archetypal California girl, Jeannette Black, and as further evidence of Norris's continuing search for the possibilities for successful and creative urban life. While Condy Rivers of *Blix* makes a propitious beginning in his career as writer, the compulsive exaltation of "work" and the "sterner note" which marks the eastern cities to which Condy moves at the end suggest that Norris found Condy and his San Francisco sketches lacking in worldly significance. (III, 174) For Norris, who wanted writers to "go a-gunning" for stories, while he portrayed in *Blix* the sedentary and tedious nature of much of the act of composition, the writer was an unpromising hero.

Ward Bennett, of *A Man's Woman* (1900), the third and last of Norris's popular romances, represents another attempt to create a significant modern-day man of action. What the book demonstrates is that the hero as fresh-air fiend has yielded to the twentieth century. Ross Wilbur's moronic escapades have become Bennett's carefully-planned polar exploring. The playboy hero is now a scientist, his thrusts into the wilderness sanctioned by nationalistic motives, and by "the City," San Francisco as base-camp, in which he is regarded as agent of civilization and where he is saluted with the inevitable diapason at the book's conclusion. Still, the genre is about played out for Norris; his modern-day hero is driven to the literal end of the earth in order to find a suitable environment for heroic action in nature. Norris's next novel was to demonstrate that the story "as big as all outdoors" was much closer to home.[18]

The expansive conception of *The Octopus* (1901) is intimated in its opening pages where Norris sets forth the poet Presley's attempt to write, in "thundering . . . hexameters," the epic Song of the West. Presley's efforts so far, we are told, "had only touched the keynote. He strove for the diapason, the great song that should embrace in itself a whole epoch, a complete era, the voice of an entire people." (I, 7) But while he conceives of his Song of the West as arising from valleys, plains, mountains, ranches, ranges, and mines, the sweep of events carries him not toward the back country and the frontier life which he envisions but away from it and toward the city. Presley, who dreams of the Romance of the wide open spaces, is diverted from his anticipated subject by the dull but persistent commonplaces and irritating realities of freight rates and railroad-farmer bickerings. Searching for material for his epic poem in the wheat ranching country of California's Great Central Valley, Presley encounters the main characters of Norris's large and boldly-drawn work. There are the two other young men central to the novel, the rancher, Annixter, and the shepherd and mystic, Vanamee.

Magnus Derrick leads the ranchers, Osterman, Broderson, Harran Derrick, Annixter, and others in the fight against the monopolistic power of the Pacific and Southwestern Railroad, while Magnus's brother, Lyman, betrays the ranchers' interests by siding with the railway in order to boost his own political ambitions. Other figures of importance are the Valley working-class family the Hoovens, the railroad engineer Dyke, the dairymaid Hilma Tree, who later marries Annixter, and the San Francisco captains of industry, Cedarquist and Shelgrim. Still it is the character of Presley, the easterner who comes west with hugely romantic expectations about the frontier but who is drawn to the city and eventually to the wide world itself, who most occupies our attention and who embodies and records Norris's purpose in the novel, as he outlined it to Howells, of illustrating the movement of contemporary civilization from an agricultural to an industrial society.[19]

Hanging in Lyman Derrick's office, in a scene midway through *The Octopus,* is a railway map of the Pacific and Southwestern Railway lines in California. The system of red lines upon a white background presents us, in Norris's relentless symbolizing, with a country sucked white by a sprawling monster, "its ruddy arteries converging to a central point." (II, 5) The central point is, of course, the city of San Francisco, and, as the actual center of the Octopus, the headquarters and meeting-point of the company's rail lines. It also provides the narrative direction for the novel, as the setting shifts from the Central Valley to San Francisco to follow the lives of those who have been drawn to it. The book's action thus demonstrates the tilt of western history toward the city and the industrial future. At the conclusion, those left behind in the Central Valley ranch country are the dead, Annixter, Harran Derrick, Broderson, Hooven, and the dying or broken, Hilma Annixter, Osterman, Magnus Derrick, and his wife. The vibrant Dyke, who fled like McTeague to the Sierras, has been hunted down and imprisoned. His mother and daughter, when we last see them, are preparing to leave for San Francisco, the old woman already anticipating her own death and the girl facing an uncertain future suggested by the fate of Mrs. Hooven and her daughters in the city. Presley's last visit to the ranch country near the end of the novel reveals an empty and desolate countryside. Annixter's abandoned ranch suggests the exhaustion of rural possibilities: "a vast stillness" hangs over it. "No living thing stirred. The rusted windmill on the skeleton-like tower of the artesian well was motionless; the great barn empty; the windows of the ranch house, cook house, and dairy boarded up." (II, 342) Of the characters who remain on the land only the mystic Vanamee remains whole. He is a potentially tragic figure as is suggested by his characteristic presentation—like McTeague in the desert—as a speck in an immense landscape, a tiny, solitary figure in a limitless natural expanse. But he is allowed finally to join his phantom lover, and as a kind of earth-father to voice the cosmic optimism with which the novel uneasily closes.

If *The Octopus,* thus described, resembles a conventional pastoral in which rural goodness is opposed by the destructive city, a closer look offers a useful corrective. The wheat ranchers, as Norris makes clear, are not Jeffersonian yeomen lovingly tilling their broad acres but cash-croppers, out for quick profit. "To get all there was out of the land, to squeeze it dry, to exhaust it, seemed their policy. When, at last, the land worn out, would refuse to yield, they would invest their money in something else; by then, they would all have made their fortunes." (II, 14) The city, on the other hand, stands identified as the emblem of the future. As the center of the Octopus, it shares the ambiguity of that central symbol: although it can be temporarily subverted for evil purposes it nevertheless participates in the general movement for good toward which, the novel's final sentence claims, all things inevitably work. Indeed, Norris's familiar metaphor of the life-force as cosmic machine is applied both to the Octopus and to nature itself. The Octopus is "a vast power, huge, terrible . . . , the leviathan, with tentacles of steel clutching into the soil, the soulless Force, the iron-hearted Power," etc. (I, 48); nature is "a vast power, huge, terrible; a leviathan with a heart of steel, knowing no compunction, no forgiveness, no tolerance; crushing out the human atom with soundless calm, the agony of destruction sending a jar, never the faintest tremor through all that prodigious mechanism of wheels and cogs." (I, 174)[20] As participant in the life-force, the city shares in the positive connotations of that force. Once again, as in the earlier novels, the city's potentialities for destruction or degradation are balanced by its opportunities for creative or progressive endeavor. As in *McTeague* and *Vandover,* those who are unprepared to take part, with Rooseveltian vigor, in the "hard, huge struggle" of city life must be cast aside. (II, 277) What drives Mrs. Hooven to starvation and her daughter Minna to prostitution is not the city so much as their inability to adapt to its ways, or to overcome "the blind, unreasoned fear" that they feel toward the city. (II, 288) Country-bred and ignorant of urban life, they are unaware "that there were institutions built and generously endowed for just such as they"; even were they aware, the "dogged sullen pride of the peasant" might cause them to turn from seeking aid. (II, 278) While one urbanite, Gerard, the railroad vice-president, lives in baronial splendor atop Nob Hill and treats his dinner guests to Blue Point Oysters on pyramids of shaved ice and asparagus brought by special train, another, Shelgrim, the road's president, is a heroic manifestation of the work ethic, whose "enormous shoulders are fit to bear great responsibilities and great abuse," and who dresses almost shabbily, puts in long hours in his office, and treats an alcoholic employee with compassion and understanding. (II, 281) If Mrs. Cedarquist typifies the city's bored and gullible socialites, her husband carries Norris's higher hopes as a creative and energetic knight of commerce, a visionary entrepreneur who correctly predicts that the great markets for American wheat will eventually shift from Europe to Asia, and who, at the conclusion of the novel, serves the life-force by building the line of clipper ships to carry the wheat to the Orient. In Cedarquist's daring pioneering venture with the wheat ships he joins the Higher Business to the life-force and thereby assumes an important place in the evolution of Norris's new man. A logical outgrowth of Norris's earlier modern metropolitans, although sketched less fully, Cedarquist also prepares us for the more substantial heroic urbanite, Curtis Jadwin, of *The Pit*.

If Cedarquist is, as Lyman Derrick calls him, one of the city's "representative men" (II, 16), he seems to represent a distinct minority of the novel's urban characters. But if the city is frivolous, or hard, or foolish, or unconcerned, as it is depicted at various points in the narrative, these representations are subsumed under the larger impressions which the novel conveys of the inevitable movement of modern life toward urban resolutions. San Francisco as the contemporary city is indeed, as it appears on the railroad map, "that center from which all this system sprang" (II, 5), a statement which is not an indictment but a recognition of modern urbanism. The representative man of the great Central Valley, the farmer Annixter, is no bucolic tiller of the soil but a contemporary executive-type who has mastered not only scientific agriculture, but finance, law, political economy, and civil engineering (I, 22–23). (Indeed all three of the novel's young heroes are college graduates and thus "new" western men.) The typical settlement of the valley is not the creeping village, but the brisk little city of Bonneville, saluted by the author as "full of the energy and strenuous young life of a new city," with its "whirring electric cars" and "zinc-sheathed telegraph poles" (I, 184, 203). Thus, city and country merge in *The Octopus*, linked by compelling new patterns of production and distribution. What we are left with is a sense of the modern world-city, an interdependent and interconnected system like the ticker-tape machines which tie the offices of the wheat ranches not only with San Francisco, but with other great cities of the country and the world, and by which the ranches become "merely the part of an enormous whole." (I, 51)

Despite Cedarquist's admirable advice to Magnus Derrick to send his wheat to the Orient, thus moving with the course of empire and helping to break up the monopolistic control over wheat prices by the Chicago speculators, Norris's determination, in his proposed trilogy of the wheat, to trace the actual historical pattern of movement from production to marketing to consumption required that he follow the flow of the wheat to Chicago in *The Pit*. Although Norris was born in Chicago in 1870 and lived there until his family moved to San Francisco in 1884, the midwestern metropolis had little hold upon him. " 'Bawn 'n raise' in California," he wrote to interviewer Isaac Marcosson in 1898 in response to a request for personal information, and in the autobiographical *Blix* Condy Rivers says of himself, " 'Bawn 'n rais' in Chicago; but I couldn't help that, you know.' "[21] Clearly, Norris wished to be considered a westerner and a San Franciscan. But Chicago, although Norris had in an earlier *Wave* article dismissed the city as hopeless for a fictional setting, responds to his need, in *The Pit*, for a city which takes its commerce seriously and in prodigious quantities as San Francisco did not.[22] Chicago is the heart and center of the commercial America, the "great grey city"; plundering the midlands ruthlessly, supreme exemplar of the "true power and spirit of America," where "the vast machinery of Commonwealth clashed and thundered from dawn to dark and from dark till dawn." (IX, 55–58) In the prose-poem of five or six pages which introduces the reader to Chicago, Norris repeatedly calls forth images of violent movement and strident sound to establish the city as a maelstrom of powers and forces and to prepare us for the frantic action to take place within the wheat pit. Anticipating Sandburg, Norris trumpets Chicago as "gigantic, crude with the crudity of youth, disdaining rivalry; sane and healthy and vigorous; brutal in its ambition, arrogant in the new-found knowledge of its giant strength . . . , formidable, and Titanic." Chicago is the San Francisco of *The Octopus*, enlarged and galvanized for combat, a fit setting for Curtis Jadwin, the last and most ambitious of Norris's king-of-the-mountain urbanites. (p. 58) *The Pit* explores whether any man, even the strongest and best-equipped, can withstand the pressures at the vortex of modern industrialism.

Jadwin is consistently depicted as a modern warrior and Norris drives home the business-as-battle analogy at length throughout the novel.[23] The Pit becomes, each day, the scene of warfare; at the close of trading, the littered floor of the wheat exchange is covered with "the debris of the battlefield," while at night, "the wounds of the day were being bound up, the dead were being counted, while, shut in their Headquarters, the captains and commanders drew the plans for the grapple of armies that was to recommence with daylight." (pp. 98, 36)

Jadwin's climactic effort to corner the wheat is done in Norris's big bow-wow style in the sustained metaphor of a complex and carefully-planned military attack; in final defeat, Jadwin is still the Good, Grey Commander, beaten but unbowed. At the height of the great battle, Norris effectively positions his hero Jadwin at the very center of the series of concentric circles which form the novel's industrial panorama. Standing in the midst of the crowded and roaring Pit, dramatized throughout the work as a whirlpool of furious activity which his efforts to corner the wheat have agitated to an absolute frenzy, all in the midst of Chicago, the larger vortex of the nation's power and energy, Jadwin is the ultimate assertion of Norris's heroic urbanite.

It is, in Norris's cosmogony, a position that no man can hold for long; Jadwin has finally gone beyond the limits of heroic personal will. In his attempt to control the entire flow of the wheat he has unwittingly thwarted the life-force itself. The inevitable "bourdon" of the massed wheat arises like "the first rasp and grind of a new avalanche . . . , a diapason more profound than any he had yet known" rises to a crescendo. (p. 357) Having disturbed the laws of "Creation and the very earth herself," Jadwin has marked himself for destruction, and the "infinite immeasurable power," that "appalling roar of the Wheat itself coming in, coming on like a tidal wave," overwhelms and engulfs him. (pp. 358, 372) Thus Norris defines in *The Pit* the limits to urban individualism. Jadwin's great "corner" was ultimately destructive not only to himself but to the poor who could not buy the bread from his cost-inflated wheat, to the farmers who were ruined by his manipulation of wheat prices, and to the institutions and individuals caught in the shock waves of his collapse. Like Poe's mariner, Jadwin has descended into the Maelstrom, and, like him, although he escapes he is shaken and altered by his experience. At the conclusion, a chastened Jadwin leaves Chicago for the West with Laura, who has undergone, in her husband's defeat, the proper Norris conversion from dilettante to man's woman. Behind them remain Jadwin's young admirer and protege, Landry Court, who, now married to Laura's younger sister, has retired to the relative sanctuary of a railroad office position after vowing that he will speculate no more.

In Jadwin's defeat and in his retreat to the nourishing West for rootholds are suggested a change in Norris's previously-held attitudes toward East and West. Earlier in his career, as he dramatized in *Blix* and in his satiric thrusts at the banalities of San Francisco society in *The Octopus*, he held that one must go East to make his way, that his western metropolis lacked the high seriousness, the sterner cult of work, of its eastern counterparts. But his own later experiences in New York, as seen in his revealing short story, "Dying Fires," brought him to the opposite conclusion, that the eastern city was hostile to work and unstimulating and unrewarding to the serious artist.[24] Immediately after finishing *The Pit*, Norris with his wife left New York for San Francisco, convinced that his move from West to East had been a mistake. The final sentence of *The Pit* suggests in its gloomy images, a similar deflation of the promise of Chicago. Our last view, seen through Laura Jadwin's eyes as she and Jadwin ride through the city to the railway station is of the Board of Trade building, "black, monolithic, crouching there without a sound, without a sign of life, under the night and the drifting veil of rain." The words repeat exactly those at the end of the book's opening chapter, expressing Laura's "first aversion" to the great city. (pp. 37, 71) Despite her attraction to the city's power and force, revealed in the paean to Chicago in the book's second chapter, Norris allows the note of ugliness and rejection to be the final judgment—not an exuberant Chicago but a silent, lifeless charnel-house. Thus Jadwin and Laura's move west is not banishment but the familiar American gesture of lighting out for the territories, toward "the new life," as Norris indeed terms it in a closing chapter thick with statements and images of rebirth and renewal. (p. 401) *The Pit*, then, reveals that Norris was enough of a westerner to continue to weigh the options to modern industrial urbanism even as he recognized its inevitability.

The Pacific Slope, the revisionist historian Earl Pomeroy reminds us, was from the beginning a region primarily urban rather than rural.[25] In our study of western literature, which has found its primary archetype in the solitary individual set against a wilderness landscape, the novels of Frank Norris challenge us to widen our perspective, to take into account new identities which are both western and urban. Norris's novels reveal an attempt to combine the primitivistic and sensate qualities of western life with a complex urban society which he saw as the product of an inescapable evolutionary advance. From his novels emerges a vital western metropolis which finds its appropriate citizens in those who respond to the compelling rhythms of both city and western setting.

Notes

1. Letter from Norris to Isaac Marcosson, December, 1898. *The Letters of Frank Norris,* ed. Franklin Walker (San Francisco: The Book Club of California, 1956), p. 23, hereinafter abbreviated as *Letters.*

2. *McTeague* (Garden City, New York: Doubleday, Doran and Co., The Argonaut Manuscript Limited Edition of Frank Norris's Works, 1928), VIII, p. 283, hereinafter abbreviated as *Works.* All subsequent references to Norris's novels and

stories are from this edition and will be limited to volume and page number and included in the text.

3. *Letters,* p. 19.

4. I am indebted to Donald Pizer's lucid and thorough explanation of Norris's conception, gained primarily from his teacher at Berkeley, Professor Joseph Le Conte, of the notion of progressive evolution. See Pizer's *The Novels of Frank Norris* (Bloomington, Indiana: Indiana University Press, 1966), pp. 3–22. An earlier study of this idea is also valuable, Arnold Louis Goldsmith's "The Development of Frank Norris's Philosophy," *Studies in Honor of John Wilcox,* eds. A. Doyle Wallace and Woodburn O. Ross (Detroit: Wayne State University Press, 1958), pp. 174–94.

5. I disagree here with a principal thesis of Warren French's *Frank Norris* (New York: Twayne Publishers, Inc., 1962), pp. 60–61, *et passim,* and with the judgments on Norris's attitude toward the city in James R. Giles's "Beneficial Atavism in Frank Norris and Jack London," *Western American Literature,* 4 (Spring 1969), pp. 15–28.

6. "Salt and Sincerity," IV (August 1902). In *The Literary Criticism of Frank Norris,* ed. Donald Pizer (Austin, University of Texas Press, 1964), p. 220, hereinafter abbreviated as *Literary Criticism.*

7. Norris's conception of the "Great March" is found in his essay "The Frontier Gone at Last," in *Literary Criticism,* pp. 111–117.

8. *Vandover and the Brute,* although not published until 1914, was Norris's first-written novel. The writing of *McTeague,* published in 1899, also antedates *Moran's* publication in 1898.

9. *Letters,* p. 22. Actually, Norris had already written much of what was later to become *McTeague* and *Vandover and the Brute* during the year 1894–95, when the author was at Harvard. See *A Novelist in the Making,* ed. James D. Hart (Cambridge, Mass.: Harvard University Press, 1970), pp. 16–22.

10. For a fuller discussion of Norris's use of the San Francisco scene in *Vandover, McTeague,* and *Blix,* see James D. Hart's informative introduction to *A Novelist in the Making* (n.9) and Kevin Starr's *Americans and the California Dream* (New York: Oxford University Press, 1973), pp. 260–65.

11. A provocative essay on McTeague as frontier hero is George W. Johnson's "The Frontier Behind Frank Norris's *McTeague,*" *Huntington Library Quarterly,* 26 (November, 1962), pp. 91–104.

12. This scene is tastefully omitted from the Argonaut and other early Doubleday editions.

13. See Norris's "A Neglected Epic," in *Literary Criticism,* p. 122.

14. Despite its frequent occurrence throughout his works, Norris's "bourdon" or "diapason" has received little attention from critics. Howells is obviously playing with the concept when he praised Norris as one who "heard nothing or seemed to hear nothing but the full music of his own aspiration, the rich diapason of purposes securely shaping themselves in performance." ("Frank Norris," *North American Review* [December, 1902] 125 p. 777). In his study of Norris, Ernest Marchand calls attention to the figure and gives some examples of its use, but does not analyze it. (*Frank Norris* [Stanford: Stanford University Press, 1942], pp. 178–79). Beyond this, the diapason or bourdon receives only passing mention from Norris's critics.

Although it is doubtful that Norris was consciously alluding to it, his descriptions of "the vast and minor note of Life" bear a close resemblance to the ancient belief in the music of the spheres, a harmony arising from the order of the universe and the right relationship of human beings to this order. For a full discussion of this concept (and for evidence that the familiar reference to the diapason in Dryden's "A Song for St. Cecilia's Day" does not reflect Norris's purposes) see John Hollander's *The Untuning of the Sky* (Princeton, New Jersey: Princeton University Press, 1961.) A more likely source for Norris's figure is the "diapason" stop on the pipe organ, which sounds a range of octaves and harmonies. There may have been an organ in the family's mansion in Chicago during Norris's youth. In any event, Jadwin's house in *The Pit* is drawn from the Norris mansion, and the great pipe organ is a focal point of the novel. (See Franklin Walker, *Frank Norris* [Garden City, New York: Doubleday, Doran and Co. Inc., 1932], pp. 12–14, hereinafter abbreviated as Walker.) Furthermore, Norris occasionally mentions the word "organ" in his descriptions of the bourdon/diapason.

15. See, e.g., *Blix* (III, 160, 163–64), *A Man's Woman* (VI, 62, 64, 239), *Vandover* (V, 199, 202), *The Octopus* (II, 254), "The Guest of Honor" (IV; 155, 165), "Salt and Sincerity" IV, (*Literary Criticism*, pp. 219–20). A particularly revealing instance of Norris's tendency to blend nature and city under the greater unity of the life-force is seen in his feature article, written for *The Wave*, of a Santa Clara carnival:

> There was another voice, that of the sea, mysterious, insistent, and there through the night, under the low, red moon, the two voices of the sea and the city talked to each other in that unknown language of their own; and the two voices mingling together filled all the night with an immense and prolonged wave of sound, the bourdon of an unseen organ, the vast and minor note of Life.

Norris, *Frank Norris of "The Wave"* (San Francisco: The Westgate Press, 1931), p. 111.

16. C.f. the exhausted Presley, confiding to Cedarquist at the end of *The Octopus*, "There's no 'go,' no life in me at all these days. I am like a clock with a broken spring." (II, 274)

17. Similarly, in Norris's short story, "The Guest of Honor," the entrance of a character representing death is accompanied by a stilling of the background bourdon of city life. (IV, 158)

18. *Letters*, p. 35.

19. Howells, "Frank Norris," *North American Review*, p. 772.

20. Donald Pizer correctly interprets the conflict in the novel as not between nature and technology but between those who oppose the natural life-force and those who ally themselves with it. See his *The Novels of Frank Norris* (n.4), pp. 148 ff. My reading of the novel follows Pizer on this crucial point and on the importance of Cedarquist as a spokesman for Norris's ideas.

21. The letter to Marcosson is in *Letters*, p. 22; Condy's remarks are in *Works*, III, p. 10.

22. For Norris's dismissal of Chicago and praise of San Francisco see *Literary Criticism*, p. 28, and Norris's short story, "The House With the Blinds," *Works*, IV, p. 11.

23. For Norris's equating of the contemporary business tycoon with the warrior see his "The Frontier Gone at Last," *Literary Criticism*, pp. 111–17. An important earlier reading of Norris's treatment of business as contemporary adventuring in *The Octopus* and *The Pit* is Walter F. Taylor's *The Economic Novel in America*

(Chapel Hill, North Carolina: The University of North Carolina Press, 1942), p. 300 ff.

24. For further treatment of Norris's disenchantment with New York, see Walker, pp. 296–97, and *Literary Criticism*, pp. 22–24. Evidence of Norris's wish to return to San Francisco as early as March of 1899 is seen in *Letters*, p. 31.

25. *The Pacific Slope* (New York: Alfred A. Knopf, 1965), pp. 120 ff.

INDEX